The Second Decade

The Second Decade

*Prospects for European Integration after
Ten Years of Transition*

Sdu Publishers, The Hague

Ministry of Economic Affairs of the Netherlands
Directorate-General for Foreign Economic Relations

Editorial board: Guido Biessen (Editor-in-Chief), Jan Deelstra, Edith
Heijting, Pieter Karsdorp, Harry Oldersma, Stephan Raes, Thijs de Ruyter
van Steveninck, Nicolette Tiggeloove, Taco Westerhuis.

Design by Wim Zaat, Moerkapelle
Typeset by Peter Verweij Grafische Producties, Zwanenburg
Printed and bound by Wilco bv

ISBN 90 12 08807 0

Contents

Europe in transition

The fall of the Berlin Wall, on 9 November 1989, is one of the most impressive events that I can remember. It was an enormous breakthrough, after the Second World War, perhaps comparable only to Man's first walk on the moon. On 9 November 1989 an artificial barrier was brought down that for decades had kept Western and Eastern Europe apart. A dynamic period followed, with a series of events cascading one after the other. New states were born, existing structures were radically changed and new markets were developed. Economic crises were followed by economic growth. Eastern Europe became the scene of a number of bloody conflicts but at the same time a number of countries in the region succeeded in finding the road to prosperity.

The process of transition in Central and Eastern Europe still goes on. Ten years after the Wall came down, it is a good thing for us to pause and ask ourselves where we stand now. First and foremost, it can be said that East and West have every interest in steady consolidation of their mutual relations. Prosperity and stability in Europe are only possible if all the European states co-operate together with respect for one another's national cultures. A great deal has already been achieved. Five countries have already made good progress with their preparations to join the European Union. In a comparatively brief space of time, these countries have delivered an outstanding performance by carrying through large-scale economic and institutional reforms. To mention just one example: ten years ago the private sector contributed less than 10% to Poland's Gross Domestic Product. Now that figure has risen to 65%. These reforms have also helped to give a substantial boost to prosperity in these countries.

Besides the five candidate members of the European Union, other countries can also report successes. But there are also countries where the transition process appears to be coming to a standstill or even going into reverse. Where do we stand at the moment? What difficulties lie ahead for the countries of Central and Eastern Europe? What can we – as governments and as trade and industry in Western Europe – do to help remove those bottle-necks? What opportunities and threats are there? And perhaps the most important question of all: what is the prospect for Europe in the twenty-first century?

These and other questions are discussed in this book. Experts examine the transition process in Central and Eastern Europe from various angles. I can recommend this book sincerely to everybody who is interested in Europe.

A. Jorritsma-Lebbink,
Minister of Economic Affairs

Introduction

Guido Biessen and Sweder van Wijnbergen

A decade ago, the Berlin Wall came tumbling down. The tremendous task of transforming a centrally planned economy into a market economy was embarked upon. On 4 November 1999, the Ministries of Economic Affairs and Foreign Affairs of the Netherlands will hold a conference for high-level officials in order to commemorate this historic event and to evaluate the implementation of this tremendous task. This book seeks to underpin the conference. The authors attempt to throw some light on the present status of the transition process and present prospects for the future. The publication is intended as a contribution to the understanding of key policy issues and policy dilemmas.

In the literature on transition it is often claimed that the transition from a centrally planned economy to a market economy is a complex and historically new process. The process involves many interdependent issues, which create dilemmas and contradictions. Summers (1992) has grouped the issues in four main categories, namely macroeconomic stabilisation, price and market reform, enterprise reform and restructuring, and institutional reform. Other authors have categorised the issues in a similar fashion. The concurrence of the many issues involved creates dilemmas and underscores the complexity of transition.

However, some of the issues are not specific to transition, and have been dealt with in other countries at different points in time. In 1947, Verrijn Stuart had already written an article entitled 'From an Administered to a Free Economy', which addressed the dismantling of the Dutch centrally administered system of prices and wages. Analogously, the Polish stabilisation programme was not inspired by new theoretical insights, but drew on well known anti-inflation programmes applied in other regions in the world (Gomulka 1992, p. 357). Nevertheless, it is clear that establishing a fully fledged market economy from scratch is a tremendous task, and indeed, as Bos, Gelauff and De Mooij note in Chapter 3, the transition process in the Central and Eastern European Countries (CEECs) deepened our knowledge of the functioning of a market economy.

CHAPTER I

Accomplishments in the first decade

The achievements during the first decade of transition were mixed. One should
bear in mind that the CEECs are not a homogeneous group of countries.[1] Although
there were large similarities in the way the traditional planned system was implemented in the countries in question, there were differences as well. Reform policies within the system of central planning, in order to mitigate flaws in that system, differed between the respective countries, making the group more heterogeneous. This holds *a fortiori* for the transition process. The issues involved are to
a large extent similar, but the way these issues are handled varies from country to
country. As a result of differences in the initial conditions and policies pursued
during the transition process, the outcomes differ widely.

In general, remarkable progress has been achieved. With respect to macroeconomic stabilisation, the inflation rates for all countries in transition dropped from
extremely high levels in the early 1990s at the outset of transition, to two-digit
numbers in the second half of the 1990s. However, in some countries a reversal
could be observed. Stabilisation did not come without social hardship. Initial stabilisation efforts in almost every country were accompanied by a sharp fall in
recorded GDP. The fall in output was accompanied by the emergence of sharply
rising unemployment, increasing income inequality and poverty. Meanwhile, in a
large number of countries, growth has resumed. The past performance with
respect to fiscal stabilisation is rather diverse. The countries that seek membership of the EU are, in general, making good progress, while countries like Russia
and Ukraine still suffer from chronic budget deficits. The latter countries appear
to be unable to raise tax revenues in a significant way.

Price liberalisation and external liberalisation go hand in hand. In order to
bring domestic prices more in line with world market prices, domestic enterprises must be exposed to foreign competition. This process of opening up was successful, in the sense that most CEECs were able to increase volumes of trade, and
to divert trade flows to a considerable degree to the West. With the process of
opening up to the world market, most CEECs were confronted with deteriorating
current account deficits. To some extent, these were financed by the increasing
inflow of foreign direct investment. However, in a number of countries the sharply
rising deficits, financed by short-term capital, are worrisome. The rising current
account deficits may prove to be unsustainable and may increase the vulnerability of the economies in question.

---

1. Throughout this book, the term CEECs refers to all Central and Eastern European countries
in transition, unless defined otherwise. For instance, in Chapter 2, a distinction is made between
the CEECs and the countries of the Former Soviet Union (FSU). This volume focuses primarily
on the ten candidates for accession to the European Union, the CEEC-10 (i.e. Bulgaria, the Czech
Republic, Estonia, Hungary, Latvia, Lithuania, Poland, Romania, the Slovak Republic and
Slovenia), and Russia and Ukraine.

In a large number of countries, private sector development has been very dynamic and the private sector share in GDP varies from a high 75% in countries like Hungary, to a low 50% in countries like Ukraine. Privatisation of state enterprises has contributed to this development. However, here the past performance is mixed too. In some countries it turned out to be difficult to privatise loss-making enterprises. In addition, even after privatisation it appeared to be difficult to confront the former state enterprises with true hard budget constraints. The subsidies given to state enterprises or formerly state-owned enterprises constitute a large burden on the state budget.

A key issue in the transition process is an adequate entry into and exit out of the private sector. The former requires, among other things, a system of well-defined property rights. For the latter, the proper functioning of a bankruptcy system is a key requirement. In general, the legal infrastructure for a properly functioning market economy must not only be enshrined in laws, but legislation also has to be implemented effectively. Much has been achieved, especially in the first group of countries that is seeking membership of the EU. Also critical to the transition process is the functioning of financial markets. Prudent supervision by an independent central bank and effective implementation of banking legislation is of the utmost importance. Again, progress with respect to the legal framework has been substantial, but effective implementation has been rather mixed.

Challenges for the second decade

We are at the eve of the second decade of the transition process. A large number of challenges still lie ahead (for an overview see Nsouli, 1999). Let us mention just a few. First and foremost, there are a number of important social issues, which need to be addressed. Increased poverty, rising income inequality, unemployment, declining life expectancy (especially in the Commonwealth of Independent States, (CIS), deteriorating health care, sharply increasing organised crime and corruption are severe problems, and issues that eventually may erode popular support for further reforms. Emphasis must be put on the rule of law. Tax evasion or tax exemptions need to be avoided, in order to improve the fiscal position. Financial systems need to be strengthened and capital markets further developed, in order to strengthen the intermediary role of the financial sector between saving and investment. Reform of pension funds is a related topic. In addition, the infrastructure is obsolete, and huge investments are required here.

A large challenge is the coming enlargement of the European Union. The ten Central and Eastern European countries which have the perspective of becoming members of the EU, the CEEC-10, have agreed to introduce and implement the whole body of existing European legislation, the *acquis communautaire*. This spurs them to adopt and implement a legal framework to suit the new conditions. Taking over EU legislation and EU practices takes a huge effort and requires a great deal of adjustment, but has a large positive effect on the proper functioning of markets. The prospect of EU membership has also increased their attractiveness to foreign investors. The coming enlargement is not only a challenge for the CEEC-10, but also for the EU. As both economic and political benefits of the enlargement are huge, the EU has the obligation to adapt its institutional setting in such a way that it has the ability to absorb newcomers without hampering the functioning of the institutions.

Outline of the book

Part I presents the actual situation in the transition economies. The three chapters in this part deal with the progress regarding stabilisation issues, the progress in terms of institutional change, and the implications of transition for international economic co-operation, foreign trade and investments in Central and Eastern Europe. In Chapter 2, Stern and Wes (EBRD) discuss the progress with respect to macroeconomics. The authors focus on inflation and monetary issues, fiscal imbalances, external imbalances, the overall investment climate and growth prospects. They conclude that there are important challenges with respect to the fiscal aspects of transition, external imbalances and rising real exchange rates. In Chapter 3, Bos (Netherlands Social and Economic Council), Gelauff and de Mooij (CPB Netherlands Bureau for Economic Policy Analysis) address the progress in the transition process in terms of institutional change in both the private and the public sector. They identify four main co-ordination mechanisms for economic behaviour, i.e. control, competition, common values and co-operative exchange. The authors analyse the development in institution building, necessary to improve the effectiveness of these mechanisms. Opening up and reintegration into the world economy is a crucial aspect of transition. In Chapter 4, Biessen, Oldersma and Tiggeloove (Ministry of Economic Affairs of the Netherlands) discuss the process of opening up, and the impact of transition, on foreign trade and investments in Eastern Europe. Special reference is made to the Dutch position on the emerging Central European markets.

Part II deals with the enlargement of the European Union. The timing of the entry of the Central European countries is a topical issue. Questions arise as to when the countries will be ready for accession to the EU, or when they will be ready to join the monetary union. Equally important is the question whether the EU will be ready to absorb the newcomers. Both the EU point of view and the Central European perspectives are considered. In Chapter 5, van den Broek (European Commission) gives an overview of the thorny process of enlargement. He discusses the preconditions the candidate countries need to fulfil, and addresses the possible delays for the coming round of enlargement. These delays may stem from those candidate countries that do not completely fulfil the criteria, or from the EU when the institutional setting is not adapted to absorb newcomers. Rollo and Smith (University of Sussex) address the necessity of temporary exemptions and transitional periods for the adoption of parts of the *acquis communautaire* in Chapter 6. The authors argue that not all key EU policies are equally important for an effective operation of the internal market, and that transitional periods are consistent with the single market. In Chapter 7, Wellink (De Nederlandsche Bank) deals with the present and future monetary relations between the candidate Member States and the euro area, with an emphasis on the 'fast track' countries. Wellink warns that completely fixing the exchange rates after EU membership may not be desirable, as the countries are still in a process of restructuring, and the resulting productivity increases may result in an upward pressure on their currencies. An interesting case is the Portuguese experience in joining the EU. In Chapter 8, Mateus (Banco de Portugal) discusses the Portuguese example of accession to the EU, which holds some important lessons relevant for the Central European countries. Remarkably, the author observes that most Portuguese negotiators are now of the opinion that the derogations, that were the subject of negotiations, were too many and too broad. In Chapter 9, Rosati (National Bank of Poland) addresses the Polish perspective on the enlargement process of the EU. Rosati draws attention to the political benefits of the enlargement of the EU. An important phenomenon, which attracts little attention, is the diminishing popular support for the enlargement in Poland. In Chapter 10, Inotai (Institute for World Economics of the Hungarian Academy of Sciences) deals with the Hungarian view on the enlargement process. Inotai identifies as the most important problem areas for the negotiation process, agriculture, environment, free movement of labour, the Schengen agreement, structural funds and the EMU. The author argues that the national government should have a clear selection mechanism, in order to evaluate the priorities in domestic demands for derogation.

Part III addresses Russia and Ukraine. Although these countries are not likely to join the EU in the foreseeable future, open economic relations with the EU are important for future development. While a bilateral (EU) approach might be important to enhance the Russian and Ukrainian international economic relations, a multilateral approach is at least as important. In Chapter 11, Gros (Centre for European Policy Studies) addresses the 'lost decade' of Russia. The author highlights the developments in Russia in the past decade of transition. Reforms were carried out only partially, leading to mistakes and contradictions. However, according to the author, shortcomings were addressed slowly and he foresees a lengthy and imperfect, but at the same time progressive, development. In Chapter 12, Pynzenyk (Parliament of Ukraine) discusses the economic situation in Ukraine. While the author finds it hard to be optimistic, at the same time he argues that Ukraine is closer to true economic reforms than ever before. It is interesting to note that both Gros and Pynzenyk question the effectiveness of international aid. In Chapter 13, Michalopoulos (World Bank) discusses the prospects and obstacles for Russia and Ukraine to join the WTO. The author evaluates their trade regimes as not being particularly restrictive, but identifies weaknesses in the functioning of market institutions as the main obstacle to become effectively integrated in the world trading system. In Chapter 14, Biessen and Engering (Ministry of Economic Affairs of the Netherlands) conclude.

References

Gomulka, S. (1992), 'Polish Economic Reform, 1990-1991: Principles, Policies and Outcomes', *Cambridge Journal of Economics,* Vol.16, pp.355-372.

Nsouli, S.M. (1999), 'A Decade of Transition; An Overview of the Achievements and Challenges', *Finance and Development,* International Monetary Fund, Vol.36, Nr.2, pp.2-5

Summers, L. (1992), 'The next decade in Central and Eastern Europe', in: Clague, C. and G. Rausser, *The Emergence of Market Economies in Eastern Europe.* Cambridge, MA, Blackwell.

Verrijn Stuart, G. (1947), 'Van Geleide naar Vrije Economie (From administered to a free economy)', *Economisch Statistische Berichten,* pp.233-237.

Part I

Accomplishments in the First Decade

Macroeconomic Progress

Nicholas Stern and Marina Wes

2.1 Introduction

The scale and speed of economic change in Central and Eastern Europe and the former Soviet Union (FSU) have been remarkable. Ten years after the onset of the transition process most economic activity is market oriented and the majority of national income is generated by the private sector. Furthermore, the new democratic systems have shown impressive advances and resilience in difficult times.

However, we must take care to avoid focusing only on regional aggregates. Many of the real lessons from the last ten years emerge only when we look at the differences in experiences between countries. The region was far from homogeneous prior to 1990.[1] Some countries had introduced limited market reforms well before the general collapse of communism at the end of the 1980s, whereas others had attempted to adhere rigidly to strict state control of economic activities. Some countries had industrial and economic structures that were more 'difficult' to reform (dependence on thoroughly uncompetitive capital goods industries, or large-scale collectivised agriculture); some had heavy debts; some are rich in mineral resources; and some have close geographic proximity to Western developed market economies. Further, historical and cultural backgrounds vary enormously. Partly as a result of these differences, countries have differed enormously in macroeconomic outcomes. Some have enjoyed several years of GDP growth, falling inflation and rapid growth in investment and capital inflows, while others have failed to achieve a sound and secure stabilisation and have yet to see much signs of recovery.

The variation in macroeconomic performance across the region has much to tell us, both about the process of transition and the role of policy in that process. Although initial conditions are of great importance, history, culture and geography do not determine everything. All countries in the region have had real policy choices since the onset of the transition process. Decisions had to be taken quick-

---

1. Throughout this chapter, the 'region' refers to the EBDR's 26 countries of operations, namely Albania, Armenia, Azerbaijan, Belarus, Bosnia and Herzegovina, Bulgaria, Croatia, the Czech Republic, Estonia, FYR Macedonia, Georgia, Hungary, Kazakhstan, Kyrgyzstan, Latvia, Lithuania, Moldova, Poland, Romania, the Russian Federation, the Slovak Republic, Slovenia, Tajikistan, Turkmenistan, Ukraine and Uzbekistan.

ly and the territory was uncharted. The early decisions have had profound effects on what followed.

For the countries of the region, the basic questions of macroeconomic policy (fiscal and monetary policy, the balance of payments and the exchange rates) all have special difficulties and challenges, which are intrinsic to the transition process. The purpose of this chapter is to examine the progress in the macro-economies of the transition countries from the perspective of those difficulties and challenges. As discussed below, they include fiscal problems arising from changing structures of government expenditures and revenues and the challenge of raising investment in the process of restructuring and growth.

In the first years of transition all countries faced rapid inflation and falling output as a result of a combination of: difficulties in asserting monetary and fiscal control in new economic circumstances, monetary overhang, an erosion of the tax base, and the dislocation of a rigid system. However, some countries asserted monetary and fiscal control more quickly than others.

Fiscal imbalances

Building a new tax system is crucial to the transition. In a command economy, the government has direct control over the resources it wishes to use. In a market economy, on the other hand, most goods and services are generated in the private sector, and if the government wishes to use resources it must finance their acquisition, primarily through taxation. The creation of an efficient and effective tax system is therefore an important priority of the transition. The response to this challenge has varied greatly and in particular in the CIS tax revenues have been limited by poor administration, erosion of the tax base, the development of barter and various forms of corruption and tax evasion.

There are also deep challenges on the expenditure side of the budget, the importance of which has been illustrated recently by the crisis in Russia. The origins of the collapse of Russia's financial markets were in the country's flawed fiscal position, which was in turn undermined by the very weak structural reforms. Although the government's stabilisation programme in the mid-1990s managed to bring down inflation, the reform programme failed to address the underlying structural causes of the macroeconomic imbalances. The government replaced monetary financing of the deficit with borrowing both on a newly created Treasury bill market and on international capital markets. But it seemed unable or unwilling to support this borrowing with the necessary fiscal strengthening. Channels of soft financing to enterprises remained significant, keeping bankrupt firms alive, and providing subsidies to avoid change rather than to foster change. Informal and off-budget subsidies were pervasive. At the same time, weak administration, political pressure and corruption weakened tax revenues. As the Russian crisis has illustrated, relying on debt finance and in particular foreign portfolio investment is unsustainable if the underlying causes of government imbalances are not tackled.

Monetary overhang

Inflationary pressures were repressed under the communist regimes, leading to yet another hidden economic imbalance. Excess demand, accumulated both in the household sector and among enterprises, was not evidenced by inflation, but rather by the widespread shortages of both consumer and investment goods and by considerable financial savings that were scarcely remunerated.

The onset of the transition process thus led to significant price increases in all transition economies. In most countries the initial jump in inflation came from a combination of price liberalisation and a loss of macroeconomic control largely due to the collapse of the tax base, without a corresponding reduction in expenditure. Inflation was thus fuelled by large fiscal and quasi-fiscal deficits, and the absence of other sources of finance led to the monetary financing of budget deficits. By 1995 however, inflation had come down rapidly across the region, down to single-digit levels at end-year in six Central and Eastern European countries (CEECs). 1995 also saw very significant improvements in the CIS, and double-digit inflation became the norm the following year. Moving to single-digit inflation has proved more challenging, however, and as discussed below, there are worrying signs of inflation reversals in several CIS countries.

External imbalances

Sustained growth in the transition economies will be associated with rising investment demand. Just as in Western Europe following World War II, capital inflows are an integral and natural part of financing that demand and the process of reconstruction. Capital inflows can also promote the transition process by bringing new technologies and management approaches, by setting standards, tightening financial discipline and raising the intensity of competition.

However, although moderate current account deficits are in principle 'desirable', they also create obligations that will have to be served. The emerging market crises were a clear reminder of that simple but basic fact. Further, open capital markets can act to soften perceived budget constraints. The experience of Russia shows the dangers of opening up rapidly to foreign portfolio investment before the financial and fiscal positions are robust. It is striking that Poland, with the strongest overall growth of any country in the region and a sound transition, has maintained some restrictions on short-term portfolio flows.

Real exchange rates

An important phenomenon in transition economies has been that of rising real exchange rates. These are to be expected during the transition process – markets produced low valuations on factors of production during the early years of transition, given the considerable uncertainty over future productivity and capacity to compete in world markets. As the transition progressed and trade and production began to be reoriented, real exchange rates have appreciated quite rapidly. However, this appreciation can lead to a lack of competitiveness if productivity does not increase sufficiently fast.

Investment climate and growth prospects

Growth will require sound investment, both domestic and foreign, and this will in turn require a favourable investment climate. Private investors take decisions on the basis of potential risk and reward, and will be deterred from making investments if the investment climate is weak. That is at the heart of the difference between a command and market economy. Macroeconomic stability is an essential element of a favourable investment climate. High inflation creates uncertainty, distorts price signals and diverts entrepreneurial energies to short-term financial engineering or manipulation. A strong investment climate also involves much deeper conditions than macroeconomic stability. It requires effective markets, sound financial institutions and a government that refrains from arbitrary bureaucratic interference and provides administrative and legal support for the basics of economic life. In short, a sound investment climate is provided by strong progress with structural reform and institution building.

At present, and in spite of significant progress in large parts of the region, the institutions, policies and practices which are needed to underpin entrepreneurship and long-term commitment of investors still have many weaknesses (for instance in state structures and behaviour, in financial systems, and in corporate governance (see Chapter 3)). The combination of high levels of skills and significant technological deficits in transition economies creates a good potential for growth. However, there is also a strong possibility of becoming trapped by government behaviour which is antipathetic to markets and entrepreneurship, resistant to change, and biased towards vested interests. Economic performance and outlook have been undermined most severely where the investment climate is the weakest.

Outline

The chapter begins by summarising the main 'stylised facts' over the last ten years. In the next section, we examine the behaviour of GDP growth, output inflation and other important macroeconomic variables for 26 transition economies in Central and Eastern Europe and the CIS. Section 2.3 analyses some of the links between macroeconomic performance and structural and institutional reforms, noting in particular the origins of the macroeconomic reversals that have occurred in a number of countries. Section 2.4 discusses the role of international capital in the transition process. Section 2.5 looks forward by considering growth prospects in the transition economies. Section 2.6 concludes.

2.2 The experience in the first decade

GDP growth

The early years of transition were very difficult for all countries. The collapse of the old system had an extremely disruptive effect on the production and exchange of goods, and was followed by severe recessions throughout the region (see Figure 2.1 and Table 2.1). The decline in output in the early years was accompanied by falls in employment and labour force participation, sharp increases in unemployment, and declining productivity and investment.[2]

There were a number of reasons for the deep recessions in the early transition period, important among them being the breakdown of a cumbersome economic system that was highly integrated across the former command economies. Payment mechanisms switched suddenly to hard currency, with prices moving towards world levels. Crucial inputs became unavailable or unaffordable. The effects were accentuated by the 'over-integration' of the Soviet economic system. At the same time, competition, including from imports, intensified with many enterprises being ill-equipped to compete in these unfamiliar circumstances. Thus the fall came from both supply and demand factors.

Figure 2.1: Index of real GDP
(Weighted averages for selected regions of Central and Eastern Europe, the Baltic States and the Commonwealth of Independant States; Base year: 1989=100)

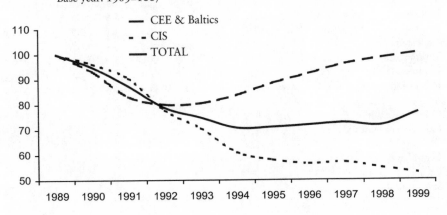

Source: EBRD

---

2. Unemployment experiences differ widely across the region. A glance a the official statistics suggests that the CIS has managed to avoid the big increases that occurred in the CEECs. However, this conclusion is false: official employment statistics in the CIS are generally based on official registration, and many unemployed do not bother to register as benefit payments are negligible or non-existent.

Table 2.1: Growth in real GDP in Central and Eastern Europe, the Baltic States and the CIS

	1990	1991	1992	1993	1994	1995	1996	1997	1998	1999
Albania	-10.0	-27.7	-7.2	9.6	9.4	8.9	9.1	-7.0	8.0	5.0
Bulgaria	-9.1	-11.7	-7.3	-1.5	1.8	2.1	-10.9	-6.9	3.5	1.0
Croatia	-7.1	-21.1	-11.7	-8.0	5.9	6.8	6.0	6.5	2.7	0.0
Czech Republic	-1.2	-11.5	-3.3	0.6	3.2	6.4	3.9	1.0	-2.7	0.0
Estonia	-8.1	-13.6	-14.2	-9.0	-2.0	4.3	4.0	11.4	4.0	3.0
FYR of Macedonia	-9.9	-12.1	-21.1	-9.1	-1.8	-1.2	0.8	1.5	2.9	-4.0
Hungary	-3.5	-11.9	-3.1	-0.6	2.9	1.5	1.3	4.6	5.0	3.0
Latvia	2.9	-10.4	-34.9	-14.9	0.6	-0.8	3.3	6.5	3.6	2.6
Lithuania	-5.0	-5.7	-21.3	-16.2	-9.8	3.3	4.7	6.1	4.4	2.5
Poland	-11.6	-7.0	2.6	3.8	5.2	7.0	6.1	6.9	4.8	3.0
Romania	-5.6	-12.9	-8.8	1.5	3.9	7.1	4.1	-6.6	-7.3	-3.0
Slovak Republic	-2.5	-14.6	-6.5	-3.7	4.9	6.9	6.6	6.5	4.4	1.0
Slovenia	-4.7	-8.9	-5.5	2.8	5.3	4.1	3.3	3.8	4.0	3.8
Central and Eastern Europe and the Baltic States 1/	-6.7	-10.8	-3.8	0.4	3.9	5.5	4.0	3.7	2.3	1.5
Armenia	-7.4	-17.1	-52.6	-14.8	5.4	6.9	5.8	3.1	7.2	4.0
Azerbaijan	-11.7	-0.7	-22.6	-23.1	-19.7	-11.8	1.3	5.8	10.1	5.0
Belarus	-3.0	-1.2	-9.6	-7.6	-12.6	-10.4	2.8	10.4	8.0	2.0
Georgia	-12.4	-20.6	-44.8	-25.4	-11.4	2.4	10.5	11.0	2.9	2.0
Kazakhstan	-0.4	-13.0	-2.9	-9.2	-12.6	-8.2	0.5	2.0	-2.5	-2.5
Kyrgyzstan	3.0	-5.0	-19.0	-16.0	-20.0	-5.4	7.1	10.4	1.8	2.0
Moldova	-2.4	-17.5	-29.1	-1.2	-31.2	-3.0	-8.0	1.3	-8.6	-5.0
Russia	-4.0	-5.0	-14.5	-8.7	-12.7	-4.1	-3.5	0.8	-4.6	-3.0
Tajikistan	-1.6	-7.1	-29.0	-11.0	-18.9	-12.5	-4.4	1.7	4.0	3.0
Turkmenistan	2.0	-4.7	-5.3	-10.0	-18.8	-8.2	-8.0	-26.1	4.2	20.0
Ukraine	-3.4	-11.6	-13.7	-14.2	-23.0	-12.2	-10.0	-3.2	-1.7	-3.0
Uzbekistan	1.6	-0.5	-11.1	-2.3	-4.2	-0.9	1.6	2.4	2.0	1.0
Commonwealth of Independent States 2/	-3.7	-5.9	-14.1	-9.3	-13.8	-5.1	-3.5	0.9	-3.5	-2.7
Central and Eastern Europe, the Baltic States and the CIS	-5.0	-8.0	-9.7	-5.1	-6.2	-0.6	-0.2	2.0	-1.3	-0.9

Notes:
1/ Estimates for real GDP represent weighted averages for Albania, Bulgaria, Croatia, the Czech Republic, Estonia, FYR of Macedonia, Hungary, Latvia, Lithuania, Poland, Romania, the Slovak Republic and Slovenia.
2/ Here taken to include all countries of the former Soviet Union, except Estonia, Latvia and Lithuania. Estimates of real GDP represent weighted averages. The weights represent EBRD estimates of nominal dollar-GDP lagged one year.
Sources: Data for 1990-97 represent the most recent official estimates of outturns as reflected in publications from the EBRD, national authorities, the IMF, the World Bank, the OECD, PlanEcon and the Institute of International Finance. Data for 1998 are estimates, data for 1999 are projections.

It must, however, also be remembered that for a number of reasons outputs in the transition period have probably been underestimated relative to the preceding period. As a result, the resumption of growth may have been quicker than the official statistics imply. The reasons for underestimation include: (i) an incentive to underreport outputs and revenues for tax reasons now, whereas previously the planning system encouraged overreporting; (ii) weaker statistical coverage of new enterprises; (iii) old price indices which undervalued newer products; (iv) higher quality; (v) better matching of outputs and demand; and (vi) the emergence of a significant informal economy. These reservations about the data are substantial and thus more attention should be paid to broad trends than to detail on particular figures. Yet, the general impression of a deep depression is unlikely to be misleading. There are a number of other indicators, including electricity consumption and living indicators, which, whilst they have their own difficulties, tell broadly similar stories.[3]

Although output fell everywhere across the region, there is a notable difference between the CEECs and the CIS, as highlighted in Figure 2.1. In Central and Eastern Europe the average level of output reached a minimum in 1993, and has since begun to grow, generating a U-shape for output. At the lowest point, output had fallen 25% below the 1989 level. Albania, Poland, Romania and Slovenia showed positive growth in 1993 and 12 countries showed positive growth in 1994. Indeed Poland had started to grow in 1992, and Poland and Slovenia have by now surpassed the output levels recorded in 1989. Using a panel of 26 transition economies from 1990-1996, Berg *et al.* (1999) find that the main driving factor behind the depth of the initial output decline was initial conditions. Trade dependency and over-industrialisation play a particularly prominent role in the initial output decline, and account for more than three-quarters of the impact of initial conditions on the output decline in year 0. They find no evidence that, controlling for other factors, structural reforms initially accentuated the economy-wide recessions.

In the CIS, the fall in output has generally been larger, and in some countries reported output fell by as much as two-thirds. While Russia's modest output recovery in 1997 was largely responsible for the first year of positive growth in the region as a whole, the crisis of August 1998 has caused a substantial downturn in the economy and a temporary return to high inflation. The fall-out from the Russian crisis is affecting economic performance in the rest of the region, in particular in neighbouring CIS economies with weak macroeconomic fundamentals and strong trade links to Russia. The output profile in the CIS as a whole over the past ten years is therefore closer to an L-shape than to a U-shape.[4]

---

3. For further discussion see EBRD Transition Reports 1994 and 1995. Kaufmann and Kaliberda (1996) construct estimates of output that draw, among other things, on electricity consumption. They conclude that the overall GDP decline during 1989-94 was 17% in the CEECs and 33.4% in the former Soviet Union.

Inflation and monetary issues

Table 2.2 presents end-year inflation rates for the transition economies during the 1990s. An inverse-U shape pattern is common across countries, but countries differ dramatically in the scale of inflation during the early years. Inflation rates have been extremely high at times in the transition process, especially in the former Soviet Union, in particular during the early 1990s. All countries in the CIS experienced inflation of more than 1,000% in the year of maximum inflation, and more than 10,000% in Armenia, Turkmenistan and Ukraine. In only three countries (the Czech Republic, Hungary and the Slovak Republic) did annual inflation remain below triple digits throughout the transition process.

Inflationary pressures had been repressed under the old regime (witness the shortages and queues that were pervasive across the region). In most countries there was an initial jump in inflation, associated with the 'monetary overhang' and a loss of macroeconomic control at the same time as prices were liberalised. This loss of macroeconomic control resulted largely from the collapse of the tax base, without a corresponding reduction in expenditure.[5] Inflation was thus fuelled by large fiscal and quasi-fiscal deficits, and the absence of other sources of finance led to the monetary financing of budget deficits.

By the end of 1992, major results in stabilising inflation had been achieved only in some of the CEECs. Macroeconomic control began to be restored in much of the region in 1993 and 1994, in many cases with the help of IMF programmes. Once undertaken, inflation stabilisation was usually rapid and impressive falls in inflation took place in 1994 and 1995. By 1995 most countries had inflation below 50% *per annum*, and in six cases annual inflation rates had come down to single-digit levels. In the early transition, government securities markets were virtually non-existent and access to foreign finance was limited. The development of a broader range of financing options alongside fiscal consolidation were key elements underlying subsequent disinflation attempts.

In many ways, the context for disinflation was quite favourable. Inflation had not persisted for long, backward indexation was limited (except in Poland and Slovenia where indexation has contributed to keeping these countries in the moderate inflation range), financial sector fragility did not undermine monetary con-

---

4. A few years ago, some saw the CIS as following a similar path to that of the CEECs, but with a two to three year lag, taking into account the later start (see for instance Fischer *et al.*, 1997). However, events in the CIS during 1998 have cast doubt on this.

5. The tax base had been, under the old regime, essentially the profits and turnover of the large state enterprises. With the general disruption of the economy, including the collapse of the CMEA, and the beginning of competition, output and profits fell sharply. At the same time, incentives to evade taxes increased strongly and the ability to monitor them through the banking system deteriorated sharply. Together, the implications for overall revenue collections were disastrous, with falls in the order of 15-20% of GDP in two years.

Table 2.2: Inflation in Central and Eastern Europe, the Baltic States and the CIS
(Percentage change in average retail/consumer price level)

	1990	1991	1992	1993	1994	1995	1996	1997	1998[1]	1999[1]
Albania	0	35	226	85	23	8	13	32	21	8
Bulgaria	26	334	82	73	96	62	123	1,082	22	7
Croatia	610	123	666	1,518	98	2	4	4	6	4
Czech Republic	11	57	11	21	10	9	8	9	11	5
Estonia	23	211	1,076	90	48	29	23	11	11	8
FYR of Macedonia	n.a.	n.a.	1,664	338	127	16	3	1	1	2
Hungary	29	35	23	23	19	28	24	18	14	9
Latvia	11	172	951	108	36	25	18	8	5	3
Lithuania	8	225	1,021	410	72	40	25	9	5	24
Poland	586	70	43	35	32	28	20	15	12	7
Romania	5	161	210	256	137	32	39	155	59	45
Slovak Republic	11	61	10	23	13	10	6	6	7	10
Slovenia	550	118	207	33	21	14	10	8	8	8
Central and Eastern Europe and the Baltic States										
Median 2/	17	120	210	85	36	25	18	9	11	8
Mean 2/	156	133	476	232	56	23	24	105	14	11
Armenia	n.a.	n.a.	n.a.	3,500	5,273	177	19	14	9	3
Azerbaijan	8	107	912	1,129	1,664	412	20	3	-1	-7
Belarus	n.a.	n.a.	971	1,188	2,200	709	53	64	73	265
Georgia	n.a.	79	887	3,125	15,606	163	39	7	4	20
Kazakhstan	n.a.	79	1,381	1,662	1,892	176	39	17	7	11
Kyrgyzstan	n.a.	85	855	772	229	53	30	26	13	15
Moldova	4	98	1,276	789	330	30	24	12	8	25
Russia	n.a.	93	1,526	875	311	198	48	15	28	95
Tajikistan	4	112	1,157	2,195	350	609	418	88	43	14
Turkmenistan	5	103	493	3,102	1,748	1,005	992	84	17	36
Ukraine	4	91	1,210	4,735	891	377	80	16	11	28
Uzbekistan	3	82	645	534	1,568	305	54	72	34	29
Commonwealth of Independent States										
Median 2/	4	92	971	1,425	1,616	251	44	17	12	23
Mean 2/	5	93	1,028	1,967	2,672	351	151	35	21	45
Central and Eastern Europe, the Baltic States and the CIS										
Median 2/	10	95	871	534	137	40	24	15	11	10
Mean 2/	105	115	729	1,065	1,312	181	85	71	17	27

Notes:
1/ 1998 estimate, 1999 projection.
2/ The median is the middle value after all inflation rates have been arranged in order of size. In Table 2.2, the mean tends to exceed the median, due to outliers caused by very high inflation rates in certain countries

Sources: Data for 1990-97 represent the most recent official estimates of outturns as reflected in publications from the EBRD, national authorities, the IMF, the World Bank, the OECD, PlanEcon and the Institute of International Finance.

trol and the credibility of disinflation, and political economy factors favoured disinflation in some countries (Cottarelli and Doyle, 1999). Where the old economic interest groups were discredited and disorganised, a political window of opportunity and an opening for 'extraordinary politics' appeared, which eased the introduction of stabilisation and reform programmes (Balcerowicz, 1994).[6] Although quite common in Central and Eastern Europe, such openings were rarely apparent in the countries of the FSU.

However, even countries that have been consistent in their stabilisation commitments have nevertheless had difficulties in reducing inflation to levels typical (at present) of Western market economies. After the initial stabilisation phase, further disinflation has often been slow especially in some of the more advanced transition economies. For instance, it took more than four years to bring inflation in Poland down from 60% to below 15%.[7] In Hungary, where inflation reached its peak in 1991 (at 35%), the 1998 level was 14.3%. Similar to experiences in some developing countries, it has been far easier to bring inflation down from annual triple-digit rates to rates between 10% and 20% a year, than to move beyond that success.

Although past empirical studies have shown that stabilisation is a necessary (but not sufficient) condition for the recovery of output (Havrylyshyn and Botousharov 1995, and Fischer *et al.* (1997)), Christofferson and Doyle (1998) suggest that there is no systematic evidence that disinflation (the change in inflation, rather than the level of inflation) was associated with declines in output. When annual inflation begins to run in the hundreds there can be little doubt that it depresses growth and lowers efficiency.[8] On the other hand, at lower rates of inflation there is less evidence of any clear pattern of covariation between inflation and growth – both in transition and in market economies. Inflation is associated with weaker output only above a certain threshold rate. Havrylyshyn *et al.* (1998) suggest that inflation levels higher than the range of 20-30% hurt growth significantly. These results are consistent with Bruno and Easterly (1998), although others find the threshold to be somewhat lower. For instance, Ghosh (1997) identifies a 10% threshold for inflation, above which growth is unlikely to occur, while Christofferson and Doyle (1998) find a threshold of about 13%.

---

6. Whoever happens to rise to power in the exceptional aftermath of the collapse of communism is endowed with an unusually large stock of political capital. The population is willing to accept temporary hardship in the anticipation of rewards to come. Former elites will take time to regroup and new interest groups are not yet in existence.

7. Important factors in explaining the persistence of double-digit inflation include the continuing adjustment of relative prices, the choice of exchange rate regime, and the policy preferences of national authorities about inflation. In addition, the upgrading of product and service quality that has been associated with the opening of borders and the growing private sector tends to be difficult to reflect in price surveys. Higher product prices may therefore, in some cases, simply reflect quality improvements.

8. Lougani and Sheets (1997) suggest that a country with 500% inflation in one year looses about two percentage points of GDP the following year and four percentage points of GDP in the longer run.

Public finances

A distinguishing feature of the first ten years of transition is the severe and continuing pressure on government budgets, and the resulting fiscal imbalances that
have arisen in most countries in the region (Figure 2.2). Over the past decade,
there has been a U-shaped path in government deficits, and deficits have generally been much greater in the CIS than in the CEECs. This pattern is closely related
both to the output collapse across the region and to the process of structural
reform in the public sector. On the revenue side, transition from a command to a
market economy requires balancing the decline in profit and turnover taxes from
the contracting state sector with increased revenues from other sources. This
demanded a major shift in the tax base, as well as the creation of a healthy and
growing private sector, tasks that are often far from complete – especially in many
CIS economies.

Figure 2.2: Government balances as a percentage of GDP
(Unweighted averages for selected groups of Central and Eastern Europe, the
Baltics and the Commonwealth of Independant States)

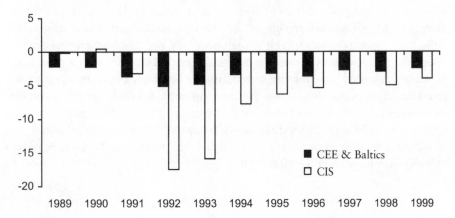

Source: EBRD

On the expenditure side, the transition-related pressures have been equally severe,
although the nature of these pressures in the more advanced transition economies
of Central Europe differs from those in the CIS. In the former, budgetary outlays
on social security increased significantly in the early stages of transition and have
led to the accumulation of large contingent liabilities in state pension systems. In
the CIS and some Eastern European countries, while price liberalisation allowed
a reduction in most budgetary subsidies, various forms of 'off-budget' support
(directed credits, tax and energy payment arrears) have emerged that undermine
the fiscal position of the consolidated government. Fiscal deficits are often associated with the implicit subsidisation of loss-making enterprises.

Large and persistent fiscal imbalances have continued to jeopardise macro-economic stability and growth, especially in the CIS. The perseverance of soft budget constraints has contributed greatly to these deficits. Without the enforcement of hard budget constraints, liberalising markets, freeing prices and privatising state enterprises is almost pointless. The government should refrain from extending credit, directly or indirectly, to the non-financial enterprise sector. Unless hard budget constraints can be imposed on the enterprise sector, stabilisation is virtually guaranteed to go by the board. Explicit or implicit government subsidies distort the incentives faced by firms and will sooner or later show up in the fiscal deficit. There is thus a close link between structural reform at the enterprise level and fiscal reform.

During the early transition period, fiscal deficits were associated with substantial inflation. The development of a broader range of financing options alongside fiscal consolidation were key elements underlying subsequent disinflation attempts. The development of securities markets has allowed a number of countries to finance fiscal deficits in a non-inflationary way, at least in the short run. Public debt levels have increased rapidly in Russia and Ukraine, as they did earlier in Hungary. In Russia and Ukraine, foreign portfolio investors have accounted for a substantial share of new Treasury bill placements. However, as the Russian crisis has illustrated, relying on debt finance and in particular foreign portfolio investment is unsustainable if the underlying causes of government imbalances are not tackled.[9] In emerging markets, fiscal deficits are often seen as a sign of macroeconomic vulnerability causing higher borrowing costs in international markets. Under these conditions, the failure to maintain fiscal discipline can carry substantial costs, once adjustment becomes unavoidable because of a cut-off from external finance. In several transition economies, the level of external debt is such that the government has to be extremely cautious about borrowing abroad to fund current or capital expenditure.

External balance

Current account deficits have been a feature of transition economies for several years. (Figure 2.3). An examination of the unweighted average for each region reveals three distinct phases: an initial sharp increase, as exports slumped and imports became more widely available; a decrease in 1993-94, as stabilisation took hold and output and exports started to recover; and then an increase over

---

9. The inflow of capital into the government securities market will initially push up prices and allow interest rates to fall. Government debt can be refinanced cheaply, while the interest burden on current budgetary outlays is gradually reduced. Yet, if confidence in the government's ability to repay on time and over time is shaken, or if the attractiveness of government paper is reduced relative to other domestic or foreign assets, the cost of servicing the stock of accumulated government debt can increase very rapidly.

1995-98, reflecting the surge in imports and increased capital inflows into the region. Over the past decade, the same path is observed in both the CEECs and the CIS, although the size of the deficits is always bigger in the CIS.

In principle, current account deficits arise naturally in a country in transition where growth has resumed, both from reduced savings rates, as consumer confidence and expectations of rising future incomes increase, and from rising demand for investment to replace existing, mostly obsolete capital stock. Nevertheless, persistently high current account deficits raise doubts about the ability of a country to pay off long-term liabilities in the future. A deficit greater than 5% of GDP is sometimes used as a rule-of-thumb warning sign; 17 out of the 25 countries exceeded this measure in 1998.

Figure 2.3: Current account balance as a percentage of GDP
(Unweighted averages for selected groups of Central and Eastern Europe, the Baltics and the Commonwealth of Independant States)

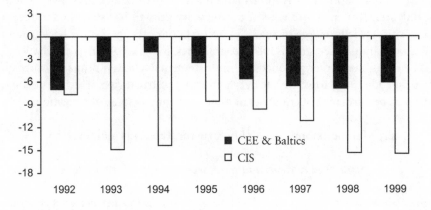

Source: EBRD

Real exchange rates and competitiveness

Another characteristic feature of macroeconomic developments in the transition so far has been the real appreciation of exchange rates.[10] Other things being equal, an increase in the real exchange rate (an appreciation) makes it harder for a country to sell its goods abroad, and in this sense makes a country 'less competitive'. On the other hand, real exchange rate appreciation may reflect productivity increases in the traded goods sector, which enhance a country's competitiveness.[11]

---

10. It is defined as the ratio of the domestic price level to the foreign price level, where the latter is converted to domestic units at the nominal exchange rate.

Exchange rate policy in transition economies was initially targeted primarily at providing price stability. Hence, the majority of countries throughout the region have opted against a fully floating exchange rate, as attempts were made to stabilise inflationary expectations using a nominal exchange rate anchor. Given the substantial currency depreciation and the low level of the real exchange rate experienced at the start of the transition, the subsequent real appreciation does not seem to have affected negatively the external balance in most transition economies (EBRD *Transition Report* 1997). However, as inflation rates have generally come down, the focus of exchange rate policy in many countries has shifted towards sustaining external equilibrium.

Real exchange rate appreciation has been associated with rising unit labour costs in foreign currency terms. The EBRD *Transition Report* 1998 argues that productivity growth has been highest in Central Europe. These productivity improvements have limited the increase in unit labour costs associated with appreciating real exchange rates. However, further disinflation and wage moderation will be required if competitiveness is to be maintained. In many other countries, including Bulgaria, Romania and Russia, productivity growth has stagnated in recent years. This has led to large increases in unit labour costs against the background of exchange-rate-based stabilisation programmes. In these countries, the challenge will be to sustain earlier productivity improvements achieved primarily through labour shedding and to accelerate deep enterprise restructuring, which lies behind the better performance of countries at a more advanced stage of transition.

2.3 Macroeconomic instability, structural reforms and reversals

Structural reforms and macroeconomic performance

In the transition economies, there has been a clear relationship between economic performance at the aggregate level and macroeconomic control. As illustrated in Table 2.3, starting the transition with widely different initial conditions, countries have also differed greatly in the speed and nature of the reform process. Those countries that have shown the strongest commitment to reform are generally also the ones which have simultaneously reduced inflation faster, suffered the smallest GDP and fiscal revenue falls, and witnessed an earlier resumption of growth. The respective medians of all of the indicators for each of the two groups of countries depict consistently the better performance of the faster reformers. For example, the median contraction of GDP at the trough for the advanced reform-

---

11. An increase in productivity in the traded sector will tend to attract scarce resources into that sector, driving up their prices. This would in turn affect production costs in the economy as a whole, which implies a real appreciation of the exchange rate. However, in this case, the impact of the real appreciation on the competitiveness of domestic goods is offset by productivity increases in the tradables sector.

Table 2.3: Progress in transition and macroeconomic performance in Central and Eastern Europe, the Baltics and the CIS

	Central and Eastern Europe and the Baltic States	Commonwealth of Independent States
Private sector share of GDP in %, mid-1998 (EBRD estimate) 1/	65	50
Governance & enterprise restructuring 2/	2.5	2.0
Price liberalisation	3.0	3.0
Banking reform & interest rate liberalisation	3.0	1.5
Maximum annual inflation rates 3/	295.5	5,163.9
Ratio of lowest registered GDP to 1989 GDP	63.2%	40.6%
Annual government expenditures as a % of GDP:		
1993	41.9	46.4
1995	42.0	26.7

Notes:
1/ The 'private sector shares' of GDP represent rough EBRD estimates, based on available statistics from both official (government) sources and unofficial sources. The underlying concept of private sector value added includes income generated by the activity of private registered companies as well as by private entities engaged in informal activity in those cases where reliable information in informal activity is available.
2/ The numerical indicators in rows 2-4 are intended to represent the cumulative progress in the movement from a centrally planned economy to a market economy in each dimension. The index may range from a minimum of 1 (negligible change from the old policies) to a maximum of 4+ (standards and performance typical of advanced industrial economies).
3/ The figures correspond to the median of the annual inflation rate of the year in which inflation peaked.

Source EBRD, *Transition Report 1998*

ers is about one-quarter whereas that for less advanced transition countries is about one-half. The same striking result applies to annual inflation.[12]

In the previous section, it was argued that the main force behind the initial output decline at the onset of the transition process was adverse initial conditions. Berg *et al.* (1999) suggest that output recovery has been driven mainly by structural reforms. In particular, the difference in macroeconomic performance be-

12. Within the CIS, there are a few exceptions to this rule. For instance, as shown in Table 2.1, the output decline in Belarus and in Uzbekistan has been much smaller than in those countries of the CIS that have been more committed to structural reforms over the first decade of transition. This may suggest that delaying reforms can help to limit a strong decline in output. Nevertheless, those countries that have shown the strongest commitment to reforms have recovered most quickly.

tween the CEECs and the FSU (and particularly the timing of the recovery) is most-ly explained by differences in structural reforms, rather than initial conditions. Furthermore, de Melo *et al.* (1997) argue that the efficacy of reforms is not low-er under unfavourable initial conditions.[13] However, unfavourable initial condi-tions can have an indirect effect on performance through their impact on policy choices.

There is some evidence that the impact of structural reform on growth has been different during the so-called 'transition recession' (in the first half of the 1990s) and in the recovery phases. Relatively early work by de Melo *et al.* (1996) calcu-lates the profiles followed on average by inflation and real growth in countries in transition during the years both prior to a reform breakthrough and after. Radi-cal reformers suffer an initial fall in real income of about 13% and a jump in infla-tion to 14% per month during the year following the 'big bang'.[14] Nevertheless, they are able to (i) resume positive growth four years later; and (ii) control infla-tion to just below 3% per month during the fifth year. By contrast, the countries that postponed reform, are able in the beginning to limit real income losses and to maintain low 'official' inflation (typically with the help of price controls).

Havrylyshyn *et al.* (1998) also suggest that in the early period 1990-1993 reforms had a 'U-curve' effect on output, and that limiting reforms helped pre-vent a strong decline in output. However, in the 1994-97 period, the effect of reforms on recovery and growth was unequivocally favourable. Even while acknowledging differences in initial conditions, those countries that moved ahead most quickly and firmly with the implementation of reforms have generally seen the most rapid economic recovery and growth. Those with least reform did most poorly.

A particularly important dimension of reform relates to the financial sector. The extent to which banks in a transition economy can mobilise and allocate cap-ital efficiently and prudently is an important determinant of how well its real economy performs. It is important that banks fulfil their role in mobilising the domestic savings to fund the investment that is necessary to advance the transi-tion and to sustain growth. They can allocate funds to the kind of investment that contributes strongly to structural change and enhanced productivity, particularly by the private sector and by small and medium-sized enterprises. Banks can also provide monetary payments without which markets can operate only at high costs.

---

13. On the contrary, they find evidence that the effectiveness of liberalisation is higher at higher levels of macroeconomic and structural distortions.

14. Larger output falls during transition were associated with higher rather than lower inflation. As stressed by Gomulka (1998), this points to a limited role in output falls of stabilisation-oriented policies, and to an important role of (supply-side and demand-side) shocks that induced both large output falls and high inflation rates.

It is important therefore to know how well financial institutions are performing as intermediaries. As discussed in the EBRD *Transition Report 1998*, the evidence suggests that macroeconomic instability is associated with low levels of activity, high interest margins, and in some cases, high rates of profitability. One response of banks operating in difficult environments has been to accumulate holdings of government securities. While these instruments often yield high returns, these returns reflect the underlying risk associated with macroeconomic stabilisation efforts. In particular, the returns include premiums for the risk of an outburst of inflation or an outright government default, as in the case of Russia in 1998.

Macroeconomic reversals

It was suggested earlier that although stabilisation is a necessary condition for recovery, it is not sufficient. In practice, inflation stabilisation in the CEECs was accompanied by a burst of structural reforms, a pattern not evident in the CIS. A lesson of experience that has been sharply re-emphasised over the past few years is that failure to move forward in reforms beyond the initial steps can eventually destabilise economies and jeopardise earlier achievements. Setbacks in economic stabilisation can be traced to delays and inconsistencies in enterprise and institutional reform. The financial cost of delay burdens budgets and weakens banks, and can ultimately disrupt payment systems and undermine confidence in local currencies.

While comprehensive structural reform was not a precondition for inflation stabilisation, progress in reforms is essential for the maintenance of macroeconomic stability. In this context, and as suggested above, the establishment of hard-budget constraints and the associated termination of inter-enterprise and tax arrears are particularly important. The failure of disinflation attempts, such as in Albania, Bulgaria, Romania and Russia are in part due to the absence of such reforms. Structural weaknesses in public enterprises, in the financial system, in governance structures and in the state, were behind the major episodes of reversals in 1993-1998 (Table 2.4).

In all these countries delays in structural reforms have impeded macroeconomic stabilisation and caused setbacks by inducing additional money creation to finance quasi-fiscal deficits caused by writing off bad debts and clearing of inter-enterprise debt. The absence of structural reform can lead to a proliferation of off-balance-sheet liabilities, thereby increasing the quasi-fiscal deficit. This was the case in Bulgaria, and particularly in Russia, where the lack of restructuring contributed to the increased use of barter and a proliferation of arrears. The financial weaknesses of enterprises had serious adverse effects on the government's fiscal position and ultimately on investor confidence in the government's ability to meet its domestic and international obligations.

Albania, Bulgaria, Romania and Russia stand out as cases where substantial disinflation was reversed in 1997/98. Two factors contributed to the Bulgarian economic crisis. First, for several years the banking system had refinanced the losses of the essentially unreformed state enterprise sector. When liquidity problems developed towards the end of 1995, confidence in the banking sector eroded quickly. Second, money creation spilled over into a loss of international reserves.

Table 2.4: Inflation and output performance in transition economies

	Year(s) in which inflation peaked	Stabilisation programme date	Exchange rate regime adopted at the date of stabilisation	Year in which output was lowest	Ratio of lowest registered GDP to 1989 GDP
Central and Eastern Europe and the Baltic States					
Albania	1992 / 1997	Aug 92	Flexible	1992	60%
Bulgaria	1991 / 1997	Feb 91	Flexible	1997	63%
Croatia	1993	Oct 93	Fixed	1993	60%
Czech Republic	1991	Jan 91	Fixed	1992	85%
Estonia	1992	Jun 92	Fixed	1994	61%
FYR of Macedonia	1992	Jan 94	Fixed	1995	55%
Hungary	1990	Mar 90	Fixed	1993	82%
Latvia	1992	Jun 92	Flexible/Fixed[1]	1995	51%
Lithuania	1992	Jun 92	Flexible/Fixed[1]	1994	53%
Poland	1990	Jan 90	Fixed	1991	82%
Romania	1993 / 1997	Oct 93	Flexible	1992	75%
Slovak Republic	1991	Jan 91	Fixed	1993	75%
Slovenia	1991	Feb 92	Flexible	1992	82%
Commonwealth of Independent States					
Armenia	1993	Dec 94	Flexible/Fixed[2]	1993	31%
Azerbaijan	1994	Jan 95	Flexible/Fixed[2]	1995	37%
Belarus	1993 / 1998	Nov 94	Flexible/Fixed[2]	1995	63%
Georgia	1993	Sep 94	Flexible/Fixed[2]	1994	25%
Kazakhstan	1992	Jan 94	Flexible/Fixed[2]	1998	61%
Kyrgyzstan	1993	May 93	Flexible/Fixed[2]	1995	50%
Moldova	1992	Sep 93	Flexible	1998	32%
Russia	1992 / 1998	Apr 95	Flexible/Fixed[1]	1998	55%
Tajikistan	1993	Feb 95	Flexible	1996	39%
Turkmenistan	1993	Jan 97	Flexible	1997	42%
Ukraine	1993	Nov 94	Flexible	1998	37%
Uzbekistan	1994	Nov 94	Flexible	1995	83%

Notes:
1/ The Latvian currency was pegged to the SDR in February 1994. Lithuania adopted a currency board in April 1994. Russia announced an exchange rate corridor in July 1995. All three countries had flexible exchange rate regimes prior to these dates.
2/ As of 1995, these countries adopted a *de-facto* peg to the US dollar.

Source: Fischer *et al.* (1996), EBRD and national authorities

In Romania, the political commitment to the agriculture and energy sectors has pervaded policy-making, and has undermined initiatives to implement sustained structural and fiscal reform. The Albanian experience, where the emergence of pyramid schemes and the inadequate control of unlicensed deposit takers led to a financial crisis, reveals the cost of delayed financial sector reform. The Russian crisis has emphasised yet again that in the absence of necessary institutional reforms, the economy is vulnerable to macroeconomic instability, which in turn incurs a heavy cost on growth. Sustainable macroeconomic stabilisation in Russia cannot be put in place without accelerating the pace of restructuring in Russian firms, and clarifying the rules under which firms are to be governed.

2.4 International capital flows and contagion

International capital flows into the transition economies can make a significant contribution to realising the region's growth potential. The potential productivity (and profitability) of new capital is likely to be higher than in more mature market environments. The physical and human capital stock in transition economies is large by the standards of middle-income countries but inefficiently employed and partly obsolete. Restructuring investment, combined with improved management and Western technology, offers opportunities for raising the yield of some of the existing capital at relatively low cost. At the same time, domestic financial systems are still unable to offer much support to investors and savings are limited, especially during the recovery from the transition recession when future earnings expectations stimulate consumption.[15] Capital flows have contributed significantly to lowering financing costs. Net capital inflows and associated current account deficits can therefore play a useful role in the region's development if channelled into quality investment.

A country's current account deficit measures the net savings it imports from the rest of the world. To the extent that these savings supplement, rather than substitute for domestic savings, they enhance the investment potential of a country. Moderate current account deficits in countries in transition should be the normal development to expect in the coming years. As growth resumes, expectations of future incomes increase, thereby reducing savings rates in line with inter-temporal consumption smoothing, and second, since much of the existing capital stock has been rendered at least partially obsolete by changing relative prices and new technology, the demand for investment is high during the second phase. This is reinforced by a collapse in investment in the early stages of transition precipitated by a lack of funds and a high degree of uncertainty, leading to the dilapidation of the capital stock, and thus the need for larger investments during the second

---

15. In some countries, FDI has played an important role in addressing the capital shortage related to low domestic savings and limited financial intermediation.

phase of the transition process. As a result, private investment demand is likely to exceed domestic savings during transition, leading to current account deficits.

Both domestic savings and investment have declined from 30% of GDP at the onset of the transition to 15% now, in line with the average for developing countries (Figure 2.4). A significant share of investment is being financed through a current account deficit, *i.e.* by relying on foreign savings. Note that, since Russia has been running a current account surplus and its GDP accounts for roughly half of the region's GDP, the picture for the region excluding Russia is one of much stronger dependence on current account deficits. Of the 26 countries of operations of the EBRD, more than two-thirds recorded current account deficits in excess of 5% of GDP in 1997, and seven countries in the region as a whole had

Figure 2.4: Gross domestic savings and investments as a percentage of GDP

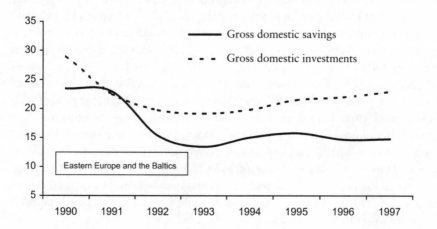

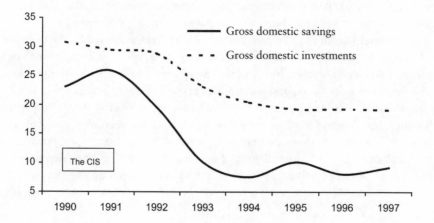

Source: World Bank, *World Development Indicators*

deficits in excess of 10% of GDP. In 1997, only Bulgaria and Slovenia among Eastern European countries, and Russia among the CIS, had a current account surplus, albeit for different reasons.[16]

Although a current account deficit can help transition economies in their reform path, it also increases their vulnerability. Foreign investors' willingness to continue to finance external deficits across the region will depend on their assessment of the ability of transition economies to generate current account surpluses in the future, which would allow them to pay off their accumulated foreign liabilities. This in turn depends on their valuation of the strength of the fiscal system, the competitiveness of enterprises and the stability of the financial system. The 'tequila' crisis of 1995 in Mexico showed the fragility of relying heavily on portfolio investment and short-term borrowing. At the time, the East Asian model was viewed as more robust, given the higher share of foreign direct investment (FDI) in the financing. In the aftermath of the Asian crisis, however, it has become clear that running high current account deficits – other things being equal – leads to fragility whatever the financing.[17]

Institutional investors in emerging markets typically use a 5% threshold as leading indicator of possible balance-of-payments crises. However, in assessing the meaning of this indicator in the countries of Eastern Europe and the CIS, there are two important differences with countries in Latin America or Asia. The first is that, unlike Latin American countries, most economies in transition had very small foreign debt stocks at the outset. The exceptions were Bulgaria, Hungary, Poland and to a lesser extent Russia. As a result, the headroom for borrowing/absorbing FDI – and thereby balancing current account deficits – of these countries was initially larger. A second key difference between transition and developing countries is that in the latter, the process of capital accumulation is such that physical capital leads and human capital lags. In transition economies the relation is just the reverse. Consequently, moderate current account deficits are desirable as long as the corresponding external resources are allocated efficiently according to market signals. The fact that the wealth in human capital of the region is relatively high (together with the other two points noted above) probably means that a given current account deficit to GDP in a transition economy is, *ceteris paribus*, more sustainable than in other developing countries.

In the context of incomplete structural reforms, international capital flows carry considerable risks and may indeed magnify underlying macroeconomic and

---

16. In the case of Bulgaria, this reflects a collapse in imports associated with the severe economic decline in 1996 and early 1997, whereas Slovenia's surplus is a counterpart of controls on capital flows. Russia's was due in large part to substantial exports from natural resources and depressed imports.

17. Data for the region suggest that FDI only represents between one-third and one-quarter of the net capital flows into the region (Lankes and Stern, 1998). In 1997, total FDI into the region as a whole, Russia included, was around 18 billion dollars, while Mexico alone with a population of one quarter of that of the region – attracted 13 billion dollars in the same year.

structural weaknesses. As mentioned earlier, in a number of transition economies, macroeconomic policy is complicated by the existence of large structural imbalances. Tensions within the macroeconomic policy mix of several countries, including Poland in 1995 and the Czech and Slovak Republics and Russia in 1996-97 have been a major reason for the attraction of short-term portfolio flows. Significant uncovered interest differentials emerged as the result of tight monetary policies and pegged exchange rates, combined with a loose fiscal stance. In Russia, for instance, returns on investments in government securities in mid-1997 averaged 50% in foreign currency terms. Even higher returns were offered in some other CIS economies. Macroeconomic policy inconsistencies in these countries often result from severe structural imperfections.[18] Thus, for at least part of these flows, it was the *absence* of transition combined with a reasonably liberal access for foreign investors that made investment attractive. In addition, the financial institutions and markets that intermediate part of these funds are still highly immature in many countries in transition. This heightens the risk of bank failures and associated dangers of volatility in capital flows.

While it will be vital for the region to maintain the achievements in establishing current account convertibility, a sequencing of capital account liberalisation may therefore need to be considered. A gradual approach to financial market integration could conceivably allow economies at earlier stages of transition to reap some of the benefits of exposure to international capital, particularly in its longer-term varieties, while limiting the downside of volatility. The empirical evidence on capital controls suggests that, during the early stages of international financial integration, specific controls on short-term capital inflows have been able to affect temporarily the level and the composition of capital flows.[19] In practice, restrictions on capital flows have taken many forms and have varied greatly in effectiveness.

Contagion

The level and quality of private capital flows depends crucially on perceptions of risks and returns. These, in turn, depend not only on basic endowments and

---

18. For instance, fiscal deficits are often associated with the implicit subsidisation of loss-making enterprises. Because many of the necessary structural reforms require time, these economies are particularly vulnerable to inflows of short-term risk capital exploiting tensions in the resulting macroeconomic policy mix.

19. The efficacy of capital controls depends on a large number of factors, such as the size of misalignment motivating inflows and outflows, the types of cross-border flows targeted by the controls, the size of trade flows (determining the scope for under and over-invoicing as well as for altering leads and lags on trade credit), the structure of the domestic financial system, the state of technology and the efficiency of the controlling bureaucracy (for more detail see World Bank, 1997). In general, domestic residents may be more prepared than foreign residents to evade restrictions, making controls on outflows less effective than controls on inflows.

potential opportunities but also on the ability to respond to opportunities in an effective, market-oriented fashion, or more generally the 'investment climate' in recipient countries. One reflection of the importance of the investment climate is that the level, location, and motive of FDI into the transition economies are all strongly associated with progress in transition. For instance, leaving out the three oil and gas economies of Central Asia (Azerbaijan, Kazakhstan and Turkmenistan), the rank correlation coefficient for 22 countries between the EBRD's average indicator of transition in 1998[20] and cumulative FDI *per capita* over the period 1989-98 is almost 0.9. This provides strong support for the conclusion that it is the reform process which opens opportunities for profitable investment and which, through its impact on risks and returns, motivates investors to take advantage of them. It also suggests that direct equity investors have carefully evaluated the economic environment and made informed choices.

The recent crisis in emerging markets, and the path of contagion in the transition economies, has further reinforced this pattern. Financial contagion has not affected the region across the board. Indeed, the Central European countries that have made the greatest progress in market reforms and in controlling macroeconomic imbalances, have been among the most resilient 'emerging markets' in 1998. After an initial, somewhat indiscriminate, reduction of emerging market exposure by international investors following the Russian devaluation and debt default of August 1998, there has been increasing differentiation across countries.

FDI in fact increased in 10 countries in Central Europe, and for this part of the region rose from 9 billion dollars in 1997 to 16 billion dollars in 1998. In Russia it fell by 2.6 billion dollars over this period and remained relatively constant at low levels in the rest of the CIS (see Chapter 4). FDI tends to be less volatile than other types of capital flows in the face of macroeconomic instability. However, all types have reflected broadly a similar pattern. Countries in Central Europe are experiencing a gradual revival of portfolio investment and commercial bank lending, and a near-return to pre-crisis bond yields, whereas much of the CIS remains reliant on official funding to cover financing gaps. There could hardly be clearer evidence that in Eastern Europe and the former Soviet Union domestic policies and reform orientation are key determinants of the size and sustainability of capital inflows.

Fries, Raiser and Stern (1999) analysed the vulnerability of transition economies to macroeconomic and financial instability following the market turmoil in East Asia. They revealed considerable differentiation across the region. Those countries at earlier stages of transition which were affected by emerging market turmoil had significant structural weaknesses in fiscal policy, including low general government revenues and high deficits. In many of the more advanced countries, such as Estonia, weaknesses in the financial sector contributed to the speed and intensity with which market turmoil spread. Central to the stable financing

---

20. See *Transition Report 1998*, EBRD London, for methodology.

of fixed investment in the transition economies is the creation of a legal, regulatory, and institutional framework, which is supportive of long-term finance.

2.5 Going forward

Growth prospects

Across the world, episodes of rapid economic growth, taken as sustained annual rates of growth in GDP *per capita* above 3% for two to three decades, have been quite rare. In general, these episodes are associated with growth phases in which relatively underdeveloped countries have caught up with the more advanced economies of the time, including recovery from major dislocation and in particular from the destruction of war. This process typically involves modernisation of relatively backward economies through high rates of investment and significant improvements in productivity.[21]

In transition economies, the positive relationship between market-oriented reforms and short-term growth suggests further potential for growth through the more efficient use of existing resources. However, over the medium term, the growth rates of transition economies will be determined both by structural change and restructuring, and by investment in plant and equipment and the introduction of new technologies.

Growth will be driven by the new private sector. After being virtually non-existent in most of the region during central planning, small and medium enterprises (SMEs) are increasingly an important driving force of growth. In most countries of Central and Eastern Europe, companies with less than 50 employees account for the largest share of newly created jobs. While definitions vary and the quality of statistics is poor (a reflection perhaps of the limited interest of the authorities in many countries), the share of registered SMEs in total employment now appears to vary from less than 10% in countries like Azerbaijan and Belarus to more than two-thirds in the more advanced Central European countries and the Baltics, comparable to the EU average of about 70%.

As discussed at some length in EBRD's *Transition Report 1997*, transition economies are generally well-placed for rapid growth after their initial period of transition because of their high level of acquired skills and the significant initial technological deficits. These factors point to long-term average annual growth rates in the range of 4 to 7% for most countries. To realise this potential, peace, order, stability, and a market-oriented government will be a prerequisite. The establishment of institutions that will create incentives for high investment and

---

21. Episodes of rapid growth since the late nineteenth century are confined primarily to Western Europe and Japan after the Second World War and to East Asian economies in the recent past.

rapid productivity growth will be required. If further improvement in institutions does not materialise, long-term growth prospects will look much less favourable.

Policies and institutions for macroeconomic stability

As highlighted earlier, the evidence shows clearly that the level, location and motive of foreign investment are all strongly associated with progress in transition. It is the reform process which opens opportunities for profitable investment and which, through its impact on returns and risk, motivates investors to take advantage of them.

Therefore, in order to establish a favourable climate for investment and market-oriented growth, the countries of the region must press ahead with structural reforms. The first phase of liberalisation and privatisation has established a market economy of sorts. The deeper challenges of the next phase are to make these nascent market economies function more effectively and to build on the foundations established in the first phase. Institutional and governance issues will be crucial elements of the next phase.

The challenges of the next phase are closely interconnected and include:

- State structures and behaviour which provide weak support for, or which are hostile to, an open competitive market economy, including bureaucratic interference, vexatious and ill-designed tax systems and weak tax administration, precarious fiscal positions, weak regulatory and supervisory structures for banking/finance, infrastructure, environment, competition *etc.*, weak legal systems and corruption.
- Systematic problems in markets, including weak financial systems which can be manipulated by insiders or governments, poorly developed capital markets, oligopolistic practices from special groups which acquired (or 'grabbed') powerful positions in the first phase of transition, clogged payment systems and extensive use of barter, and barriers to entry and expansion for SMEs.
- Systematic problems in enterprises and in infrastructure, including infrastructure that functions poorly (in terms of revenues, cost and delivery) and is inadequately oriented to the needs and principles of a market economy, ownership structures and practices which lead to weak corporate governance, and unsound business practices.
- Social issues, including the growth of poverty, extreme inequalities in income and wealth, deterioration in health care and public health, declining life expectancy in many CIS countries, problems in reallocating and restructuring pension responsibilities, serious problems of housing, and crime.

Although some of these challenges are also faced by countries outside the region, they are challenges that are intrinsic to the transition. Most of them arise in some shape or form in all countries of the region but are, in many respects, deeper and more intractable in the CIS. They are interconnected and they all relate to interconnections between public and private sectors as well as to the functions of the individual sectors. They continue to create an investment climate that, notwithstanding the great opportunities in the region, can be very discouraging and difficult.

The prospects for investment and growth, indeed for the transition itself, depend on the response to the challenges described above. The central and critical influences will be the policies and behaviour of governments in the transition countries themselves. It is they who will have to strengthen the foundations for a favourable investment climate through progress in structural reform and institution building efforts. However, the domestic private sector also has a strong responsibility to pursue the sound business practices that underpin a healthy market economy. Furthermore, countries outside the region and International Financial Institutions have a major role to play in fostering market-oriented development. In particular, they must promote the private sector development that in turn promotes stability and long-term growth.

2.6 Conclusions

Looking forward, managing the fiscal aspects of transition will remain a crucial challenge for macroeconomic policy and structural reforms alike. For a number of countries, particularly in the CIS, the problem of low revenue collection reflects a lack of tax discipline in three dimensions, in all of which corruption plays an important role. First, tax evasion is widespread, especially in countries with a large informal economy. Many payments are by cash and unrecorded.[22] Barter is also widespread in the CIS and tax collection on such transactions is often impossible. In addition, evasion is facilitated by the ambiguous and complicated tax codes of many countries in the region. Second, tax avoidance is very common. Numerous tax concessions and tax breaks leave companies much room for manoeuvre and civil servants with great discretion. In many countries in the region, the tax authorities have become an important instrument of harassment by tax officers, which has a damaging impact on entrepreneurial activity. Third, many governments remain lenient with enterprises that have large tax debts. This problem is particularly acute in Russia, where tax arrears have grown from 3.2% of GDP at end-1994 to 12.2% of GDP at end-1997. Also, in 1997 about 20% of federal tax revenues were paid in barter or through offsets.

Increasing tax revenue in the CIS is important not simply to control deficits but also to provide revenues to meet obligations to pensioners and government workers, to maintain health and education expenditures, and to invest in rebuilding crumbling infrastructures. Without the revenues, the fabric of the state and of social expenditures cannot be sustained. It is not, however, just a question of rais-

---

22. Despite the ban on cash payments over a certain amount in many transition economies.

ing revenues. Significant efficiency gains can also be made on the expenditure side, for instance in the area of implicit subsidies.

The fiscal challenges in the CEECs are also severe, although somewhat different in nature. Tax revenues are much higher than in the CIS, but expenditures are burdened by high levels of pension and other social payments. The challenge is to change those commitments in a way that can relieve fiscal pressures while limiting social hardships. While a 'first pillar' of publicly provided pensions should be a central element of any pension system, there can also be an important role for a 'second pillar' of private and mandatory pensions. Such a move will facilitate the reform of underfunded public pensions systems as well as contribute to the development of local capital markets and the institutions that contribute to them. It would be dangerous, however, to underestimate the time scale, complexities and the costs involved in building the second pillar. Other key elements in the reform of pension systems involve changes in retirement ages, benefit levels and eligibility rates.

Most countries in Central and Eastern Europe are working towards accession to the EU. Ten countries have formally applied for EU membership, with accession, at least for some, likely to take place in the first decade of the next century. Membership of the EU carries a number of responsibilities in terms of minimum environmental and regulatory standards and harmonisation of taxes, and therefore implies changes in revenue and expenditure. These required changes provide further impetus to the process of fiscal reform.

A second macroeconomic challenge arises from increased investment demand and associated external imbalances. For sustainable growth in the medium term, national savings rates have to follow the upward trend of investment rates. However, on the available evidence, savings rates are not generally rising. While recognising the advantages of foreign direct investment and foreign savings during a period of reconstruction, the ability to service debt-associated inflows must be created alongside the investment. At the heart of the policy response to the challenge of sustaining growing investment and high capital inflows throughout the region must be sound fiscal policy (yielding public savings), measures to raise private savings, a favourable investment climate for equity investments, and strong financial institutions and corporate governance to provide productive use of investment.

A third challenge is that of rising real exchange rates, which put strong pressure on productivity improvements. Although a rising real exchange rate is to be expected during the transition, this appreciation can lead to a lack of competitiveness if productivity does not increase to match it. The increase in productivity must come from further reforms and investments.

As illustrated throughout this chapter, there is an intricate and mutually reinforcing relationship between macroeconomic performance and structural reform. Stabilisation policies interact closely with liberalisation policies, with structural reforms, and with institution-building efforts. Although macroeconomic stabilisation is a necessary prerequisite for growth, it is not a sufficient condition. As has been illustrated by the reform reversals in Bulgaria (1996/97), Romania (1997) and Russia (1998), structural reform and the functioning of market institutions (including the elimination of soft-budget constraints) are essential if macroeconomic stability is to be sustained.

A few years ago, some economists (*e.g.* Fischer *et al.*, 1997) predicted that the CIS would follow a similar path to that of the CEECs, but with a two to three year lag, taking into account the later start (1991/92 as opposed to 1989/90). This was at a time when it looked as though growth in the CIS, just positive in 1997, would become established. With hindsight, we can now see that this was unrealistic. The institutional foundations and social capital in the CEECs are much stronger than in the CIS. The prospect of joining the EU also offers a powerful incentive for institutional change. The enterprises of the CEECs have shown their ability to compete on world markets and their growth prospects seem much more secure than those of the CIS. For Russia and the CIS on the other hand, the forces for sustained growth are not yet firmly established.

References

Balcerowicz, L. (1994), 'Common Fallacies in the Debate on the Transition to a Market Economy', *Economic Policy* No.19, pp.18-50.

Berg, A., E. Borensztein, R. Sahay and J. Zettelmeyer (1999), 'The Evolution of Output in Transition Economies: Explaining the Differences', IMF *Working Paper*, forthcoming.

Bruno, M. and W. Easterly (1998), 'Inflation Crises and Long-Run Growth', *Journal of Monetary Economics*, No.41, pp.3-26.

Christoffersen, P. and P. Doyle (1998), 'From Inflation to Growth: Eight Years of Transition', IMF *Working Paper*, WP/98/100.

Cottarelli, C. and P. Doyle (1999), 'Disinflation in Transition: 1993-97', IMF *Occasional Papers*, forthcoming.

De Melo, M., C. Denizer and A. Gelb (1996), 'From Plan to Market: Patterns of Transition', *World Bank Policy Research Paper*, No.1564.

De Melo, M., C. Denizer, A. Gelb and S. Tenev (1997), 'Circumstances and Choice: the Role of Initial Conditions and Policies in Transition Economies', *World Bank Policy Research Working Paper*, No.1866.

European Bank for Reconstruction and Development, *Transition Report*, London, various issues.

Fischer, S., R. Sahay and C.A. Végh (1997), 'From Transition to Market: Evidence and Growth Prospects', in S. Zecchini (ed.), *Lessons from the Economic Transition: Central and Eastern Europe in the 1990s*, pp.79-102, Kluwer Academic Publishers.

Fries, S., M. Raiser and N. Stern (1999), 'Stress Test for Reforms: Transition and East Asian Contagion', *The Economics of Transition*, Vol. 7, No.2, pp.535-567.

Gomulka, S. (1998), 'A comment on David Begg', in C. Cottarelli and G. Szapary (eds.), *Moderate Inflation: The Experience of Transition Economies*, IMF and Bank of Hungary, Washington, D.C.

Ghosh, A. R. (1997), 'Inflation in Transition Economies: How Much? And Why', *IMF Working Paper*, WP/97/80.

Havrylyshyn, O. and P. Botousharov (1995), 'Five Years of Transition' *Bank Review*, No.4, Bulgarian National Bank.

Havrylyshyn, O., I. Izvorski and R. van Rooden (1998), 'Recovery and Growth in Transition Economies 1990-97: A Stylized Regression Analysis', *IMF Working Paper*, WP/98/141.

Kaufmann, D. and A. Kaliberda (1996), 'Integrating the Unofficial Economy into the Dynamics of Post-Socialist Economies: A Framework of Analysis and Evidence', *World Bank Policy Research Paper*, No.1691.

Lankes, H. P. and N. Stern (1998), 'Capital Flows to Eastern Europe and the Former Soviet Union', *EBRD Working Papers*, No.27.

Loungani P. and N. Sheets (1997), 'Central Bank Independence, Inflation and Growth in Transition Economies', *Journal of Money, Credit and Banking*, Vol.29, pp.381-399.

World Bank (1997), *The Road to Financial Integration: Private Capital Flows to Developing Countries*, Washington, D.C.

Transition and Institutional Change

Marko Bos, George Gelauff and Ruud de Mooij

3.1 Introduction

Ten years of transition in Central and Eastern Europe have substantially deepened our understanding of the functioning of a modern market economy. They have revealed its systemic complexity and the difficulties of creating it from scratch. The transformation process entails far more than simply liberalising the economy and discarding the system of central planning. A consensus has grown that the development of a new institutional infrastructure is an essential element of the systemic change, and that it takes time and effort to create such an infrastructure (*e.g.* Stiglitz, 1999, p.6). As Nellis (1999, p.18) puts it: "... capitalism requires much more than private property; it functions because of the widespread acceptance and enforcement in an economy of fundamental rules and safeguards that make the outcomes of exchange secure, predictable and widely beneficial. Where such rules and safeguards are absent, what suffer are not only fairness and equity but firms' performance".

This chapter addresses the progress in institution building in twelve Central and Eastern European countries (CEECs), namely the ten candidate members of the European Union as well as Russia and Ukraine. The approach chosen is more general than the one used in the negotiations for accession to the European Union (EU), which takes as a reference point the *acquis communautaire*, *i.e.* the set of rules and common policies of the EU. In particular, Section 3.2 develops an analytical framework to explore the link between institutions and economic performance. Accordingly, we judge the institutional developments in the twelve CEECs from a more general economic perspective. After examining some recent institutional developments in CEECs in Section 3.3, Section 3.4 discusses challenges for the future, thereby focussing on path dependency and on accession to the European Union.

3.2 Institutions and economic performance[1]

Institutions are "the rules of the game in a society", "the humanly devised constraints that shape human interaction" (North, 1990, p.3). These constraints can be formal rules (regulations) and contracts as well as conventions and self-imposed codes of behaviour. Institutions can be created or may simply evolve over time. They provide the rules of the game for organisations (like government agencies, firms and trade unions) that structure human interaction to some common purpose. The evolution of organisations is influenced by the institutional framework; in turn organisations tend to influence the evolution of the institutional framework.

This section discusses why institutions matter for economic performance. To structure the discussion on institutions, Sections 3.2.1-3.2.4 successively review the four mechanisms that can co-ordinate economic behaviour in a market economy, namely:

- competition: rivalry between agents striving for something not obtainable by all;
- control: the power of an agent to take decisions and impose these on others;
- common values and norms: congruent sets of preferences within a group of economic agents;
- co-operative exchange: bargained cooperation between independent agents with different preferences.

Institutional design can be regarded as the selection of a set of institutions that support a particular co-ordination mechanism. The four co-ordination mechanisms all have their potential strengths and weaknesses. Section 3.2.5 discusses trade-offs involved in institution building.

3.2.1 Competition

Competition involves the most elementary co-ordination mechanism in a market economy. Guided by the invisible hand of the market mechanism, competition ensures that people choose those actions that, in equilibrium, appear to be in their common interest. In ideal circumstances, competition achieves efficient allocation, adequately conveys information about relative scarcities through price signals, and provides incentives for individual flexibility.

In a stylised neo-classical framework, competition does not need many institutions to function well. Secure property rights and a well-functioning market mechanism go a long way to achieving efficient allocation and welfare maximi-

---

1. This section heavily draws on Chapter 2 of the CPB Netherlands Bureau for Economic Policy Analysis (1997).

sation. In reality, however, it is difficult to find the neo-classical economic agent who is rational and equipped with perfect foresight. Indeed, ample examples exist of economic agents who make systematic reasoning errors because their human cognition is limited. In principle, agents should be able to oversee all relevant contingencies, assign probabilities to each of these contingencies and take a fully informed decision or write a comprehensive contract. In practice, it would be irrational to act in such a way because deliberation takes time and effort. Economising on deliberation costs explains why people generally apply a heuristic approach to decision making. This means that people are boundedly rational. Accordingly, economic agents possess only limited knowledge of their environment and the actions of other agents: imperfect foresight and information asymmetries characterise economic exchange.

Besides costly deliberation, transaction costs complicate the co-ordination of decisions among economic agents. *Ex-ante* transaction costs comprise the costs of gathering information on the relevant conditions affecting the transaction and the resources devoted to itemising and writing possibly detailed actions in complex contracts. *Ex-post* transaction costs consist of the costs of monitoring, enforcement and possible default. Transaction costs make it infeasible to design comprehensive contracts which specify all parties' obligations in all possible future states of the world and which are interpretable and perfectly enforceable in court. Hence, contracts are incomplete.

Imperfect foresight, information asymmetries and incomplete contracts constitute important reasons why market competition may fail as a co-ordination mechanism. Furthermore, markets may fail in producing an optimal outcome in the presence of externalities or market power. Therefore, the functioning of a market economy in real life can be improved by the implementation of institutions. These institutions may facilitate each of the three alternative co-ordination mechanisms discussed below.

3.2.2 Control

The co-ordination mechanism of control means that one party can impose its will on another party, *e.g.* government intervention. This provides certainty to private agents. For instance, due to legal rules and regulations, participants need not perform long search actions or incur large costs to guard against the opportunism of others.

Yet, control is not the ultimate answer to market failures: there may be government failures as well. Command and control measures often take away incentives and may invoke rent-seeking behaviour. Compliance costs and the costs of gathering information may prohibit the exercise of effective control. Controllers may give in to interest groups or may pursue private interests, which distorts the intentions of the control measures. The past performance of transition countries illustrates the limits of the control mechanism to guide economic behaviour.

3.2.3 Common values and norms

Common values and norms pertain to congruent sets of preferences within a group of people and form the guiding co-ordination principle within communities. Repeated interaction promotes spontaneous solidarity, consensus, and common values and norms. Social norms can be interpreted as implicit social contracts to co-operate, embedded in customs and rituals. Agents voluntarily aim at a mutually beneficial outcome.

Yet, common values and norms and solidarity may take a long time to develop, while they can be destroyed quickly. In particular when circumstances change rapidly, social norms may cease to be adequate, information asymmetries may intensify and the ability of members of the group to monitor the behaviour of others may decline. Free riders threaten the internal coherence and consensus within a community. Members may take advantage of information asymmetries by pretending to act in the interest of the community, while in reality they pursue their own goals and exploit the solidarity of other members (moral hazard).

3.2.4 Co-operative exchange

Co-operative exchange takes an intermediate position compared with the other co-ordination mechanisms. It involves bargained consultation and cooperation between a limited number of otherwise independent parties. Parties may be private firms, but also organised interest groups or even the government. For instance, a supplier and a procuring corporation can enter into a co-operative-exchange arrangement which focuses on product design. Likewise, unions and employers' organisations bargain about wages but may co-operate on the organisation of a vocational training program. Consultation and co-operation enhance learning processes and improve the problem-solving capabilities of the parties concerned; they provide a way to internalise externalities.

Apart from the issues that parties co-operate upon, their relationship may be competitive. This provides incentives to stay alert and innovative, to exploit market opportunities and to adjust quickly to a changing environment. However, it also implies that a party may exploit information asymmetries or may abuse the co-operative stance of the other party. In addition, co-operative exchange can turn into collusion when the parties use their relationship to restrict entry in the relevant market. Furthermore, although co-operative exchange may improve internal flexibility, *i.e.* the ability of parties to adjust the subject matter of their co-operation quickly, it typically exacerbates external rigidities. Indeed, switching between partners is more difficult and sometimes the co-operative-exchange relationship takes precedence over market opportunities.

3.2.5 Trade-offs in institution building

The four co-ordination mechanisms discussed above all have their potential strengths and weaknesses (see Box 3.1). The comparative strengths of each of the co-ordination mechanisms manifest themselves differently in different social, technological and economic conditions. For instance, competition may generally be more appropriate in a heterogeneous society, and co-operative exchange or common values and norms more easily develop in a homogeneous society.

For each co-ordination issue, the performance characteristics of each co-ordination mechanism should be judged on the basis of social preferences and circumstances. In principle, this leads to an optimal outcome. In practice, however, it is not possible to derive a single clear-cut optimal institutional configuration for a modern market economy. A more fruitful way of thinking is therefore in terms of trade-offs: *e.g.* between diversity and economies of scale, between external flexibility and commitment or between incentives and solidarity. These trade-offs reflect the fact that 'solving' one problem through institutional adjustment may create new problems. Accordingly, institution building is typically a process of social innovation, consisting of trial and error in search for the optimal trade-off.

Shifts in social preferences or in circumstances can change a country's performance characteristics and therefore their position on the trade-offs. This may call for institutional adjustments. However, shifting between co-ordination mecha-

Box 3.1: Mechanisms that co-ordinate economic behaviour in a market economy

	Potential strengths	Potential weaknesses
Competition (market)	allocation, information dissemination, incentives, experimentation	rent seeking, transaction costs, commitment, income distribution
Control (legislation, regulation, court order)	enforcement, certainty, policy implementation	incentives, rentseeking, information and compliance costs, capture by interest groups
Common Values and Norms (family, volunteer group, church, team)	motivation, commitment, internal flexibility	free riders, external rigidity, lack of privacy
Cooperative Exchange (supplier relationship, industrial relations, research joint venture)	mutual learning, incentives, internal flexibility	enforcement, abuse of cooperation, external rigidity

nisms is a complex and lengthy process, because institutions are interrelated and rooted in society and reforms can be encumbered by entrenched entitlements and vested interests. Furthermore, institutional change can be costly because the government might lose its reputation, which may discourage risky private investments. Indeed, private agents often base their (long-term) decisions on the expectation that institutions will remain unchanged in the future.

The discussion above gives rise to two major challenges for transition countries in institution building. First, there are certain minimum conditions on institutions that underpin each of the co-ordination mechanisms. The next section elaborates on how the institutional framework in transition countries has evolved in the light of these minimum conditions. Second, transition countries face trade-offs in institution design. Indeed, in determining the transition path towards an institutional framework, countries also determine their position on the trade-offs. It is of critical importance to clearly face these trade-offs, especially in the light of the difficulties in changing an institutional framework at a later date. The next section illustrates some of these trade-offs in the process of institution design.

3.3 Institutional change in Central and Eastern Europe

This section provides an overview of institutional change in the transition countries. We discuss the institutional developments on the basis of the functioning of each of the four co-ordination mechanisms derived in Section 3.2: competition, control, common values and norms and co-operative exchange.

A comprehensive review of the institutional structure in each of the twelve CEECs is beyond the scope of this chapter. Instead, we identify common trends in the process of institution building and highlight the performance of countries in some specific cases. Accordingly, we give a rather general judgement of institutional change in CEECs.

Extensive use is made of the EBRD transition indicators, presented in its most recent *Transition Report* (see Tables 3.1, 3.2 and 3.4). These indicators can be used to make a rigorous comparison of the process of market-oriented transition. As noted by the EBRD (1998), the numerical indicators are intended to serve only as summaries of a detailed qualitative analysis of progress and do not cover all the relevant aspects of the transition process. The indicators range from 1 to 4+, where 1 denotes the poorest possible performance on a particular issue, and 4+ stands for good performance, *i.e.* performance similar to developed countries in Western Europe. At the bottom of the tables and in the main text, we provide a more detailed explanation of what is meant by good and bad performance.

3.3.1 Competition

Competition was virtually absent in the CEECs before the transition but forms the heart of any market economy. For markets to be introduced, transition economies needed to liberalise prices and trade, promote the functioning of markets, harden the budget constraints of firms and fundamentally reform the financial sector. These aspects will be discussed below.

Prices, markets and trade

Price liberalisation is important to inform market participants about the relative scarcity of goods and resources and will induce the right incentives which will lead to an efficient allocation. At an early stage of the transition, countries have liberalised most prices, although state procurement remained important for housing rents, transport and public utilities. Among the most advanced countries, Estonia is a notable exception, still controlling prices for goods and services that account for one-quarter of the CPI basket (EBRD, 1999, p.19).

The Europe Agreements have triggered a drastic liberalisation of the import regimes of the CEECs and are designed to establish duty-free trade in industrial goods with the EU. Liberalisation of trade and foreign exchange have now resulted in WTO membership for a number of CEECs, although Lithuania, Estonia, Russia and Ukraine have not yet received membership. Trade liberalisation has resulted in a substantial degree of economic integration of most CEECs with the industrialised world, thereby reaping the gains from increased specialisation, import of new technologies and enhanced competition.

Privatisation, corporate governance and hard budget constraints

In the twelve transition countries studied, the private sector now produces between 50% and 75% of GDP (see Table 3.1). This is a big step forward within a decade. The simple fact of being privatised, however, does not guarantee that a firm is subject to hard budget constraints and effective corporate governance – conditions for the efficient use of resources. Indeed, budget constraints are softened by state aids, soft loans, inter-enterprise arrears and ineffective bankruptcy enforcement.

The sheer size of it already makes the privatisation of large and medium-sized enterprises in transition countries a difficult exercise. The transition indicators in Table 3.1 reveal that, in many countries, less than half of the large former state-owned enterprises are in private hands (indicated by a ranking less than 4). The privatisation of these firms is complicated by factors like the divergent and partially conflicting objectives of privatisation[2], the absence of a mature, well-functioning capital market and of a modern legal infrastructure. Various methods of

---

2. The World Bank (1996, p.52) distinguishes five objectives: better corporate governance, speed and feasibility, better access to capital and skills, more government revenue, and greater fairness.

Table 3.1: Transition indicators for 1998 for privatisation and liberalisation

	EBRD transition indicators						
	Liberalisation			Privatisation			
	Prices[a]	Trade[b]	Competition policy[c]	Large firms[d]	Small firms[d]	Corporate governance structure[e]	Private sector share in GDP (1997, in %)
Poland	3+	4+	3	3+	4+	3	65
Hungary	3+	4+	3	4	4+	3+	75
Czech Republic	3	4+	3	4	4+	3	75
Estonia	3	4	3-	4	4+	3	70
Slovenia	3	4+	2	3+	4+	3-	50
Latvia	3	4	3-	3	4	3-	60
Lithuania	3	4	2+	3	4	3-	70
Slovak Republic	3	4+	3	4	4+	3-	75
Bulgaria	3	4	2	3	3	2+	50
Romania	3	4	2	3-	3+	2	60
Russia	3-	2+	2+	3+	4	2	70
Ukraine	3	3-	2	2+	3+	2	50

4+   reflects the performance of an advanced industrial economy.

[a] 3 =   good progress in price liberalisation, state procurement is phased out.

[b] 2 =   some liberalisation of trade; non-transparent exchange rate regime.
3 =   removal of most trade restrictions; more transparency; current-account convertibility.

[c] 2 =   legislation/institutions are set up; some reduction of entry restrictions; some action on dominant firms.
3 =   more action to promote competitive environment, break-up of dominant conglomerates.

[d] 2 =   small firms: substantial share privatised; large firms: comprehensive scheme ready for implementation.
3 =   small firms: nearly comprehensive programme implemented; large firms: more than 25% in private hands.
4 =   small firms: complete privatisation; large firms: more than 50% in private hands.

[e] 2 =   credit and subsidy policy moderately tight; weak enforcement of bankruptcy legislation.
3 =   actions to harden budget constraints and promote effective corporate governance; privatisation combined with tight credit and subsidy policy and enforcement of bankruptcy legislation.

Source: EBRD, 1998

privatisation have been applied but none of them is without drawbacks (Bos-Kar-czewska, 1993). Hence, the privatisation process is full of trade-offs; these, how-ever, are rather often not explicated.

Nellis (1999, pp.17-18) summarises the critique on the practice of privatisation in CEECs as follows: "In many transition countries, mass and rapid privatisation turned over mediocre assets to large numbers of people who had neither the skills nor the financial resources to use them well. Most high-quality assets have gone, in one way or another (sometimes through the 'spontaneous privatisation' that preceded official schemes, sometimes through manipulation of the voucher schemes, and perhaps most often and acutely in the non-voucher second phases), to the resourceful, agile and politically well-connected few, who have tended not to embark on the restructuring that might have justified their acquisitions of the assets. (...) These outcomes have been most pronounced where the post-transition state structures have been weak and fractured, allowing parts of the government to be captured by groups whose major objective is to use the state to legitimise or mask their acquisition of wealth".

This critique applies primarily to the transition countries with the weakest insti-tutional infrastructure but is not irrelevant to the more advanced countries. As there is no real alternative to privatisation of state-owned enterprises – would it really be better to keep them in the hands of a weak and venal state? – the obvi-ous solution is to create the institutional preconditions for a successful privatisa-tion in the longer run: effective corporate governance, effective financial institu-tions, and an effective public administration. The voucher privatisation, most broadly applied in the Czech Republic, does not seem to provide a way out. It does not solve the problem of monitoring the managers' performance; it only shifts it from the enterprise level to the level of the voucher investment funds (Stiglitz, 1999, p.11).[3]

Bankruptcy procedures have been effective only in a few transition countries. In some transition countries, most notably Russia, financial discipline has deteri-orated recently.

Financial markets

Financial institutions and markets play a crucial role in the allocation of resources in a market economy. Indeed, they form the intermediary between supply and demand for capital, establish hard budget constraints on enterprises and sub-stantially lower the cost of market transactions. The challenges for transition

---

3. Frydman *et al.* (1997), however, conclude on the basis of a 1994 survey that privatisation funds do as well at revitalising privatised companies as other outside owners, finding no evi-dence that they are less effective than 'strategic' investors.

Table 3.2: Financial transition indicators

	Non-performing loans in % of total loans (1997)	Transition indicators	
		Banking sector[a]	Insurance sector[b]
Poland	10	3+	3+
Hungary	4	4	3+
Czech Republic	29	3	3
Estonia	1	3+	3
Slovenia	12	3	3
Latvia	10	3-	2+
Lithuania	28	3	2+
Slovak Republic	33	3-	2+
Bulgaria	13	3-	2
Romania	57	2+	2
Russia	4	2	2-
Ukraine	11	2	2

4+ reflects the performance of an advanced industrial economy

[a] 2 = liberalisation of interest rates and credit allocation.
   3 = progress in bank solvency; prudential supervision and regulation; significant presence of private banks and lending to private enterprises.
   4 = well-functioning banking sector.
[b] 2 = formation of securities exchanges, market makers and brokers; rudimentary legal and regulatory framework.
   3 = emergence of non-bank institutions; substantial issuance of securities by private firms and corresponding institutions established.

Source: EBRD, 1998

countries in this field are huge. Securities markets have to be created from scratch. Banks have to change their role from a passive bookkeeping authority (the mono-bank) towards an active financial intermediary. This requires new reporting and accounting systems, effective prudential regulations and supervision by the government, and the development of new skills and practices by employees. Moreover, state banks need to be restructured, re-capitalised and privatised.

In spite of the progress made in recent years, the financial sector in most transition economies is still underdeveloped compared with that of market economies at a comparable level of economic development. It is characterized by a lack of financial intermediation and weak central bank supervision. In many countries, large banks still provide soft loans at artificially low interest rates, often to large loss-making enterprises. The share of non-performing loans by banks in the Czech Republic, Lithuania and the Slovak Republic exceeds 25% and in Romania even 50% (see Table 3.2). At the same time, the total volume of credits to enterprises remains rather small (EBRD, 1998).

In Bulgaria and Romania, extensive state control has impeded the necessary restructuring of the banking and insurance sectors. More generally, competition in the financial sector is limited in most countries, owing to the dominance of a small number of large banks of which the managers have maintained close connections with government officials: also in this respect, corporate governance structures remain inefficient. Securities markets are even less well developed in their function of debt and equity financiers to the private sector or as a means to encourage enterprise restructuring.

Some countries have now restructured or privatised a number of state-controlled banks or replaced them by new private profit-oriented banks. In particular, Hungary has made considerable progress in bank privatisation, enforcing banking laws and regulation and effectively carrying out prudential supervision. Hungary and Poland have attracted many foreign banks which have stimulated competition and significantly improved the performance of the financial sector. Some 60% of the Polish banking market is now controlled by foreign banks.

In Russia, the banking system has basically collapsed. Most leading banks are technically insolvent, but closures remain scarce (Jack, 1999). The payment system has been restored to some extent, but it is highly inefficient. Financial discipline is low. Inter-enterprise arrears are now estimated to amount to 45% of GDP; a large part (some 60%) of total sales are through non-monetary transactions (barter). Non-payments to public utilities are a major source of soft budget constraints and distort competition (EBRD, 1999, pp.20-21). The non-cash economy is stimulated by the state accepting tax payments in kind. Likewise, a large part of gas and electricity bills is either not paid or settled in kind; in August 1998 only some 10% was paid in cash (Commander and Mumssen, 1998, pp.12-21).

3.3.2 Control by the government

The transition requires a true metamorphosis of the role of the government, from the central planning of economic activities towards the provision of an institutional framework that inspires confidence. As argued by Tanzi (1999, p.20), "To function well, market economies need governments that can establish and enforce the 'rules of the game', promote widely shared social objectives, raise revenues to finance public sector activities, spend the revenues productively, enforce contracts and protect property, and produce public goods". The state's capacity for reform may be an important determinant of the speed with which formal institutions are adopted and of the role that inherited informal institutions can play in socio-economic co-ordination (Raiser, p.6).

Quality of public administration; corruption

Transactions in the private sector require legal security and good governance in the public sector. However, the functioning of public administrations and the management of government are a major cause of concern in most CEECs. It is important to raise the levels of efficiency, consistency and transparency. The lack of competent, adequately-trained staff in the regulatory authorities seems to be a major problem. Entrenched patterns of practice have to be broken by changing incentive structures and by investments in human capital.

The level of corruption and the size of the underground economy may be taken as indicators for the advance of good governance. As Table 3.3 shows, especially Latvia, Bulgaria, Russia and Ukraine perform relatively poorly in this respect. In particular Russia and Ukraine suffer from a high level of regulation, a weak legal system and a large degree of bureaucratic discretion. This combination causes a downward spiral in a growing underground economy, falling state revenues, eroding publicly provided services (including the remuneration of public officials and the morale of the civil service), increasing tax rates which further reduce the incentive for official registration etc. Eliminating corruption needs a series of reforms, including greater transparency of the public administration, the political will to remove corrupt officials, tax reform (including simplification), a more independent judiciary, and the promotion of alternative dispute resolution mechanisms (Johnson and Kaufmann, 1999, p.19).

Poland provides the example for improvement. Before 1989, it had earned a bad reputation. But Poland has managed to reduce corruption by replacing politicians at various levels, curtailing the power of important lobby organisations, and by workers' councils firing managers from large state-owned enterprises (Johnson and Kaufmann, 1999, p.3). Since 1996, however, administrative and political corruption as perceived by business and others is again on the increase. On

Table 3.3: The informal sector and corruption

	Share of unofficial economy (% of total GDP, 1995)	Corruption Perceptions Index 1998 (0: highly corrupt; 10: highly clean)
Poland	12.6	4.6
Hungary	2.9	5.0
Czech Republic	11.3	4.8
Estonia	11.8	5.7
Slovenia	n.a.	n.a.
Latvia	35.3	2.7
Lithuania	21.6	n.a.
Slovak Republic	5.8	3.9
Bulgaria	36.2	2.9
Romania	19.1	3.0
Russia	41.6	2.4
Ukraine	48.9	2.8

Sources: first column Johnson and Kaufmann, 1999; second column Transparency International the 1998 Transparency International Corruption Perception Index, Poland and EU-member state Italy share the 39TH position among 85 countries. Among the CEECs, Estonia is the highest ranking at 26, above Belgium, while Hungary (rank 33) and the Czech Republic (rank 37) are close to Greece (Transparency International, 1998).

Legal infrastructure

A critical condition for a well-functioning market economy is an appropriate legal infrastructure which secures the property rights of private agents. In general, comprehensive legislation and enforcement of law are vital elements for developing entrepreneurship and attracting foreign direct investment. To illustrate this, commercial law such as bankruptcy law and company law is elementary to protect the rights of shareholders and provide clarity on the rights of debtors and creditors. In order to facilitate transactions in the private sector properly, these laws must be both extensive (*i.e.* approach the rules and laws of the more developed countries) and effective (*i.e.* should be clear, accessible and adequately supported administratively and judicially) (see Table 3.4).

Likewise, legal rules governing banking and securities are critical for the functioning of the financial sector. Taxation laws and regulations are crucial for the functioning of the private sector as a whole. Moreover, competition law should promote an appropriate functioning of markets in the private sector and restrict the abuse of dominant positions.

Although the legal system in the CEECs is somewhat less well developed than that in Western Europe, significant progress has been made during the first decade of transition. Indeed, the extent to which legal rules and regulations have been introduced is amazing. Nevertheless, the proper implementation and enforcement of law remain a great cause for concern. In particular, Latvia, the Slovak Republic, Romania, Russia and Ukraine suffer from inadequate law enforcement, while rules are sometimes unclear or contradictory. Even Slovenia, Estonia and the Czech Republic suffer from serious problems in enforcing regulation on banking and securities (see Table 3.4).

Competition laws have been implemented in most CEECs along the lines of the EU framework, with the exception of Bulgaria. Although the administrative structures and the enforcement of competition legislation have improved in the most advanced CEECs, actions to reduce the abuse of market power have been limited, owing to inadequate staffing and political interference. This makes the competition laws less effective, especially in Slovenia, Romania, Bulgaria and Ukraine (*cf.* Table 3.1).

Table 3.4: EBRD legal transition indicators for 1998

	Commercial legal rules on pledge, bankruptcy, company formation and governance		Banking laws and regulation		Securities laws and regulations	
	extensiveness[a]	effectiveness[b]	extensiveness[a]	effectiveness[b]	extensiveness[a]	effectiveness[b]
Poland	4	4	4	3	4	4
Hungary	4	4	4	4	4	4
Czech Republic	4	4	3	3-	4-	3
Estonia	3	4	3	3	4	2+
Slovenia	3	3	4	3	3+	2+
Latvia	3+	2	3	3	3	3
Lithuania	4	3	3-	2+	3	2
Slovak Republic	3	2	3	2	3	2
Bulgaria	4	4	4	4-	4	3
Romania	4-	2	3	2+	3	3
Russia	4-	2	3-	2+	3	2
Ukraine	2	2	2+	2	2	2-

4+   reflects the performance of an advanced industrial economy

[a] 2 =   limited legal rules; conflicting interpretations and inconsistencies; poor registration and enforcement.
3 =   amended legislation performs better but leaves room for improvement.
4 =   comprehensive legislation.

[b] 2 =   legal rules unclear or contradictory; few procedures to make laws operational and enforceable.
3 =   legal rules reasonably clear, administration or juridical support generally inadequate or inconsistent.
4 =   legal rules clear, administration, registration and juridical support reasonably adequate.

Source: EBRD (1998)

Financial sector regulation

The future growth, in size and complexity, of the financial sector will have to be met by a fundamental strengthening of the regulatory and supervisory framework (EBRD, 1998, Chapter 6). In recent years, transition countries generally have made substantial progress in this area. Most frontrunners to EU-accession now have comprehensive and reasonably effective banking regulations and an independent central bank (although some refinement is still needed, see Table 3.4). The slow developer in this group is the Czech Republic; Bulgaria has performed much better in this respect, having upgraded its regulations in the wake of its recent banking crisis. In many countries, the shortage of banking supervisory staff and the lack of use of international standards for accounting seriously harm the effective implementation of rules for banking. The extensiveness of securities laws may now be broadly comparable to that of banking; their effectiveness is generally less (except for the most advanced countries, Hungary and Poland). Among the frontrunners towards EU-accession, Slovenia and Estonia in particular will have to improve the effectiveness of their legal rules: they are now lagging behind Bulgaria.

Taxation and social security systems

Most of the candidate member states of the EU have substantially improved their revenue collection and reduced their fiscal deficits. Nevertheless, some of the CEECs need to fundamentally change their tax and social security systems. Low revenue collection in Russia, Ukraine, Bulgaria and Romania, for instance, reflects the weakness of tax administrations and a lack of fiscal discipline – rather than low tax rates. Tax evasion is stimulated by high tax rates, very complicated legislation and opportunities for tax avoidance. In Russia, the shift away from corporate taxation towards personal income taxation has failed. In fact, unduly high corporate taxes have discouraged investments or have driven companies into the informal economy. Ex-post tax bargaining (over tax arrears) and the acceptance of payments in kind (at overvalued prices) substantially soften the budget constraints of firms. Ukraine has recently simplified its tax system on corporations as an incentive to shift activities back to the formal sector (see Table 3.3 for estimates on the size of the unofficial economy).

In social security, most countries rely on a pay-as-you-go pension system. The ageing of the population and the generous use of early retirement schemes – used as a way of avoiding the painful consequences of industry restructuring – put an enormous pressure on the financial sustainability of this system. To tackle this problem, Hungary and Poland have recently implemented pension reforms that gradually introduce a three-tier system of a public pay-as-you-go scheme, a fully funded system (pension funds) and voluntary additional savings for retirement (OECD, 1998 and 1999). In the longer run, this is expected to increase private savings for retirement and relax the pension liabilities on the budget. In other countries, pension reform is also urgently required.

More generally, the design of a new social insurance system entails a trade-off between incentives and solidarity. In many cases, interdependent risks and adverse selection caused by asymmetric information limit the possibilities for co-ordination by competition. Social security providing compulsory insurance can encourage people to take some risk in developing new activities that may benefit society, like moving to a new job or starting a new business. Compulsory risk-sharing through control may, however, cause moral hazard and reduce incentives for economic agents too.

3.3.3 Common values and norms

Common values and norms fundamentally influence human behaviour. They play a crucial role in facilitating economic exchange by supporting self-enforcing rules-of-the-game. This self-enforcement – based on mutual trust and goodwill – is an important quality, because the transaction costs of covering all contingencies in contracts and having their breach enforced in court are prohibitive. Moreover, common values and norms tend to foster trust in third-party enforcement through the state: "A society in which cheating is the norm in bilateral transactions is also less likely to benefit from impartial and incorruptible third-party enforcement" (Raiser, 1997, p.7). Hence, they form a vital element of any mature market economy.

One of the legacies of totalitarian rule in CEECs is the underdevelopment of a civil society in which individuals seek co-operative solutions to problems of collective choice. "In general, East Europeans are 'sceptics' (...) That scepticism concerns not just political institutions such as government, parliament, political parties, civil servants or the police, but generally applies to civil institutions as well. This suggests that the region has inherited a relatively low level of social capital". (Raiser, 1997, p.23)

Surveys show that trust is lowest in Ukraine and Bulgaria (Russia was not surveyed).[4] It is higher among the more advanced transition economies. This difference can be partly explained by different legacies from the communist past: *e.g.* in Poland the civil opposition in the form of the Catholic Church and the independent trade union Solidarnosc. But the firm and credible commitment of the post-communist governments to far-reaching reforms has also made a difference. It is plausible to expect a strong complementarity between the level of trust and the effectiveness of government policy in the form of either a virtuous or a vicious circle.

3.3.4 Co-operative exchange

In Western Europe, industrial relations constitute an example of co-operative exchange between non-governmental organisations: trade unions and employers' organisations. This co-operative exchange can form the basis for a social partnership.

For the former centrally planned economies, the creation of a balanced system of industrial relations turns out to be a huge challenge. Both sides of industry are still in the process of building their organisation and defining their position and identity. In general, employers have been less successful than employees in creat-

---

4. Survey responses collected from 10,087 individuals from nine CEECs in 1993. Ratings were asked for 15 political and civil institutions. See Raiser (1999, pp.22-25).

ing independent organisations that are effectively able to represent the interest of their (potential) membership. This can be explained by the great diversity of interests among employers (including the managers of state-owned enterprises). Moreover, the rules of the game of collective bargaining have to be elaborated and forums for a social dialogue have to be developed (Slomp, Van Hoof and Moerel, 1996; Deppe and Tatur, 1997; Ockenga, 1997; Tóth, 1997).

In various CEECs, including Hungary, the Czech and Slovak Republics, Poland, Bulgaria and Romania, tripartite advisory bodies have been created to facilitate the social dialogue. The third party in these councils or committees is the government. A positive interpretation of this construct is that it "may serve to facilitate the shift from government control to national co-ordination by peak organisations" (Slomp, van Hoof and Moerel, 1996, p.347). At the same time, the major role of the government in the tripartite council and the absence of an alternative forum for bipartite consultations keep trade unions and employers' organisations in a dependent position. The negative side of this kind of tripartism[5] is that it tends to consolidate the prevailing orientation of both sides of industry towards a still dominating state, politicising industrial relations and creating a new form of state-led corporatism. The challenge for these organisations is to first develop their autonomy in direct union-employer bargaining (in particular at sector level) and in social partnership in their own domain (primarily wage-setting). This form of self-regulation at various levels may then provide a good basis for co-ordination of social and economic policies with the government (*cf.* Langewiesche, 1997).

In Russia, creating real autonomy for prospective social partners is even more of a fundamental problem. Relatively few employers are members of an association. Moreover, most of these are more like a trade association, lobbying for government support for specific sectors in close collaboration with the branch trade unions. At enterprise level, Russian trade unions are still dependent on management;[6] the trade union president is part of the management team, responsible for social and welfare services. The (traditional) trade unions enjoy comprehensive legal protection, are involved in monitoring health and safety regulations but are not in a position really to represent their members and to negotiate on behalf of them to resolve conflicts (Clarke, 1997).

---

5. A comparison with the basic institutional structure of the Dutch consultation economy can be illustrating. The Social and Economic Council (SER) is a tripartite advisory body to the government on social and economic policies, the third party being independent experts (not representing the government). The Labour Foundation is the private body that is created by social partners for bipartite consultation at the national level. This Labour Foundation meets regularly with a government delegation to exchange information and to co-ordinate policies (tripartite consultation).

6. Management is still admitted to trade union membership, and a substantial number of enterprise directors belong to a trade union branch.

3.4 Challenges for the future

The transition to a modern market economy entails the rebuilding of the institutional framework of an economy and a society. That is a wide-ranging and complicated task, involving many intricate interdependencies and trade-offs. Progress in institution building is necessarily gradual. At the beginning of the process, however, the rapid implementation of a critical mass of reforms is essential to fundamentally change the behavioural patterns of people and firms. It has to be clear to all economic agents that the 'rules of the game' have changed and that this is not just another of those partial, ill-fated reform attempts of the past. A comprehensive liberalisation of prices and economic activities is crucial to force the transition from a sellers' to a buyers' market; the imposition of hard budget constraints is needed to provide incentives for improving efficiency.

That is the element of shock therapy. Frictions and inconsistencies are inevitable, because not all institutional preconditions can be created in time. Stern (1997, p.53) is right in emphasising: 'shock therapy' *versus* 'gradualism' is a false dichotomy and an unhelpful way of presenting things. Some things can and should be done quickly, others take longer. Where political and administrative structures have broken down, then gradualism may simply be a euphemism for the prolongation of uncertainty and stress.'

In the CEECs, the old institutional setting has been discredited, leaving a systemic vacuum. In principle, this situation of *tabula rasa* offers ample opportunities to experiment with new variations of institutions and to choose a setting in accordance with specific preferences and circumstances. In practice, however, experimentation entails costs because it creates uncertainty. Furthermore, the options that are really available turn out to be limited. To elaborate on the future of institutional change in the CEECs, two factors seem particularly important: path dependency (Section 3.4.1) and accession to the European Union, implying the implementation of its '*acquis communautaire*' (Section 3.4.2).

3.4.1 Path dependency

Path dependency makes institutional design dependent on history. The CEECs used to rely heavily on the control mechanism to co-ordinate economic behaviour. In the earlier stages of the transition, liberalisation of prices and activities and the privatisation of firms have given an important impetus to the development of the competition mechanism. Most countries have achieved substantial progress in introducing and reforming these two co-ordination mechanisms. Differences between countries with respect to the speed of institutional change, however, are growing and all countries still need further improvement in the institutions that facilitate control and competition in their role as effective co-ordination mechanisms. The quality of the public administration will remain a serious bottleneck, as investments in human capital take time.

The other two mechanisms, common values and norms and co-operative exchange, are on the national all-encompassing level relatively underdeveloped in all CEECs.7 This reflects a low level of inherited 'social capital', of 'trust', and is a typical example of path dependency in institutional design. It takes time and effort to implement new institutions; informal institutions change even more slowly than the formal institutional framework (Raiser, 1999, p.16). This low level of trust forms a handicap for the operation of a modern market economy and reduces the options available in institutional design.

How can policy make a positive contribution in building trust in public institutions and promoting mutual confidence among economic actors? Raiser (1999) suggests three possible lines of action: (i) the creation of constitutional safeguards for open democratic government (including the possibility of competition among government agencies and a democratically legitimised turnover of ruling elites); (ii) distributional policies that foster the perceived fairness of transition outcomes and provide a basic safety for individuals, allowing them to break free of existing social networks; (iii) and direct policy intervention to strengthen business networks which build on mutual trust by facilitating the exchange of information.

3.4.2 The European Union

Ten countries of Central and Eastern Europe have been accepted as associates and candidate-members of the European Union. Five of them – Poland, Hungary, the Czech Republic, Slovenia and Estonia – are since November 1998 involved in negotiations on the terms of accession. The other countries will be invited for the negotiations if sufficient progress has been made with respect to the so-called Copenhagen criteria. These relate to the stability of institutions guaranteeing democracy, the rule of law, human rights and the protection of minorities; to the existence of a functioning market economy, capable of coping with competitive pressures within the EU; and to the ability to take on the obligations of membership, including adherence to the aims of political, economic and monetary union.

Acquis communautaire

The accession to the EU will involve the adoption and implementation of (the essence of) the *acquis communautaire*.8 This can be helpful to countries in tran-

---

7. These mechanisms, however, can be effective in co-ordinating the interests of specific groups, *e.g.* on the basis of *nomenklatura* networks ('spontaneous' privatisation, barter). In this way, vested interests can take advantage of the weakness of the mechanisms of competition and control by the government.
8. The European Commission's interim reports on the five 'frontrunners' provided a positive assessment of progress in Estonia, Hungary and Poland, being less favourable of the Czech Republic and Slovenia owing to slower progress in adapting legislation to the *acquis*.

sition in providing a reference point for institutional change. At the same time, effectively implementing the full *acquis* will be problematic, in particular because of the institutional preconditions to be met. Indeed, introducing formal organisations and structures is one thing, but making them operational and effective is generally more difficult. The capacity and expertise of the national and local administrations and the shortage of legal experts form serious bottlenecks. Hence, integration tends to underline the importance of institutional change, including investments in the quality of the civil service.

For the associated countries, the implementation of a large part of the *acquis* clearly makes economic sense. The process of legal approximation should, however, not be seen just as a straightforward legal exercise but should also be based on an economic impact analysis. In this respect, not all elements of the *acquis communautaire* are relevant in the current stages of accession and/or transition. Some elements may even be harmful as they would complicate the necessary restructuring processes. Examples are the premature adoption and strict implementation of the convergence criteria for EMU – or more particularly the early pegging of the currency to the euro – (World Bank, 1997, p.4; Köhler and Wes, 1999) and the full implementation of a non-reformed Common Agricultural Policy (SER, 1996). Indeed, sequencing in the adoption of the *acquis* is important. Priority should be given to measures that are essential to the operation of markets, in the perspective of both integration in the internal market of the EU and the transition to a modern market economy. Typical examples concern the fields of company law, the regulation and supervision of the financial sector, the protection of intellectual property, competition policy (including the control of state aids) and public procurement as well as product-related legislation (Mayhew, 1998, Chapter 8; EBRD, 1998, Chapter 6). But some process-related regulations concerning occupational safety or environmental standards can be very costly if applied at short notice to all production facilities, old and new, while these rules may not be essential to the operation of the internal market. The use of transition periods and arrangements can offer an efficient solution for such problems (SER, 1998, pp.30-42).

Frontrunners and laggards

The decision of the EU to differentiate between a fast track group and a slower group is based on the EU's judgement of the progress being made with respect the Copenhagen criteria. However, the decision to differentiate may further exacerbate the divergence in transition between the frontrunners and the laggards. Indeed, foreign investors and the EU governments may pay due attention to the frontrunners than to the laggards. Furthermore, there tend to be self-enforcing mechanisms among the frontrunners (through cooperation and regular contacts and meetings among government officials) which further speed up the process of institutional change (Emerson *et al.*, 1999). For Poland, Hungary, the Czech

Republic, Slovenia and Estonia accession to the EU by the year 2005 now seems a realistic option. It can be expected that at least the formal institutions of these countries will have evolved to a large degree to the level appropriate for a modern market economy. Institutional change will still pose a big challenge especially in the functioning of organisations and people, but the corner has been turned.

The perspective of institutional change in other CEECs – EU-candidate member states like Romania and Bulgaria as well as the non-candidate members Russia and Ukraine – is gloomier. These countries have so far made significantly less progress in institutional change. Their lower level of social and economic development and the lower level of trust in society are serious handicaps to implementing institutional reforms. Moreover, the perspective of accession to the EU is either distant (Romania, Bulgaria) or absent (Russia, Ukraine), which weakens the potential guidance of the *acquis communautaire*.

Challenges for the EU

The Partnerships for Accession and the *acquis communautaire* of the European Union are important factors stimulating and guiding institutional reform in CEECs. Through PHARE, as well as through new programmes, financial support is given to the processes of institution building, infrastructure development and economic reform in the CEECs. For enlargement to be really successful, the EU itself will have to implement a number of reforms, including institutional reform (with respect to decision-making) and reforms in its common agricultural policy and its structural policies (CPB *et al*, 1999). Moreover, the EU should realise what the implications of the current division between frontrunners and laggards are. If this division should be allowed to turn into a more permanent split, moving the outer border of the EU only halfway east, countries like Romania and Bulgaria would have substantially reduced chances for a successful transition to a modern market economy.

References

Bos-Karczewska, M. (1993), 'Privatisering van staatsbedrijven' (Privatising state-owned enterprises), in: N. van der Lijn (ed.), *De overgang naar een markt-economie in Oost-Europa* (The transition to a market economy in Eastern Europe), Stenfert Kroese, Culemborg.

Clarke, S. (1997), 'Trade unions, industrial relations and the state in Russia', *Transfer*, Vol.3., No.2, p.377-389.

Commander, S. and C. Mumssen (1998), *Understanding barter in Russia*, EBRD Working Paper, No.37, London.

CPB Netherlands Bureau for Economic Policy Analysis (1997), *Challenging Neighbours: Rethinking German and Dutch economic institutions*, Springer-Verlag, Berlin, Heidelberg, New York.

CPB Netherlands Bureau for Economic Policy Analysis, ING and SEO (1999), *Europese Grensverlegging, Scenario's voor Midden- en Oost-Europa tot 2010* (Shifting European borders, Scenarios for Central and Eastern Europe to 2010), The Hague.

Deppe, R. and M. Tatur (1997), 'Transformation processes and trade union configurations in Poland and Hungary', *Transfer*, Vol.3, No.2, pp.242-269.

EBRD (1998), *Transition report 1998*, London.

EBRD (1999), *Transition report update April 1999*, London.

Emerson, M., D. Gros and P. Ludlow (1999), *Coming to terms with EMU and Enlargement*, CEPS, Brussels.

Frydman, R., C. Gray, M. Hessel and A. Rapaczynski (1997), *Private ownership and corporate performance: evidence from transition economies*, EBRD Working Paper, No.26, London.

Havrylyshyn, O. and Th. Wolf (1999), 'Determinants of Growth in Transition Countries', *Finance & Development*, Vol.36, No.2, pp.12-15.

Jack, A. (1999), 'Russian banks' manoeuvrings ring up few changes', *Financial Times*, 30 June 1999.

Johnson, S. and D. Kaufman (1999), *In the Underground*, Paper prepared for the IMF Conference 'A Decade of Transition: Achievements and Challenges', 1-3 February 1999, Washington, D.C.

Köhler, H. and M. Wes (1999), *Implications of the Euro for the Integration Process of the Transition Countries in Central and Eastern Europe*, EBRD Working Paper, No.38, London.

Langewiesche, R. (1997), 'Phare Social Dialogue Programmes – some lessons from 18 months of experience – a structural reflection', *Transfer*, Vol. 3, No.2, pp.437-445.

Mayhew, A. (1998), *Recreating Europe – The European Union's Policy towards Central and Eastern Europe*, Cambridge University Press, Cambridge.

Nellis, J. (1999), 'Time to Rethink Privatization in Transition Economies?', *Finance & Development*, Vol.36, No.2, pp.16-19.

North, D.C. (1990), *Institutions, Institutional Change and Economic Performance*, Cambridge University Press, Cambridge.

Ockenga, E. (1997), 'Trade Unions in Romania', *Transfer*, Vol, 3, No.2, pp.313-328.

OECD (1998), *Economic Survey Poland*, Paris.

OECD (1999), *Economic Survey Hungary*, Paris.

Raiser, M. (1997), *Informal institutions, social capital and economic transition: reflections on a neglected dimension*, EBRD Working Paper, No.25, London.

Raiser, M. (1999), *Trust in transition*, EBRD Working Paper, No.39, London.

SER (1996), *Advies Hervorming Gemeenschappelijk Landbouwbeleid* (Recommendations for Reforming the Common Agricultural Policy), The Hague.

SER (1998), *Advies Agenda 2000: de uitbreiding en financiering van de Europese Unie* (Recommendations for Agenda 2000: The Enlargement and Financing of the European Union), The Hague.

Slomp, H., J. Hoof and H. Moerel (1996), 'The transformation of industrial relations in some Central and Eastern European countries', in: J. van Ruysseveldt and J. Visser (eds.), *Industrial Relations in Europe – Traditions and Transitions*, SAGE Publications, London, pp.337-357.

Stern, N. (1997), 'The transition in Eastern Europe and the former Soviet Union: some lessons from the experience of 25 countries over six years', in: S. Zecchini (ed.), *Lessons from the Economic Transition – Central and Eastern Europe in the 1990s*, Kluwer Academic Publishers, Dordrecht, pp.35-57.

Stiglitz, J.E. (1999), *Quis Custodiet Ipsos Custodes? – Corporate Governance Failures in the Transition*, Keynote Address, Annual Bank Conference on Development Economics-Europe, 21-23 June 1999, Paris.

Tanzi, V. (1999), 'Transition and the Changing Role of Government', *Finance & Development*, Vol.36, No.2, pp.20-23.

Tóth, A. (1997), 'The role of multi-employer collective agreements in regulating terms and conditions of employment in Hungary', *Transfer*, Vol.3, No.2, pp.329-356.

Transparency International, *The Corruption Perceptions Index*, Internet: http://www.transparency.de/

World Bank (1996), *From Plan to Market – World Development Report 1996*, Oxford University Press, New York.

World Bank (1997), *Poland – Country Economic Memorandum – Reform and Growth on the Road to the EU*, Report No.16858-POL, Washington, D.C.

CHAPTER 4

Opening Up

Guido Biessen, Harry Oldersma and Nicolette Tiggeloove

4.1 Introduction

The former centrally planned economies of Central and Eastern Europe were considered to be more or less closed to world markets. Producers and consumers were sheltered from developments in the world market. Currencies were not convertible. There was no free movement of goods, people and ideas across borders. Nevertheless, the degree of openness to capital inflows was substantial in some planned economies, as is evident from the significant accumulation of hard currency debts in some countries during the 1970s and 1980s.

Since the process of transition was embarked upon, there has been a tremendous change in the external orientation of the countries undergoing transition. Not only has the level of trade increased, but also the geographical composition of trade has changed dramatically. Moreover, foreign investors have discovered profitable investment opportunities in this region.

Opening up to foreign trade and investment plays a vital role in the process of transition and reintegration in the world economy, both at the macro level and the micro level (Eatwell *et al.*, 1995). At the micro level, price liberalisation and trade liberalisation go hand in hand. Foreign trade and the reintegration in the world economy are important to establish a link between domestic prices and world market prices. Moreover, foreign trade and FDI force domestic producers to become more competitive. Imports of foreign technology and capital goods are equally important to the restructuring of the economy. What is more, FDI is generally accompanied by an inflow of modern management skills, marketing techniques and organisational know-how.

At the macro level, participation in international trade and investment promotes the process of specialisation, which enhances the competitiveness of the economy, and creates the basis for wealth creation and sustainable growth. Of course, the other side of the coin is that opening up to foreign trade and investment will lead to increased foreign competition and for certain sectors this will lead to a loss of market share in the home economy. For the economy as a whole, this may result in large current account deficits. Although the compensating inflow of foreign capital may be helpful for the restructuring process, it may create some difficulties both in the short run and in the longer term. In the short run, large inflows of short-term capital might be reversed in the aftermath of financial turbulence in emerging markets, creating short-term instability. Moreover, substantial inflows of capital can complicate an effective monetary policy, aimed at controlling inflation. In the longer term, a rapid accumulation of foreign debt might limit the future access to capital markets.

This chapter is confined to the analysis of trade and investment relations of the CEECs. In Section 4.2, volume and geographical distribution of foreign trade are discussed. Moreover, the potential for further growth of the trade links is analysed. In Section 4.3, the inflow of foreign capital is discussed. Section 4.4 will explore the Dutch position towards Central and Eastern European markets.

4.2 Foreign trade

4.2.1 Trade performance

Foreign trade of the CEECs experienced a number of important changes in the period 1989 to 1999. Figure 4.1 shows a strong rising trend in the value of merchandise trade of six CEECs since 1990. In 1998, the total dollar value of exports of six CEECs – Bulgaria, Hungary, Romania, Poland and the Czech and Slovak Republics – was more than doubled when compared with 1990. In 1998, total imports of these countries were more than twice the 1990 value. The Baltic countries have shown even faster rising aggregate exports and imports. In the same period, the value of Russian exports increased by 85%, while Ukrainian exports

Figure 4.1: Foreign merchandise trade of six CEECs*, 1990-1998
(In billions of dollars)

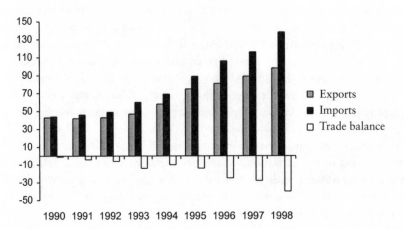

* Bulgaria, Hungary, Romania, Poland and the Czech and Slovak Republics

Source: IMF, *Direction of Trade Statistics*

jumped by almost 150%. Also, Russian imports in dollar terms more than doubled between 1993 and 1998, whereas Ukrainian imports more than tripled. Overall, import growth outpaced the growth of exports in all CEECs, with the exception of Bulgaria. As a result, the trade balances of all the countries deteriorated.

In 1996, the growth in Central and Eastern European exports started to decrease. Exports rose by 8% in dollar terms in 1996, after rapid growth (25 to 30%) in the preceding two years. The growth of exports from Poland, Hungary, the Slovak Republic, the Baltic countries, Russia and Ukraine was substantially lower, whereas exports from Bulgaria, Romania and Slovenia actually showed a decline. Although the growth of imports into the CEECs slowed down a little, imports continued to outpace exports, resulting in a further widening of the aggregate trade deficit for the region as a whole to 34 billion dollars in 1998.

4.2.2 Geographical distribution of trade

A noteworthy achievement of the transition is the reorientation of trade. Whereas previously trade of the CEECs was mainly taking place amongst themselves, and in particular with Russia, nowadays Western markets, in particular the European Union, and especially Germany, play an increasing role. The shift in the geographical pattern of exports was more pronounced for the more advanced reformers. More than 70% of the imports to the Czech Republic, Poland and Hungary now come from the European Union, while more than 60% of their exports go to the EU countries. There is evidence of a similar redirection of trade among the former Soviet republics, in particular the Baltic States. For the Baltic States, the major new trading partners are the Scandinavian countries. The redirection of exports from Russia and Ukraine towards the Western markets has been less pronounced but nonetheless significant.

4.2.3 Composition of trade

Since 1990, the structure of Central and Eastern European imports has changed. There has been an important and growing share of machinery and transport equipment in total imports. Imports of foreign technology and capital goods are, of course, important to the restructuring of the economy. It is striking that the 'leading' reform countries, in particular Poland, Slovenia and the Czech Republic have (with respectively 33%, 34% and 38% in 1996) the highest share of capital goods as a proportion of total imports. Intermediate and other manufactured goods form a high proportion of imports as well. Russian imports consist largely of agricultural products.

In 1989, manufactured exports from the CEECs were heavily concentrated in a few industries: textiles, clothing, footwear, timber and furniture, ferrous and nonferrous metals and chemicals. Though in 1996 exports still largely consisted of products from these traditional industries, there were already significant quantities of capital goods going to the European Union. Exports from the Czech Republic and Slovenia (33% and 34% respectively) show an especially high and growing proportion of machinery and transport equipment. However, some countries, like Hungary, have a high share of food and agricultural products in total exports. Exports from Russia continue to be dominated by fuels and raw materials, but the share of manufactured products has increased.

4.2.4 Potential trade

As shown above, the CEECs are in a process of trade reorientation. They are seeking to develop more extensive trade relations with the Western world, while their mutual trade has broken down to a substantial degree. This trade reorientation has already taken place against the background of the liberalisation of foreign trade sectors. The gravity model has proven to be a powerful econometric tool to describe the geographical distribution of trade flows and has been used extensively by different researchers in the past.[1] In the gravity model, normal trade is defined as the level of trade one could expect given the country's size and geographical location. All these studies indicate that there was a substantial gap between actual and normal trade in the period before transition. Actual trade was only about 20% of normal trade, and hence there was substantial room for increased division of labour between Eastern and Western Europe.[2] Here, we try to evaluate the extent of trade reorientation that has taken place in the course of transition for the three larger countries of the first group of accession candidates, *i.e.* the Czech Republic, Hungary and Poland (CECs).[3] We used a gravity model for a sample of 24 OECD countries, including the three CECs, implying that we have 552 trade flows.

The gravity model is written as:[4]

$$X_{ij} = \beta_0 Y_i{}^{\beta_1} Y_j{}^{\beta_2} D_{ij}{}^{\beta_3} P_{ij}{}^{\beta_4} u_{ij} \qquad \text{(Eq. 4.1)}$$

---

1. See Hamilton and Winters (1992), Biessen (1991), and Van Bergeijk and Oldersma (1990).
2. It must be noted that the extent of undertrading also depends on the exchange rates used in order to measure the dollar GDP's of CEECs. Mostly purchasing power parities (PPP) were used, as the official exchange rates were highly artificial. However, measuring income of the transition economies at PPP reveals higher incomes, and, consequently, their resulting normal level of trade should be higher. In order to compare the weight of countries in international relations, one should use market exchange rates (Gros and Steinherr, 1995). Here, market exchange rates are used to measure the dollar GDP's.
3. For 1991 we used data for Czechoslovakia.
4. We did not include population variables, for reasons of multicollinearity. Due to multicollinearity between national income and population it is impossible to separate the effects of population and national income. If the coefficient to log Y_i increases, the coefficient to log N_i decreases.

where:

X_{ij}	=	value of merchandise exports from country i to country j
Y_i, Y_j	=	gross domestic product (GDP) in countries i and j
D_{ij}	=	the distance between country i and country j
P_{ij}	=	dummy variables to take account of special circumstances such as membership of a customs union
u_{ij}	=	disturbance term

In Equation 4.1, the bilateral trade flow from country i to country j is determined by the potential foreign supply of country i (Y_i), the potential foreign demand of country j (Y_j), and the resistance to trade between country i and country j represented by the distance (D_{ij}) between countries i and j. It is assumed that Y_i and Y_j have a positive effect on the export flow, and that D_{ij} has a negative effect on the export flow. In addition to the variables Y_i, Y_j and D_{ij}, representing the 'normal' or 'potential' level of trade, several dummy variables (P_{ij}) are included. A neighbour dummy (Neighbour) is included, in order to evaluate whether neighbouring countries indeed have a more intensive mutual trade. Also, a dummy is introduced to take account of the potentially above-normal trade within the European Union. To take account of the special position of Germany, two separate dummies (Germany-CEC) for exports from Germany to the CECs and CEC-Germany (*visa versa*) are introduced. We have included one dummy for the export of Western Europe, excluding Germany, to the CECs (Europe-CEC), and one dummy for the other way around, the export from the CECs to Western Europe (CEC-Europe). Finally, two dummies (CEC-Non Europe and Non Europe-CEC) are included in order to evaluate trade between the non-European OECD countries in the sample (US, Canada, Australia, New Zealand and Japan).

The empirical results for 1991 and 1997 are given in Table 4.1. The regression results reveal that the variables representing the normal pattern of trade have the expected sign and are remarkably stable over time. With respect to deviations from the normal pattern of trade, a number of observations can be made:

- The Neighbour-dummy, both in 1991 and 1997, is positive and significant, revealing that countries that are neighbours indeed have a more intensive mutual trade.
- Within this sample, and with the specification chosen, the effect of the European Union is significantly positive at a 10% significance level. This conclusion is stable over time, despite the round of enlargement that took place in 1995.
- In 1991, in general, mutual trade between Western countries, both European and non-European, and the Central European countries was still substantially below the normal level of trade.
- In 1991, Germany had already regained its pre-World War II dominance in the trade of the Central European countries. This special position appears to have

been reinforced during this decade of transition.

- In 1997, European exports to Central Europe no longer deviated in a significant way from a normal export level. The gap of the 1980s had been closed. However, mutual trade between non-European OECD countries and the CECs remains significantly below normal trade levels.
- In 1997, Central European exports to the West European countries were still significantly below the normal level. So, in contrast to the performance of West European exporters in Central European markets, Central European exporters did not reach their full potential in the markets of the West. This is remarkable, as the exporters from the CECs did manage to fully grasp their potential on the German market.

Table 4.1: Regression results for a sample of 24 OECD countries

	1991		1997	
Variable	Estimate	T-ratio	Estimate	T-ratio
Constant	4.01	11.83	3.79	9.53
Y_i	0.83	34.82	0.83	33.43
Y_j	0.78	32.45	0.79	31.60
D_{ij}	-0.78	-22.94	-0.77	-20.24
Neighbour	0.83	4.76	0.79	4.42
EU	0.22	1.73	0.22	1.75
Germany-CEC	0.04	0.06	0.75	1.24
CEC-Germany	0.21	0.34	0.72	1.18
Europe[1]-CEC	-1.16	-6.23	-0.25	-1.25
CEC-Europe[1]	-0.97	-5.53	-0.73	-3.93
Non Europe-CEC	-2.31	-8.12	-1.77	-6.24
CEC-Non Europe	-1.32	-4.61	-1.67	-5.82
R^2 adjusted	0.89		0.87	

1/ Europe excluding Germany.

Using a different specification for Equation 4.1, *i.e.* incorporating dummies for all bilateral trade flows between the CECs on the one hand, and the OECD countries on the other, it is possible to reveal the relative performance of the individual countries in Central European markets during this decade of transition. Obviously, these performances vary to a substantial degree (see Table 4.2). Whereas in 1991, countries like Germany, Austria and the Netherlands already had actual trade levels above or close to their potential, countries like France, Italy, and the UK were lagging behind. In 1997, the latter countries also performed much better in Central European markets. However, with respect to imports from Central Europe, a number of countries, *e.g.* France and UK, were importing significantly below the normal level.

To sum up, the gap existing in the 1980s between the 'potential' level of trade and the actual level of trade within Europe between East and West has been narrowed

Table 4.2: Actual exports of the most important Western trading partners to the Czech Republic, Poland and Hungary, and *vice versa*, as a percentage of the estimated 'normal' level of export, 1991 and 1997

	Exports from the countries listed to CECs		Exports from CECs to the countries listed	
	1991	1997	1991	1997
Austria	104	138	98	87
BLEU	82	171	75	104
France	45	83	36	52
Germany	116	187	122	168
Italy	50	129	56	72
Netherlands	93	146	100	113
United Kingdom	34	84	34	53
United States	22	38	26	38
Japan	54	60	36	18

to a considerable degree during a decade of transition. For Germany, but also for Austria and the Netherlands, this gap was already closed in 1991. In 1997, in general, Western European countries were exporting close to their potential, but imports were still significantly below the normal level. In coming years, a further flow of goods from Central Europe to Western Europe is to be expected.

4.3 Foreign capital movements

The recent financial turmoil in the emerging markets is putting pressure on the current account balances of the CEECs. The collapse of Russian import demand following the rouble devaluation in August 1998 has intensified these pressures.

4.3.1 Current account deficits and financial instability

To start with, a current account deficit is a normal feature for an economy in transition, especially when its economic growth is high. Stern and Wes (Chapter 2) are right to suggest that current account deficits are desirable, because, indeed by definition, it means the use of foreign savings. Foreign capital inflows are important for restructuring the economy. Raising the efficiency of domestic industries requires imports of foreign technology and investment goods. However, rapidly increasing and/or persistently large current account deficits present a source of vulnerability. The question of whether present current account imbalances in CEECs are sustainable depends on factors such as:

- the types of financing (relatively stable FDI or short-term capital flows that can easily be withdrawn);
- the pattern of spending (imports of investment goods that strengthen competitiveness or goods for consumption);
- appreciation of the real effective exchange rate (*i.e.* declining competitiveness);
- total debt servicing.

Considering these factors, the size of current account imbalances presently being observed and the uncertainty of future capital inflows, concerns have arisen concerning the sustainability of several CEECs' financial positions. A currency crisis in some CEECs is certainly not unrealistic. In several CEECs external deficits have widened, owing to declines in domestic savings, often used to finance imports of goods for consumption. Furthermore, real exchange rates appreciated in nearly all transition economies (with the exception of Hungary). This is particularly true for those countries which are running large fiscal deficits as well, and which are financing persistent current account deficits with short-term credits.[5] So new currency crises cannot be ruled out.

Figure 4.2: Current account balances, 1998
(As a % of GDP

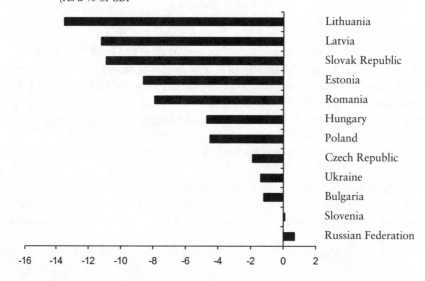

Source: EBRD, *Transition Report Update*, April 1999

Figure 4.2 shows that five countries had a current account deficit in 1998 larger than 5% of GDP, a threshold often used as a 'rule-of-thumb' warning signal. In the Slovak Republic, Latvia and Lithuania, current account deficits even exceeded 10% of GDP in 1998. Since the second half of last year, the collapse of Russian import demand has intensified pressures on the current account balances of the transition economies. In almost all CEECs, external balances deteriorated sharply in 1998. In Hungary the current account deficit more than doubled. In Bulgaria the current account balance shifted from a surplus of 4% of GDP in 1997 to a

---

5. Bear in mind that current account imbalances became unsustainable in the cases of the Czech and Slovak Republics in May 1997 and October 1998 respectively. In both cases the fixed exchange rate regimes had to be abandoned.

deficit of 1% of GDP in 1998. In the Czech Republic, following the devaluation of 1997, the current account balance improved by more than 4% of GDP in 1998. The decline in export revenues from oil caused a dramatic swing in Russia's external position in 1998. However, Russia maintained a positive current account balance owing to the collapse of imports following the rouble devaluation in August 1998. This is not a positive sign, however, as domestic savings are channelled abroad instead of being used for necessary domestic investments.

4.3.2 Foreign capital flows

The financial turmoil in emerging markets and the shift in the risk perception of international investors have raised the cost of borrowing for the CEECs. Net private capital flows into the region fell sharply in 1998. However, as analysed by Stern and Wes (Chapter 2), financial contagion has not affected the region across the board. International investors and lenders increasingly differentiate among economies on the basis of the quality of macroeconomic management and structural reform. International capital flows have been mainly going to those Central European countries which have achieved most progress in implementing structural reforms and in macroeconomic stabilisation. The changes in international capital movements were also highly differentiated by the type of capital flow. While commercial bank lending declined sharply and portfolio inflows were even negative in 1998, inflows of foreign direct investment actually rose.

4.3.3 Foreign direct investment

The resilience of FDI inflows in CEECs has underlined its importance as a major source of foreign capital. FDI plays an important role in the transition process. Until 1991, FDI flows into the CEECs were very small. Driven by waves of privatisation and liberalisation, and by economic recovery in some countries, FDI inflows into the CEECs have shown a fast rising trend in recent years, as demonstrated in Figure 4.3. Investment inflows into the region rose to a record of 19 billion dollars in 1997. The region now accounts for 5% of world inflows, compared with only 1% in 1991.

In the early years of transition, Hungary was the greatest beneficiary of FDI. Important host factors like political stability and a good environment for entrepreneurship played a crucial role. In the last few years FDI flows into Poland rose impressively. Poland – the largest and fastest growing market in Central Europe – is now by far the largest recipient of FDI flows. In Eastern Europe, the Russian Federation is the leading recipient of FDI.[6]

---

6. Foreign direct investment outflows from the CEECs are still relatively low. Investment outflows from the region reached 3.3 billion dollars in 1997. The Russian Federation accounted for the bulk of outflows (2.5 billion dollars) in 1997, followed by Hungary and Estonia.

Figure 4.3: Foreign direct investment in the CEECs, 1990-1997
(Inward flows in billions of dollars)

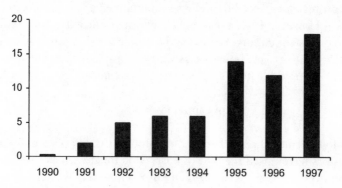

Source: UNCTAD, *World Investment Report 1998*

Figure 4.4 shows the geographical distribution of FDI in the CEECs at the end of 1997. Poland and Hungary, each with a share of 25% in the total stock, are the greatest beneficiaries from FDI. Together with the Russian Federation and the Czech Republic, these countries account for more than 80% of the total stock of FDI in the region.7

FDI in the Russian Federation is concentrated in energy, mining, food production and services. The largest investment projects were realised in oil and gas extraction. In the other CEECs, FDI growth mainly occurred in manufacturing and services. A remarkable feature is the strength of FDI in the service sector in the Czech Republic, Poland and Hungary. This is predominantly the outcome of investment in financial, telecommunication and related services.

Inward FDI in the CEECs is heavily dominated by investors from the European Union. The EU accounts for some three-quarters of the FDI stock in Poland and the Czech Republic and two-thirds of the FDI stock in Hungary.8 In Russia, the EU accounts for some 50% of the inward FDI stock.

The outlook for FDI in the CEECs is generally positive, in particular for those countries that have a strong economic performance, fast progress in structural reforms, a good investment climate and the prospect of becoming a member of the European Union. According to UNCTAD figures, FDI inflows into Central Europe reached a new record in 1998. Inflows in the CEECs, other than the Russian Federation, rose from 13 billion dollars in 1997 to 16 billion dollars in 1998.9 Prospects for FDI in Russia and Ukraine are less bright, given both economic and political instability and the lack of a clear and reliable regulatory framework.

---

7. Hungary is Central and Eastern Europe's largest recipient of FDI *per capita*, followed by the Czech Republic and Estonia.
8. Based on data from OECD (1998).
9. UNCTAD Press Release, 2 June 1999, www.UNCTAD.org.

Figure 4.4: Foreign direct investment in the CEECS, 1997
(Percentages of total inward stock)

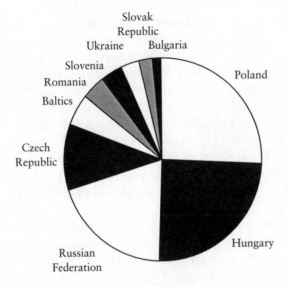

Source: UNCTAD, *World Investment Report 1998*

Deterred by financial and political instability, FDI inflows in Russia fell drastically from 6 billion dollars in 1997 to 2 billion dollars in 1998.

4.4 Dutch bilateral relations with Central and Eastern Europe

Approximately 3.8% of Dutch exports find their way to the Central and Eastern European markets[10], which cover about 2.6% of total Central and Eastern European imports. On the other hand, roughly 3.2% of Dutch imports come from Central and Eastern European markets and account for about 2.1% of total Central and Eastern European exports. Furthermore, the CEECS account for about 2% of the total stock of outward Dutch FDI.

---

10. Here we consider Poland, Hungary, the Czech Republic, Romania, Bulgaria, Albania, the Slovak Republic, Russia, the Baltic States, all the remaining republics of the former Soviet Union, Slovenia and all other former republics of Yugoslavia.

4.4.1 Trade between the Netherlands and Central and Eastern European countries

Since 1989, both Dutch exports to and imports from the CEECs have shown a remarkable growth. On average, merchandise exports and imports increased annually by 16% and 9% respectively in the period up to 1998. Exports to the CEECs started to grow soon after the fall of the Berlin Wall and kept their momentum. However, imports fell in the early period and their growth really picked up only a couple of years later (Figure 4.5). The quality of products made in Eastern Europe simply did not stand up to Dutch, and for that matter, Western standards in general. The real appreciation of most Central and Eastern European currencies during the first years of the nineties further undermined the CEECs' competitiveness. Only raw materials, especially crude oil, could find their way to the Netherlands in the first years of transition. Improvements eventually led to imports by the Netherlands picking up as well, and since 1994, imports seem to have been on the increase every month. In recent years, Dutch import growth from the CEECs outpaced export growth. Nevertheless, the trade balance between the Netherlands and the CEECs still shows a large surplus for the Netherlands.

Figure 4.5: Dutch merchandise trade with CEECs
(In billions of guilders)

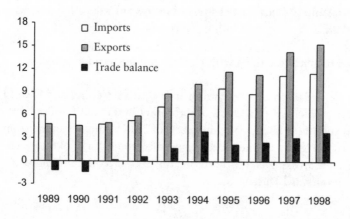

Source: Statistics Netherlands

The outbreak of the financial crisis in Russia brought trade developments to a halt. Data for the first quarter of 1999 confirm that exports to the CEECs have dropped considerably (18%), although exports to especially Hungary and the Czech Republic continued to grow. Imports were and are affected by the financial turbulence as well, but to a far lesser extent.

In 1998, Poland was the most important export market for the Netherlands in Central and Eastern Europe. In 1997, Poland was second after Russia. However, bilateral trade with Russia plunged by more than 50% after the outbreak of the financial turbulence. Russia remained nevertheless the most important Central and Eastern European supplier to the Netherlands. Of course, it's oil which is accountable for that. In the long run, Russia will almost certainly regain its position as the most important Eastern European trading partner of the Netherlands. However, in the short-term, trade relations with markets like Poland, Hungary and the Czech Republic will be more important.

During the nineties, trade patterns between the Netherlands and the CEECs changed. As Figure 4.6 shows, the share of energy in Dutch imports dropped from almost one half to little more than 15%. Imports of capital goods and consumer durables showed a remarkable growth, especially after 1993 when imports of TV's, VCR's and PC's from Poland and the Czech Republic especially, started to flow in. Finished and semi-processed products also became more important as imports increased sharply, from especially Russia. Surprisingly, the share of agricultural products in total imports has diminished remarkably during the last decade. Given the fact that most Eastern European countries have a comparative advantage for these products, one would expect these shares to rise again. Most likely the Dutch market, or better the EU market, is not really open to Eastern European agricultural producers.[11]

Figure 4.6: Dutch imports from CEECs by main categories
(Percentages)

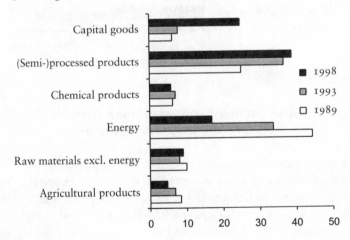

Source: Statistics Netherlands

The Netherlands' export structure changed as well. The proportion of capital goods increased over the years to the detriment of chemical products, which nev-

---

11. In Figures 4.6 and 4.7 Central and Eastern Europe excludes former Yugoslavia.

ertheless showed good growth figures recently (see Figure 4.7). The growth of capital goods exports is broad based, but very recently exports of PC's and electrical equipment in particular, soared. Agricultural exports saw their share rise to almost 30% in 1993 but basically because their growth outpaced the growth of other products. In the following years the share dropped to 25% by 1997 before falling sharply in 1998 as a result of the Russian crisis. This sharp drop is easily explained if one keeps in mind that Russia counts for more than half of total Dutch agricultural exports to the CEECs. Nevertheless, even with a share of around 20%, agricultural products still constitute an important export category for the Netherlands.

Figure 4.7: Dutch exports from CEECs by main categories
         (Percentages)

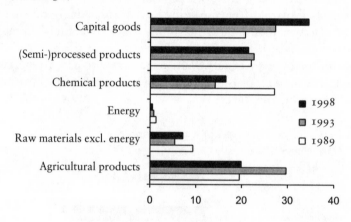

Source: Statistics Netherlands

4.4.2 Competitive position of Dutch exporters on the Central and Eastern European markets

Interesting as these developments may be, they tell us preciously little about the development of the competitive position of the Dutch exporters. To gauge whether their positions have improved or declined in Central and Eastern European markets[12], we have run a Constant Market Shares (CMS) analysis for the years 1993 and 1997[13] (see Oldersma and van Bergeijk, 1993; Jepma, 1986).

Because our main concern was the performance of Dutch exporters in the Central and Eastern European markets, we have basically split the change in Dutch

---

12. We distinguished the following Central and Eastern European markets: the Czech Republic, Hungary, Poland, Russia, the Slovak Republic, Romania, Bulgaria, Slovenia, the Baltic States and the former Soviet Union excluding Russia and the Baltic States.

exports to the CEECs into two parts in our CMS analysis. The first part represents the change which should occur if, in every sub-market,[14] the Dutch shares remained constant (the constant market share). The second part is the residual, which represents the difference between the observed change and the calculated change, assuming constant market shares. This residual is generally used as an indicator for the change in competitiveness. A positive residual indicates an improvement in competitiveness.

The assumption of constant market shares does not mean that every sub-market grows with the same percentage, nor does it mean that total market shares do not change. Let us take the Dutch export structure as an example. The trade structure of the Netherlands is, and has been for a long time, quite different from the OECD average. The Netherlands exports relatively large quantities of agricultural and energy goods and relatively few capital goods.[15] Such an export pattern has an influence of its own on export growth. All other things being equal, suppose that Central and Eastern Europe's demand for agricultural goods falls relative to the demand for capital goods. As agricultural goods make up a relatively large part of Dutch exports, a decline in the Netherlands share of total exports to the CEECs is to be expected, even if market shares in all sub-markets do not change. The same argument can be applied to the different geographical markets. So, in order to estimate the impact of competitiveness on changes in export growth rates one must take both the geographical pattern and the commodity composition into account. The CMS analysis enables us to make such a breakdown.

Assuming constant market shares in the CEECs, we can break down the change in Dutch exports to CEECs into a part that can be attributed to the overall growth of the Central and Eastern European market (the so-called scale effect),[16] a part that can be attributed to the geographical distribution of the markets in Central and Eastern Europe, a part that can be attributed to the commodity composition, and a part that must be attributed to the interaction between the geographical and the commodity compositions.[17] The residual, being the difference between the observed change and the calculated change assuming constant market shares, is

13. We have chosen 1993 because the period before that year is characterised by restructuring in CEECs, the resurgence of new nations in Eastern Europe and dismantling of old federal structures. The year 1997 was simply chosen because trade figures for 1998 were not yet available on the scale needed to run a meaningful CMS analysis. As the reference group we used a subset of the OECD. Not included are the CEECs themselves, Korea, Mexico, New Zealand, Canada, Turkey and Iceland.
14. We distinguish ten commodities and ten geographical markets, so a total of hundred (10×10) submarkets are considered.
15. This is partly reflected on the import side where the Netherlands also imports relatively many energy goods, especially crude oil, and capital goods. Agricultural and semi-processed products are imported to a lesser extent.
16. Note that in this exercise, Dutch exports are compared to the exports of the OECD to the CEECs and that neither adjustment is made for export changes from other countries to the CEECs nor for the changes in domestic production in the CEECs.

used as an indicator for the change in competitiveness. This is formally described in the following identity (Eq. 4.2):

$$\Sigma\Sigma\Delta q_{ij} = s^o\Delta Q \qquad\qquad\qquad\qquad\qquad\text{(i)} \quad \text{scale effect}$$
$$+ \Sigma\Sigma s^o{}_{ij}\Delta Q_{ij} - \Sigma s^o{}_i\Delta\, Q_i \qquad\qquad \text{(ii)} \quad \text{geographical effect}$$
$$+ \Sigma\Sigma\, s^o{}_{ij}\, \Delta Q_{ij} - \Sigma\, s^o{}_j\, \Delta Q_j \qquad\qquad \text{(iii)} \quad \text{commodity effect}$$
$$+ (\Sigma s^o{}_i\, \Delta Q_i - s^o\Delta Q) - (\Sigma\Sigma s^o{}_{ij}\, \Delta Q_{ij} - \Sigma\, s^o{}_j\, \Delta Q_j) \quad \text{(iv)} \quad \text{interaction effect}$$
$$+ \Sigma\Sigma\Delta\, s_{ij}Q^o{}_{ij} + \Sigma\Sigma\Delta s_{ij}\, \Delta Q_{ij} \qquad\qquad \text{(v)} \quad \text{competition effect}$$

where q_{ij} is the export of commodity i to country j, Q_{ij} is the export of commodity i of the reference group to country j, the share s equals q/Q, Q_j equals $\Sigma\, Q_{ij}$ over i, Q_i equals $\Sigma\, Q_{ij}$ over j and the superscript o refers to the base year.

In Tables 4.3, 4.4 and 4.5 the results of the CMS analysis are shown.[18] It is clear from Table 4.3 that the Netherlands' exports have grown in line with total exports of the OECD to the CEECs. Whereas total OECD exports to the CEECs almost doubled in the period between 1993 and 1997 (a rise of 93%, the scale effect), Dutch exports grew by about 82%. The difference is partly explained by the unfavourable commodity composition of Dutch exports. As already explained, this is attributable to the relatively large agricultural share, while Eastern European countries have a declining interest in agricultural products relative to other goods. The geographical composition was favourable for Dutch exports. This is explained by the fact that the larger Central and Eastern European markets are relatively more important to Dutch exporters than the smaller ones.

However, actual growth in exports (82%) was smaller than the calculated growth assuming constant market shares (89%). This indicates that the Dutch competitive position relative to other OECD countries has deteriorated slightly during the period 1993-97. That Dutch exporters are losing market shares in Central and Eastern European markets may be a normal development. To some extent, as shown by the gravity model, Dutch exporters had already discovered Eastern markets at an early stage, whereas some other OECD countries expanded their exports to the CEECs at a later point in time. Furthermore, it may be that Dutch producers have set up production facilities in the CEECs which are not captured in a CMS analysis. In addition, it may be that exporters have shifted to other markets or that the Dutch competitive position has deteriorated because of a real appreciation of the guilder.[19] Part of the explanation may also be that Dutch

---

17. This interaction effect is basically a correction factor. Suppose that the geographical market distribution and commodity composition reinforce each other. In both cases a plus will be recorded but the overlap has to be subtracted. So, a negative sign implies that geographical and commodity developments reinforce each other, a positive sign the opposite.
18. Calculations are based on US dollars. Using guilders instead does not fundamentally change the outcomes.

Table 4.3: Results of the CMS analysis for the Netherlands *vis-à-vis* 20 OECD countries for the period 1993-1997 (Percentage change)

Scale effect	93.2
Commodity effect	-10.1
Geographical effect	4.3
Interaction effect	1.5 +
Constant Market Share	88.9
Residual (Competition effects)	-7.4
Observed change in export value	81.5

exporters are losing market shares in the expanding Central and Eastern European markets simply because they are not able to provide the products asked for at competitive prices. Whatever the reason, the negative sign should not be taken too seriously, for the Central and Eastern European markets will certainly be promising markets in the near future.

If one takes a look at different geographical markets, some interesting features are revealed as well. Dutch export growth to a geographical market is of course a result of the overall growth of the geographical market with a correction for the commodity composition of Dutch exports to that market and a change attributable to changing competitive positions of Dutch exporters in that geographical market.

Table 4.4 shows the share of Dutch exports in different geographical markets, indicating again that Dutch exports have grown in line with total OECD exports to the CEECs. The exception is Poland, where an unfavourable commodity composition and large losses in the competitive position reinforce each other. With the exception of Russia, the commodity composition of Dutch exports is unfavourable in all other geographical markets as well. The plus for Russia can be explained by the large share of agricultural products in the exports to Russia. Obviously, in the longer run, when Russia can be expected to demand more and more capital goods, this positive influence will diminish.

If one studies the competition effects in the different markets, it is surprising to see the large losses in the Polish market. The close proximity of Germany, together with the large Polish demand for capital goods, including cars, may be accountable for that. Dutch exporters have managed to improve their positions in the Hungarian market, which seems to be correlated with developments in the capital goods markets. Exports of electronic equipment and PCs in particular show high growth figures in the Hungarian market. The plus for the Russian market is explained by the large agricultural content.

---

19. Remember that the calculation is only made for Central and Eastern European markets, not for total exports.

Table 4.4: Share of Dutch exports in OECD exports to the different markets in Central and Eastern Europe and the commodity and competition effects on these markets

	Dutch export shares		Commodity effect	Competition effect
	1993	1997	in percentage of observed change of Dutch exports in that market	
Czech Republic	4.2	4.0	-6.2	-6.9
Hungary	4.2	4.0	-24.4	12.5
Poland	7.1	5.8	-18.3	-34.6
Russia	5.7	6.1	7.0	10.1
Total 1/	5.2	4.9	-12.4	-9.1

1/ Total includes also the Baltic States, Bulgaria, Romania, the Slovak Republic, Slovenia and the former Soviet Union excluding Russia and the Baltics

Table 4.5 shows the Dutch export shares in total OECD exports to the different commodity markets in the CEECs and the geographical and competition effects for Dutch exports on these markets. Noteworthy is the fact that the share of agricultural products in total Dutch exports is not just large, but that the Netherlands share of agricultural products in OECD exports to the CEECs is large as well and has risen in recent years. Another remarkable fact is that the Dutch share in the exports of capital goods to the CEECs did not fall in the recent past. This is a result of plusses on the smaller markets and minuses on the larger, but also stresses the point that no single sector is homogeneous. In the capital sector, it seems that Dutch exporters of all kinds of electronic equipment and machinery are doing fine and that the automotive sector is not.

As noted above, the overall competitive position deteriorated to some extent. Table 4.5 however, shows large differences between sectors. For agricultural, finished and semi-processed products, the situation actually improved. Losses are recorded in the chemical sector, which is hardly surprising but can perhaps be attributed to a relative deterioration in transport possibilities.

The capital goods sector shows an expected loss, given the position and composition of the Dutch capital goods industry (relatively few cars) and a large loss for finished manufactured goods. This category is hardly a homogeneous one and the data used in this exercise indicate that this loss of competitiveness has most likely been caused by a sharp fall in the Dutch export shares for clothing and shoes. The reason behind this is not really clear and it may well be the case, given the economic developments during the period 1993-97, that Dutch exporters of clothing and shoes have shifted their attention to other more profitable markets.[20]

___

20. In 1997, total Dutch exports of clothing and shoes were 61% higher than in 1993, wheras exports to the CEECs were only 7% higher.

Table 4.5: Share of Dutch exports in OECD exports to the different commodity markets in CEECs and the geographical and competition effects in these markets

	Dutch export shares		Geographical effect	Competition effect
	1993	1997	in percentage of observed change of Dutch exports in that sector	
Agricultural products (SITC 0)	10.9	12.0	7.8	16.1
Chemical products (SITC 5)	7.0	6.6	-0.6	-13.4
(Semi-)processed products (SITC 6)	3.5	3.6	0.1	5.7
Capital goods (SITC 7)	3.3	3.3	6.5	-8.5
Manufactured goods (SITC 8)	4.9	3.9	9.4	-83.1
Total 1/	5.2	4.9	5.3	-9.1

1/ Total includes the smaller sectors SITC 1 to SITC 4 and SITC 9

It is also possible that producers from different emerging markets like Asia and/or Turkey forced them out of the Central and Eastern European markets, or that exports have been replaced by local production.

To sum up: Dutch exports to the CEECs seem to have been more or less in line with that of their main competitors. However, the CMS analysis indicates that the competitive position of Dutch exporters in the Central and Eastern European markets was under some pressure during the 1993-97 period as well.

4.4.3 Dutch foreign direct investment

It is not only trade which gives an indication for the intensifying bilateral economic relations between the Netherlands and the CEECs. The development of FDI also indicates that economic relations are becoming more intense. Up to now, it is mostly Dutch FDI in the CEECs, and not the other way around. That is not surprising given the position of the CEECs. However, one should bear in mind that other emerging markets have brought forward a large number of companies that are investing in Western countries like the Netherlands as well. It is only a matter of time before Polish and Russian companies or those of other nationalities will invest in the Netherlands on a larger scale.

Since 1989, CEECs have opened up their markets for FDI. It took a few years before Dutch companies, and others as well, really started to invest in the CEECs. In 1993, the total stock of Dutch FDI in the CEECs ammounted to little more than 0.5 billion euro, which was equivalent to a share in total Dutch outward FDI stock of less than one half per cent. At the end of 1997, Dutch FDI in the CEECs totalled a staggering 3.3 billion euro, which is equivalent to a share of 2% in total Dutch outward FDI stock. Total investments in Eastern Europe by Dutch companies at the end of 1999 should easily surpass the 6 billion euro mark.[21]

Up to 1993, trade and food were the dominant sectors in which Dutch companies invested (Figure 4.8). That is hardly surprising, given the fact that up to 1989 Central and Eastern European markets were closed to Western companies except for a few which were necessary to distribute or sell Central and Eastern European products abroad, especially in food and trade. In the years following 1993, investments found their way especially to financial, transport and communications services and the mining industry, as well as the food industry. Given the Dutch economic structure and given the sectors in which large Dutch companies are present, this is not a very surprising development and most of all a result of opening up the Central and Eastern European markets. Poland, the Czech Republic and Hungary are the main destinations for Dutch investments. Russia became a more important recipient of Dutch investments during 1997 and 1998.

Figure 4.8: Dutch FDI in Central and Eastern Europe, 1997
(Outward stocks in millions of euros, at the end of the year)

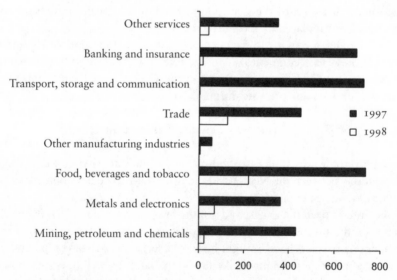

Source: De Nederlandsche Bank

---

21. Total investments in Albania, Bulgaria, the Czech Republic, Hungary, Poland, Romania, the Slovak Republic, the former European Soviet Republics and former Yugoslavia.

4.4.4 Strategic behaviour of Dutch enterprises

The different crises, which have hit several emerging markets in the recent past, clearly made investors more careful. However, several studies found that foreign investments which a company deems to be strategic are not being postponed, or if they are, then only for a short period.[22] Because Central and Eastern Europe is still seen as one of the most promising regions, certainly in the longer run, Dutch companies will go on investing in Central and Eastern Europe in the coming years. However, companies are making clear distinctions. It is important in their view to be present in Poland, Hungary and the Czech Republic. These countries have carried out an impressive restructuring of their economies. Therefore, they are not only favoured because of their promising prospects as a market to sell products in, but also because the prevailing conditions make them interesting suppliers for other markets. The distance by which nations like Russia and Ukraine are trailing the above mentioned nations is extremely great. Investments in those countries are made with a very long-term view and, as far as Russia is concerned, are related to the impressive reserves of oil and gas as well as other raw materials. However, given the turbulence in Russia it remains to be seen to what extent investors are willing to maintain their direct investments in Russia at the levels seen in the recent past.

4.5 Conclusions

Since the start of the transition period, now ten years ago, countries in Central and Eastern Europe have begun to open up their markets to foreign trade and investment. There are big differences amongst the CEECs but all have experienced strong growth in cross border trade and inflows of foreign capital. Trade flows have more than doubled during the last decade. Trade volumes still developed in an asymmetrical way, in the sense that exports to the CEECs increased more rapidly than imports from the CEECs. Central and Eastern European producers shifted their attention from their former principal trading partners in the East toward Western markets. They also shifted their attention to products with higher added value, like capital goods. With a more open view for the outside world, the CEECs became also recipients of large inflows of foreign capital, especially FDI.

Dutch producers and foreign traders have contributed their share to these developments. Trade and investment relations were intensified and already early in the nineties trade patterns between the Netherlands and the CEECs resembled a normal trade pattern as is shown by an analysis using the gravitation model. However, using a CMS analysis, Dutch exporters seem to have slightly lost some competitive power in the recent past. Part of that loss may be attributed to the increase

---

22. See KPMG (1998) and McKinsey and Company (1999).

of Dutch FDI in the CEECs. Part of it may be a reflection of the relatively strong initial position of Dutch exporters in the markets of the CEECs. Recently, Dutch FDI flows into the CEECs have risen strongly and now account for about 5% of total Dutch outward FDI flows.

Appendix 4.1: Data sources

The following data sources were used for simulations with the gravity model: The export data of the OECD countries for 1991 were obtained from OECD, *Foreign Trade by Commodities*. The source for the export data of the CEECs for 1991 was the *PlanEcon Report*, Vol. VIII, no. 27, 28, 29, July 1992. The export data for 1997 were obtained from IMF Direction of Trade Statistics. The US dollar GDPs were obtained from IMF, *International Financial Statistics*. For the sources of gravity centres and distances see Biessen (1991).

References

Biessen, G. (1991), 'Is the Impact of Central Planning on the level of Foreign Trade Really Negative?' *Journal of Comparative Economics*, Vol.15, No.1, pp.42-44.

De Nederlandsche Bank (1999), *Statistisch Bulletin Juni 1999 (Statistical Bulletin June 1999)*, Amsterdam.

Eatwell, J., M. Ellman, M. Karlsson, M. Nuti, and J. Shapiro (1995), *Transformation and Integration; Shaping the Future of Central and Eastern Europe*, Institute of Public Policy Research, Londen.

European Bank for Reconstruction and Development (1999), *Transition Report Update*, London.

Gros, D. and A. Steinherr (1995), *Winds of Change Economic Transition in Central and Eastern Europe*, Addison, Wesley Longman, London.

Hamilton, C.B. and L.A. Winters (1992), 'Trade with Eastern Europe', *Economic Policy*, Vol.14, April.

International Monetary Fund, *Direction of Trade Statistics*, various issues, Washington, D.C.

International Monetary Fund, *International Financial Statistics*, various issues, Washington, D.C.

Jepma, C.J. (1986), *Extensions and Applications of the Constant Market Shares Analysis*, Ph. D. Thesis, University of Groningen.

KPMG (1998), *Gevolgen van de Azië-crisis voor de bedrijfsstrategie van Nederlandse ondernemingen – Gesprekken met ondernemers* (Consequences of the Asia crisis for corporate strategies of Dutch companies – Interviews with leading executives), 4 November 1998.

McKinsey and Company (1999), *Versterken positie in Midden- en Oost-Europa. Samenvatting van interviews met Nederlandse top-ondernemingen* (Reinforcing the position in Central and Eastern Europe. Summary of interviews with leading Dutch executives), 8 June 1999.

OECD, *Foreign Trade by Commodities*, various issues, Paris.

OECD (1998) *International Direct Investments Statistics Yearbook 1998*, Paris.

Oldersma, H. and P.A.G. van Bergeijk (1993), 'Not so constant! The Constant market shares and the exchange rate', *De Economist*, pp.380-401.

UNCTAD (1999), *Handbook of International Trade and Development Statistics 1996/1997*, New York and Geneva.

UNCTAD (1998), *World Investment Report 1998: Trends and Determinants*, New York and Geneva.

Van Bergeijk, P.A.G. and H. Oldersma (1990), 'Détente, Market-oriented Reform and German Unification: Potential Consequences for the World Trade System', *Kyklos*, Vol.43, No.4, pp.599-609.

Part II

Enlargement of the European Union

CHAPTER 5

Time for Enlargement

Hans van den Broek[1]

5.1 Introduction

Almost ten years after the fall of the Berlin Wall, the Kosovo crisis has been a bloody reminder of what, in another context, we used to call 'the cost of non-Europe'.[2] For the current member states of the European Union, the integration process that began in the early 1950s has brought both remarkable political stability and a spectacular increase in economic well-being. Conversely, the disintegration in the Balkans during the past decade has exacerbated poverty and inter-ethnic hatred, and cost the lives of many thousands of innocent civilians. The comparison of these two polar cases may not constitute a very rigorous scientific demonstration, but it does provide a *prima facie* argument in favour of regional co-operation and progressive integration.

This chapter does not deal with the Balkans specifically. Its subject matter is the method of European integration, as it is being applied to the formal candidate countries, mostly in Central Europe. The same method of integration will ultimately apply to all countries wishing to join the EU. In line with the main thrust of this book, the current chapter will put considerable emphasis on the economic aspects of EU enlargement, but it will also try to place it in its broader political context.

Compared with the simplicity of the basic political message – European integration brings both peace and wealth – the practicalities are rather more complicated. In some important respects, the EU is a club for rich countries, whose policies, rules and institutions have attained a level of sophistication that is hard to match for less wealthy countries. It is precisely because these policies, rules and institutions operate throughout its entire territory that the EU is what it is. Casting this principle aside for the benefit of rapid enlargement – in other words,

---

1. The views expressed in this paper are those of the author, and not necessarily those of the European Commission or other EU institutions
2. The 'Costs of non-Europe' project, which led to the 'Cecchini report' of 1988 named after its chairman Paolo Cecchini, conducted a detailed assessment of the potential economic effects of completing the internal market of the European Community. It tried to quantify the gains from such a completion, and thus the 'cost' of not doing so.

allowing new entrants major and lengthy dispensation from the common rules – would help no one. The current members would suffer because the essence of what has been a successful venture would be destroyed, and the new members would not gain from joining something that has been destroyed by the manner of their joining.

We therefore face a complex set of practical questions in organising an enlargement process that is as rapid as possible, yet maintains the integrity of the Union. What are the preconditions a candidate needs to fulfil? Among the many difficult preparatory steps, which should come first? How can the incumbents assist the candidates in what is a truly Herculean effort? How can we maintain public support for integration and avoid disenchantment with the process, potentially leading to reversals? These are some of the essential questions.

Over the past few years the European Commission, true to its role as the motor of European integration and the guardian of the EU's treaties, has developed answers to these questions. So far, the EU member states have agreed that, broadly, these are the right answers. And the candidate countries have largely accepted the logic of the EU approach. They have already made very substantial strides towards accession, and thereby provided early vindication of the method.

5.2 We must be doing something right

The queue of countries hoping to join the EU is long. There are 13 candidates who have submitted applications and on which the Commission has issued formal Opinions, as can be seen from Table 5.1. With six of them, actual accession negotiations began in 1998. Six more countries are lined up for negotiations to begin in the next few years. Then there is Turkey, which the European Commission definitely regards as a candidate country even if the Council of Ministers has so far been reluctant to use this form of words. There are a few developed European countries that have, over the years, been ambivalent in their European ambitions but whose future membership cannot be excluded, such as Norway (which still holds the record for the shortest accession negotiations ever, but whose population then rejected membership in a referendum in 1993) and Switzerland. And, highlighted by the crises of recent years, there are the Balkan states, many of which clearly have the ambition to join the EU, even though everybody realises that this will take time to materialise.

If so many countries believe the EU is worth joining, we must be doing something right. A cynical view might be that most countries in the queue are much poorer than the EU, and they hope for financial gain in terms of budget transfers. Of course, such a bookkeeper's interpretation is wrong. First of all, there are powerful non-economic arguments for accession. In fact, anyone who has done any travelling to the candidate countries over the past decade will have been struck by the fact that it is mostly political and security considerations that drive these countries towards the EU, and that economic gain comes only in second or

Table 5.1: The queue for EU membership

	Application date	Commission Opinion	Start of negotiations
Turkey	14 April 1987	1989	
Cyprus	3 July 1990	1993	March 1998
Malta	16 July 1990	1993	
Hungary	31 March 1994	1997	March 1998
Poland	5 April 1994	1997	March 1998
Romania	22 June 1995	1997	
Slovak Republic	27 June 1995	1997	
Latvia	13 October 1995	1997	
Estonia	24 November 1995	1997	March 1998
Lithuania	8 December 1995	1997	
Bulgaria	14 December 1995	1997	
Czech Republic	17 January 1996	1997	March 1998
Slovenia	10 June 1996	1997	March 1998

third place. But even the strictly economic arguments are clear and uncontroversial: enlargement will not only be of huge benefit to the candidate countries, but will be advantageous to the existing member states as well.[3]

The thesis that underlies the EU's enlargement method is that enlargement is only worthwhile if all member states – old and new – play by the same rules. Having second-class member states which would have fewer obligations (and, consequently, fewer rights) would not only be of doubtful value to the new member states, it would also put at risk the essence of what makes the EU into a success. Since this is a crucial argument, it is worth elaborating briefly.

For a quintessentially political project, the EU is a surprisingly technical affair. Since the 1950s, European integration has produced 80,000 pages of legislation (which for some obscure reason is generally referred to by its French jargon term: *acquis communautaire*). This came about through a process that could be called 'integration by accretion'. It started in the 1950s with the coal and steel community – crucial industries at the time but still a rather narrow focus. It then expanded to the creation of a customs union, and a common agricultural policy. Subsequently, we discovered that an absence of customs duties does not make for a really free flow of goods and services internally, so we added the 'internal market'.

---

3. There is a surprising lack of literature investigating the economic case for EU enlargement in any great depth – perhaps because it is uncontroversial. Baldwin, Francois and Portes (1997) is one of the best-known exceptions. Its bottom line is unambiguous: 'enlargement is a very good deal for both the EU incumbents and the new members'. A more recent publication by the French Commissariat Général du Plan, '*L'élargissement de l'Union Européenne à l'Est de l'Europe: des gains à escompter à l'Est et à l'Ouest*', (Paris, 1999) reviews the existing literature and comes to the same positive conclusion.

Then we considered that this internal market would only reach its full potential with monetary union and a common currency. And all along, we added many other things on the side, from education and science to culture.

Two things are quite remarkable about this process. First, the final goal of the European integration process is decidedly fuzzy – intentionally so. While some outsiders have sometimes used grandiloquent phrases such as "A United States of Europe"[4] to indicate what we are heading for, those who wrote the Treaties have limited themselves to indications such as 'an ever closer union'. To borrow from the jargon of economists who describe how markets arrive at balancing supply and demand, it is integration by *tâtonnement*: we feel our way to each subsequent phase; we avoid unnecessary ideological and teleological debates by going one step at a time. The second remarkable feature of the process is that this ever-deeper integration has been achieved while at the same time expanding the number of member states. One of the oldest *faux débats* in the history of EU integration concerns the tension between deepening (more integration) and widening (more member states). The result is there for all to see: the EU is now far more integrated than a generation ago, and also has $2^{1}/_{2}$ times more member states.

Some parts of the *acquis communautaire* may be less appealing to the general public than others. The fact that there are 28 pages of EU legal text describing, in excruciating detail, what are the requirements for tractor headlights – including five technical drawings and diagrams[5]– is not the stuff that draws many voters to the polls during elections for the European Parliament. But on the whole, it works. Tractors with the right headlights can be bought and sold freely throughout the EU. No customs or other controls at internal borders. More generally, EU integration creates a level playing field for business, by means of internal market rules on product safety or environmental standards, competition rules, *etc*. This contributes hugely to the competitiveness of the economy, and has positive spin-offs such as making the EU into one of the main actors in world trade.

It should be emphasised that the EU budget plays only a marginal role. The budget is barely more than 1% of GDP. The key things that make the EU into what it is cost almost nothing. To take only one example: telecom liberalisation. Some years ago, the EU adopted a few legislative texts opening up national telecom-markets to competition. Since then, the Commission has produced annual reports assessing the telecom-market, with a very clear result: prices are down, service and reliability are up, and employment in the telecommunications industry is up. All at virtually zero cost to the taxpayer, and with large economic gains for business and consumers.

---

4. Winston Churchill.
5. Council Directive 78/933/EEC of 17 October 1978 on the approximation of the laws of the Member States relating to the installation of lighting and light-signalling devices on wheeled agricultural and forestry tractors. Official Journal L 325 , 20 November 1978.

Obviously, the *acquis* that has developed over the decades was created to suit the incumbent member states. This means that it is geared to the needs of relatively highly developed market economies, and places considerable demands on its institutions – not only the governmental administration, but also regional and local authorities, the legal system, supervisory and regulatory bodies, and several parts of the private sector such as lawyers, accountants, *etc*. This poses a considerable challenge for those candidate countries in Central Europe that only began to create a market economy and its attendant institutional features a decade or so ago, and that moreover, are still at a level of income where some of the more refined aspects of EU societies may be considered 'luxuries'.

5.3 The criteria

Yet, it is clear that the existing member states will want to preserve the benefits of EU integration and will resist diluting the general applicability of the *acquis*. This is why, now as well as during all previous enlargements, the principle is that candidate countries sign up to the *acquis communautaire*. In that sense, 'accession negotiations' is a misnomer: the *acquis* is not negotiable. The only real purpose of the negotiations is threefold: to determine whether the candidate country has fully grasped the meaning of the *acquis*, to verify that it is able and willing to implement it, and to discuss transition arrangements. In a limited number of areas it may be desirable either for the candidate country or for the incumbent member states that the *acquis* is phased in gradually. A short but crucial passage from the Copenhagen European Council conclusions (June 1993) is worth quoting in full:

"The associated countries in Central and Eastern Europe that so desire shall become members of the Union. Accession will take place as soon as a country is able to assume the obligations of membership by satisfying the economic and political conditions. Membership requires:
- that the candidate country has achieved stability of institutions guaranteeing democracy, the rule of law, human rights and respect for and protection of minorities;
- the existence of a functioning market economy, as well as the capacity to cope with competitive pressure and market forces within the Union;
- the ability to take on the obligations of membership, including adherence to the aims of political, economic and monetary union.

The Union's capacity to absorb new members, while maintaining the momentum of European integration, is also an important consideration in the general interest of both the Union and the candidate countries".

The three indents in the above quotation have become known as the three Copenhagen Conditions. In shorthand, they are a political criterion, an economic criterion, and what one could call an '*acquis*' criterion.

The Copenhagen text is still relatively vague and needs to be made operational. This is what the European Commission has done in recent years, starting in July 1997 with the ten Opinions on the Central European candidates' accession requests (and the accompanying Composite Paper which summarises the Opinions and draws political conclusions). Then, in November 1998 this analysis was refined considerably in the Regular Reports on the candidates' progress towards accession. By the time the current book is published, in late 1999, the Commission will have issued another set of Regular Reports.

Making the Copenhagen conditions operational has turned out to be a complex process: it requires setting up an analytical framework that determines which features will have to be looked at, then amassing a huge amount of quantitative and qualitative information, and lastly arriving at a broad judgement that takes into account this multitude of disparate factors. These range from the mundane to the abstruse. For instance, the political criterion requires that the rule of law be guaranteed. How does one measure this? One of the many things the Commission has done is to 'count the judges' – literally: how many judges are there in Estonia or Slovenia, how many judges' posts are vacant, what is their average age or their average seniority on the bench?

The second Copenhagen condition, which relates to the economy, can be broken down into two parts. First, whether a country is a functioning market economy, and second, whether it will be capable to cope with competitive pressures and market forces in the internal market.

The existence of a market economy requires that equilibrium between supply and demand be established by the free interplay of market forces. A market economy is functioning when the legal system, including the regulation of property rights, is in place and can be enforced. The performance of a market economy is facilitated and improved by macroeconomic stability and a degree of consensus about the essentials of economic policy. A well-developed financial sector and an absence of significant barriers to market entry and exit help to improve the efficiency with which an economy works.

It is difficult, some years ahead of prospective membership, and before a candidate country has adopted and implemented the larger part of Community law, to form a definitive judgement of the country's capacity to cope with competitive pressures in the Union. Nevertheless, it is possible to identify a number of features of its development which provide some indication of this capacity.

The first of these features is a stable macroeconomic framework within which individual economic agents can make decisions in a climate of reasonable predictability. There must be a sufficient amount of human and physical capital, including infrastructure. A substantial proportion of individual businesses needs to have the ability to adapt to face increased competitive pressures in the single market. Businesses need to invest to improve their efficiency, so that they can both compete at home and take advantage of economies of scale which flow from access to the single market. This capacity to adapt will be greater, the more firms have access to investment finance, the better the quality of their workforce, and the more successful they are at innovation. Moreover, an economy will be better able to take on the obligations of membership, the higher the degree of economic integration it achieves with the Union ahead of accession. The more integrated a country already is with the Union, the less will be the further restructuring implied by membership. The level of economic integration is related to both the range and the volume of goods traded with member states. Direct benefits from access to the single market may also be greater in sectors where there is a sizeable proportion of small businesses, since these are relatively more affected by impediments to trade.[6]

Both in the 1997 Opinions and in the subsequent annual Regular Reports, the Commission has assessed the economies of the candidates based on this analytical framework, and drawn its conclusions. This is not a mechanical process of totting up pluses and minuses and yielding a pass or fail mark, but requires a certain degree of judgement: the various elements that enter into the analysis are not all of equal weight, and interact with each other in various ways that are hard to model precisely.

This economic analysis has had very practical consequences for the candidate countries. Its outcome has largely determined with which countries the Union has since opened formal accession negotiations. In the Opinions, the Commission concluded that only some of the ten Central European candidates passed the market economy test, and had made sufficient progress that they should be able, in the medium term, to pass the competitiveness test as well. This was the dividing line: be a functioning market economy now, and offer reasonable guarantees of withstanding competitive pressures within about five years. If so, the economic conditions for the start of negotiations are met. Of course, there are political and *acquis* criteria as well, but – with one notable exception – it turned out that the economic test was decisive: all candidates but the Slovak Republic passed the political test, and all failed the *acquis* test (but the latter was considered normal, in the sense that alignment would take place during the course of the negotiations, prior to accession). As a result, negotiations were opened in March 1998 with the Czech Republic, Estonia, Hungary, Poland and Slovenia – and with Cyprus, but here the history is different.[7]

This judgement was broadly confirmed in the Regular Reports of 1998. Much to the disappointment of Latvia and Lithuania in particular, the Commission not-

6. This paragraph and the two preceding ones are almost straight quotes from the Commission's 1997 Opinions on the Central European candidate countries.
7. Firstly, Cyprus is not a formerly centrally planned economy. Secondly, Cyprus had already been assessed positively in a Commission Opinion several years earlier, but the start of negotiations had been delayed to allow for the completion of the Intergovernmental Conference that led to the Amsterdam Treaty. Malta was in the same situation, but decided to put its membership bid on hold after the parliamentary elections of 1996.

ed that these countries had made substantial progress in economic reform during the past year, but that there was not sufficient change in their situation to warrant an immediate start of negotiations. And much to the disappointment of the Commission, it had to note that in two countries that had passed the economic test the year before – the Czech Republic and Slovenia – economic reforms had slowed almost to a standstill.

The case of the Slovak Republic is worth a special mention in this context, not only because it is a peculiar case, but also because it highlights some of the key aspects of how the Commission assesses a candidate country's readiness for the opening of negotiations or for accession. In the Commission Opinion of 1997, the Slovak Republic was the one country that did not pass the 'political' test of the Copenhagen conditions. This in itself was sufficient ground not to propose the country for the immediate opening of accession negotiations. And what about the economic criteria? Here too, the Slovak Republic was a special case. In the Commission's view, the Slovak Republic had the potential to do well on the competitiveness criterion in the medium term, but there were doubts about the market economy criterion. There was a clear lack of transparency in the management of the Slovak economy – for instance, in the privatisation process. After the Commission published its Opinion, there was a widespread perception that the Slovak Republic was being excluded from the negotiations on political grounds only, and that once these political obstacles were removed, the country would be admitted to the group of negotiating countries instantly. This is not quite right. The Commission had doubts about the proper functioning of the market economy too – and incidentally, these doubts stemmed from considerations similar to those that led to the negative assessment of the political situation.

In late 1998, when the Commission produced its first Regular Reports, the political situation in the Slovak Republic had improved dramatically, so it came as a shock to many that the Commission still did not recommend the Slovak Republic for the immediate opening of negotiations. Again, it is important to realise why. There were two reasons. First, because the political changes were quite recent and needed to be consolidated before they would be sufficiently credible. Second, because there was a fear that the economic legacy of the previous regime could turn out to be considerably worse than expected. It has indeed been confirmed since then that long periods of government interference in the privatisation process, political manipulation of state bank operations, favouritism in tax collection *etc.* have taken their toll on the Slovak economy.

The final point that needs to be made regarding the Copenhagen criteria relates to another widespread misconception: the idea that there are 'waves' or 'groups' of candidate countries. This is wrong. It is wrong for formal reasons: negotiations are always conducted on a bilateral basis, in an Intergovernmental Conference between the EU member states on the one hand, and each candidate country on the other. It is wrong also for substantive reasons. It is quite clear that each candidate country will be judged on its own merit. The time at which accession negotiations start has a very limited bearing on when they can be concluded: that will depend on the progress that is made in the candidate country, and whether this progress can be demonstrated in such a way that all 15 incumbent member states are convinced that the candidate is able and willing to play its full part as a member of the Union.

This chapter was written several months before the Commission issues its 1999 Regular Reports, and before the Helsinki European Council of December 1999 will have to take decisions on whether to extend the accession negotiations to more than the current six candidates. Under the influence of the Kosovo crisis, there were those, in mid-1999, who pleaded strongly for an immediate opening of negotiations with all candidates. Whatever the Commission will have proposed, or what Helsinki will decide, it is quite clear that over the coming period, the state of the negotiations with each of the candidates will show quite clearly to what extent these depend on individual progress – or lack of progress. The larger the number of negotiating countries becomes, the clearer it will be that some will be able to sign an accession treaty rather earlier than others. And once such a treaty is signed, there will be precious little reason to delay its ratification and entry into force. The current crop of candidates shows substantial difference as to its readiness for accession, and their joining the EU will undoubtedly be spread in time.

5.4 What could delay enlargement on the side of the candidates?

Preparing for accession requires an extraordinarily complex and complete overhaul of government and society in the candidate countries. As was set out above, adopting the *acquis communautaire* is no mean feat – and what will count most is implementation, which is rather more demanding than legislation. This has begun to be understood at least by most of those directly involved in the accession process. It is, however, quite possible that, as the practical effects of alignment to the *acquis* become clearer to the wider public in the candidate countries, resistance to the process will increase. Currently, the level of public support for EU integration in the candidate countries is still considerably higher than in the EU itself, but this is likely to be eroded gradually. It will require very considerable political leadership skills, as well as unstinting and very focused determination on the part of the candidate country governments to convince their electorates that the profound changes that accession requires are worth the effort. This will not be easy, and it may fail on occasion, potentially leading to delays in the necessary reforms.

This is probably most true in areas outside the realm of economic policy. The most emotive and sensitive issues are those such as land ownership: opening up sales of land to EU nationals is fiercely resisted in many candidate countries. Standard economic policy (fiscal policy, monetary policy, *etc.*), although the subject of rather precise EU legislation, is likely to be less controversial, for two reasons. First, the *acquis* in this field essentially boils down to "thou shalt conduct a prudent macroeconomic policy and leave thy central bank to do its business unhindered". This is wise in any event, independently of accession to the EU. Second, no one expects the candidates to join the Euro immediately on accession – it is clearly an area where several years of phasing in of the *acquis* will be necessary.[8]

It is argued by some that it is unfair to ask the candidate countries to implement the *acquis* (almost) fully by the time of accession, on the grounds that the EU 15 do not always fully implement the *acquis* either. This is irrelevant. As was said before, the candidates will need to convince all 15 that they can broadly play by the rules. They do not want to enter into an accession process where they know in advance that the Commission has to start hundreds of infringement procedures before the European Court of Justice, accusing the new members of disregarding the Treaties. This may or may not be unfair; but it is the traditional advantage of incumbents.

There is one major economic area where a similar point can be made: the Economic and Monetary Union (EMU). Some of the current 15 member states have obtained an opt-out from EMU. This is because they were already inside the Union before stage three of EMU was reached. No future member states will have the same possibility. They will not introduce the Euro on the day of their accession, but they will have to take on the commitment of doing it a few years later.

Timing is politically very sensitive in the EU's enlargement process. This has been shown in particular by the excitement surrounding the starting dates of negotiations, but also by more recent debates on whether it would be useful to set target dates for the completion of negotiations. It should be stressed that, while this concern with dates is understandable, it is in fact less important than it may seem. As the previous sections show, accession is a gradual and complex process. The dates – start of negotiations, completion of negotiations, entry into force of the accession treaty – are merely milestones in the integration process. The process was started years ago and is well advanced. In 1998 the candidate countries definitely benefited from the fact that their trade and economic integration with the EU had been advancing already: they were largely sheltered from the impact of the Russian economic crisis. Compare this with how a similar crisis would have affected them ten years ago: the difference is startling.

5.5 What could delay enlargement on the side of the EU?

Richard Baldwin said he did not believe EU enlargement to the East would happen within a generation because the candidates were "too populous, too poor and too agricultural".[9] He has a partial point. His argument is that while the EU has in the past successfully absorbed poorer and highly agricultural countries,[10] there

---

8. This argument is developed in detail in the Composite Paper accompanying the European Commission's 1998 Regular Reports.

were never more than two or three at the same time. The current queue of candidates is so long that it would force the Union to choose: either to pay up (notably by sharp increases in 'structural' spending[11] and in the cost of the common agricultural policy) or change its main spending policies so that they become less costly. Baldwin's assessment is that the incumbent member states would not be prepared to do either. This is based on the idea that within the EU 15 there is a dichotomy between rich member states that are net contributors to the EU budget, and poorer member states that are net beneficiaries. The richer member states would refuse to see their net contributions to the EU budget increase substantially, and the poorer member states – that are still considerably wealthier than most candidates (see Table 7.2) – would refuse to lose their status of net beneficiaries. This would lead to deadlock, since enlargement can only be decided by unanimity among the EU 15. The stark simplicity of Baldwin's argument is enlightening but fortunately the reality is more complex – and this permits solutions to be found.

First, there is not such an unambiguous division into two camps among the EU 15, between rich contributors and poor agricultural beneficiaries. Some rich countries are quite agricultural; some less-rich countries are among the highest net contributors. And, crucially, some rich countries have huge geopolitical and economic interests in enlargement, and would be ill-advised to delay East European accessions based on rather narrow budgetary considerations.

Second, it is true that the queue of candidates is far longer than ever before, but as the previous sections have illustrated, it is quite unlikely that all candidates will be ready to join at the same time. The EU's eastern enlargement is very likely to be phased over a fairly long period, making it much easier to digest the budgetary consequences.

Third, it would probably be both necessary and desirable to modify some of the EU's main spending policies, even independently of enlargement. The classic example is agricultural policy. The old-style CAP, based on price guarantees and

---

9. "... the massive liberalisation entailed by EU enlargement would probably bring large long-run economic benefits to all Europe. However, the Eastern economies are currently too populous, too poor and too agricultural to enter the EU without radically altering the Union itself. Consequently, a significant enlargement of the EU to the East is unlikely to occur until the Easterners are much richer and much less agricultural. This is likely to take at least two decades for most of the CEECs" (Baldwin 1994, p. 157).

10. Being much poorer than the EU average need not be an insurmountable handicap for the candidates. Ireland's GDP per head was 60% of the EU 15 average when it joined the EEC in the early 1970s; currently it stands at 105%. Portugal's GDP rose from 45% of EU 15 average a few years prior to its accession to 69% now. And even Greece, which has done relatively less well during EU membership, at least until fairly recently, went from 50% of EU GDP in the late 1970s to 69% now. Some caution in interpreting these statistics is necessary, however. The EU is now much more deeply integrated than the European Community was when Ireland joined; it is not immediately obvious that Ireland in 1973 would have been able to implement the 1999 EU acquis.

11. EU jargon for spending on regional development policies in poorer parts of the Union.

prohibitive protectionism, has already been adjusted in a more market-oriented direction, and will have to move considerably further under pressure from trade partners – and because it makes more economic sense. As regards 'structural' spending, this is by its very nature only temporary: as soon as the underdeveloped regions to which it is targeted have become more developed, the need and justification to spend structural funds there disappear. The classic example here is Ireland, which has clearly benefited substantially from structural funds and no longer really needs them. The converse of this argument is that if structural spending does not have the desired effect, and the beneficiary region remains poor, the money should either stop flowing there, or the region in question should change its development policies, or the way in which the funds are spent should change – but the result should never be that the funds continue to be spent in a useless way. However one turns the reasoning, regions should benefit from structural funds only for a finite period.

Fourth, there is the soothing effect of economic growth. As time progresses, the EU becomes wealthier. The candidate countries become wealthier even faster, since the economic inefficiencies they inherited from central planning are such that there is scope for rapid productivity improvements during several decades. Both effects reduce the budgetary pain. Maintaining structural fund spending in Spain or Greece at current levels, even in inflation-adjusted terms, means that this spending gradually falls as a percentage of GDP.

These considerations lie at the heart of the Commission's 1997 proposals in 'Agenda 2000', which implied a greater concentration of structural spending on the regions that really need it, and a market-oriented reform of the CAP. Provided that this is done, the Agenda 2000 proposals showed that enlargement within a reasonable time frame (up to five accessions by 2002/2003) would not break the budget, and would allow for the EU budget to remain within a modest ceiling of 1.27% of EU GDP.

The decisions taken by the Berlin European Council on the Agenda 2000 proposals go a long way in this direction. The only major difference relates to the CAP, where Berlin decided to be rather less radical than the Commission had proposed. This clearly means that further reform of agricultural policy will be on the EU agenda relatively soon, not just for the sake of enlargement but also in the light of the coming Millennium Round within the World Trade Organisation. This is an element of unfinished business that, much to the European Commission's regret, is still on the table.[12]

---

12. To illustrate the discussions in this area, take the argument with Poland. The CAP used to provide adequate incomes to its farmers through guaranteed prices for some key agricultural products. Starting some years ago it has begun to move away from this, by lowering guaranteed prices and compensating the poorest farmers for the resulting loss in income by direct income support subsidies. This is much more targeted and thus more efficient and cheaper. Poland claims 'equal treatment': upon accession, it wants its farmers to qualify for these compensatory income subsidies. The EU maintains that since Polish farmers never benefited from the higher guaranteed prices in the first place, there is nothing to compensate them for.

The second main element of unfinished business relates to the EU's institutional set-up. The EU still functions with institutions and decision-making rules designed in the 1950s for a much less integrated Community of three large and three small countries. When the current 12 candidates join, we will have a Union of six or seven large and about twenty small member states. Applying the current system of weighted voting in the decision-making Council of Ministers would lead to a relative loss of influence of the larger member states that these would find unacceptable – a few large countries, accounting for almost half the EU population and well over half its GDP could be outvoted by a coalition of small countries. On the other hand, under current rules the policy-making European Commission would consist of some 35 Commissioners, which would clearly be too much of a good thing. And then there is the question of languages. There are eleven official languages today. Not only would there be twice that number after enlargement, but the number of permutations rises exponentially, as would the cost of ensuring translation and interpretation between them, and the risk of mistakes and misunderstandings.

Solutions for these institutional problems need to be found before enlargement. This will not be easy but there is no reason to doubt that it is possible and that it will be done on time. The Cologne European Council of June 1999 launched the process that will lead to an Intergovernmental Conference (IGC) in which the necessary changes to the Treaties will be negotiated. The IGC could finish at the end of 2000 or a bit later, and ratification of the new Treaty would follow in 2001 or 2002: well in time for the first accessions.

5.6 Conclusion

The *horror belli* in the aftermath of World War II provided the inspiration for European integration in the 1950s. Then, during the cold war period, the process gradually lost some of its lustre and came to be seen as a largely technocratic exercise. The fall of the Berlin Wall in 1989, the catastrophic events in the Balkans in recent years, and especially the Kosovo crisis of 1999, are salutary reminders of the *finalité politique* of European integration. The EU has been phenomenally successful in consolidating peace and stability, and in bringing wealth to its members. It was always the intention of the founding fathers that any European democracy that so desired should join the process. This is what EU enlargement is about. An EU that is capable of making a common currency but proves incapable of extending its benefits to Central and South-Eastern Europe should be ashamed of itself on moral grounds, and would be short-changing itself in economic terms.

However, like any truly great edifice, an enlarged EU needs solid foundations if it is to stand the test of time. Merely saying 'we'll build a great cathedral, come and join us for High Mass' is not enough. It requires the finest building materials, thousands of master craftsmen, time, patience and hard work to build it. This may be frustrating at times but there is no other way. Fortunately, the design of an enlarged EU is clear, much of the scaffolding has been erected. Work is well under way.

References

Baldwin, R.E. (1994), *Towards an Integrated Europe*, Centre for Economic Policy Research, London.

Baldwin, R.E., J.F. Francois and R. Portes (1997), 'The costs and benefits of eastern enlargement: the impact on the EU and Central Europe', *Economic Policy*, No.24, pp.127-176.

The Transition to EU Membership in Central and Eastern Europe

Jim Rollo and Alasdair Smith

6.1 Introduction

The Central and Eastern European transformation from communism to market democracy is a multi-faceted and long-term process. In this chapter, we discuss the role of European Union (EU) membership in that process and the implications for how the accession of the Central and Eastern European countries (CEECs) to the EU should be managed. Successful transition has both political and economic dimensions. At a political level, sustained democracy with smooth transfers of power is one important criterion; and respect for a range of human and civil rights is another.

At the economic level, one might look for a magic number, for example the proportion of economic activity in the private sector, to mark the transition from communist/state socialist mechanisms of allocation and income determination to market-led mechanisms, though the large variance in the size of the public sector in market economies makes it hard to identify the correct number. Criteria based on policy regimes might include the treatment of capital markets, access to foreign goods, services, capital and workers, the manner in which business is regulated and how far competition is encouraged. The application of any such criteria involves much judgement, and again the performance of Western market economies is quite variable.

Membership of various international organisations and the norms that such membership requires provide an important set of indicators of progress. Membership of the Council of Europe marks the meeting of important political criteria. On the economic side, membership of the WTO is associated with the acceptance of major restraints on trade policy, both in the fixing of tariffs and the imposition of pressure to dismantle non-tariff barriers. WTO disciplines on services trade are less stringent however, and many aspects of domestic regulation, such as government procurement, are not included. Many WTO members have economies which are far from a market ideal. Equally, membership of the OECD, which includes commitments to disciplines on capital market regulations, is a partial but not complete guarantee that market disciplines have primacy.

In many respects, the EU provides an uncertain benchmark by which to judge transformation. All of its members give a convincing appearance of being market-driven economies, though in all of them the state plays a significant economic role. The ratio of government expenditure to GDP varies from a low of 38% in the UK to a high of 63% in Sweden in 1996 (OECD, 1999, international comparisons table). Direct aids to industry are far from unknown. Regulation is significant in all EU member states and is a significant restraint on market activity in some. State ownership of industry is still an important feature of industrial organisation in most.

Nonetheless, the EU is well integrated into the world economy. Average tariffs after the Uruguay Round will be of the order of 3%; the EU is the largest trader in goods and services exceeding even the USA; and it vies with the USA as the largest inward and outward investor in the world (all comparisons excluding intra-EU trade and investment flows).

Above all, the EU via the single market legislation now aspires to complete freedom of trade in goods and services and free movement of capital and labour. Flanking these four freedoms are a complex of other policies, some intended to support the single market, and some independent of the single market and, as we discuss below, to a degree contradictory in outcome if not in operation.

We can regard EU membership as one, perhaps the most important, institutional recognition of the progress and the irreversibility of transition. From the beginning of the transition process the former communist states in Central Europe particularly, but now also in the Baltic and Balkan regions, have looked to EU membership as a way of anchoring democracy on the market and hence, as an integral part of their transitional strategy.

Thus EU membership is not just a passive act of recognition. It should play an active part in supporting the transition, and any discussion of the process and timing of CEECs' accession to the EU must give due weight to that objective.

The eastern enlargement of the EU is different from any previous enlargement, not only because of the fact that the acceding countries are in the process of a dramatic transition to becoming market economies (more dramatic than the rather different transitions of Greece, Spain and Portugal), but also because this is the first enlargement in which accession implies accession to the post-1992 single market. Sweden, Finland and Austria joined the EU after 1992, but in most important respects they had joined the single market via the European Economic Area before their accession to the Union.

Accession to the EU is a process rather than a single step. The *acquis communautaire* is a whole complex of policies and regulations which constitute the EU, whose different parts have different implications for the transition from communism to the market. Thus in examining the accession process, we look at how the adoption of the various policies will impact on economic transformation, and above all how the adjustment strains will manifest themselves and how such adjustment should be managed. We draw on the existing literature on this subject, particularly Baldwin (1994), Smith *et al.* (1996), Baldwin *et al.* (1996) and Rollo (1997).

The eastern enlargement of the EU will also be different from previous enlargements because the difference in income per head between the incumbents and the candidates is greater than in previous cases. Table 6.1 shows the headline data.

Table 6.1: Income per head and transition indicators

	Private sector as a % of GDP 1998	Share of agriculture in the economy 1997 in %		GDP per head 1997	
		GDP	Employment	at PPP	As a % of EU average
Bulgaria	50	12.8	23.4	4,400	23
Czech Republic	75	2.9	4.1	12,000	63
Estonia	70	8.0	9.2	7,000	37
Hungary	80	5.8	8.2	8,900	47
Latvia	60	7.6	15.3	5,100	27
Lithuania	70	10.2	24.0	5,800	30
Poland	65	6.0	26.7	7,500	39
Romania	60	19.0	37.3	4,800	30
Slovak Republic	75	4.6	6.0	8,900	47
Slovenia	55	6.3	7.8	13,000	68

Sources: EBRD 1998, European Commission 1998b, European Commission 1998c

Even in 1997, all but the Czech Republic and Slovenia had a lower GDP per head (measured in PPP), expressed as a percentage of the EU-15 average, than Greece (64% in 1979), Spain (70% in 1985), Portugal (53% in 1985) or Ireland (60% in 1972) had on entry to the EU (European Commission 1998d, Table 9, p.234). Indeed, all but the Czechs, Hungarians, Slovakians and Slovenians were poorer in 1997 than the poorest region in the existing EU (Iperios in Greece at 43% of EU average in 1997). Also of relevance is the share of agriculture in value-added and employment shown in Table 6.2. There have been concerns within the existing EU that, in Richard Baldwin's striking phrase, the CEECs are "too poor and too agricultural" (Baldwin, 1994) for immediate EU membership. More generally they have been perceived as being structurally too underdeveloped and hence too different from the existing EU.

However, the income differences between the CEECs and the EU are not just an indicator of possible obstacles to EU membership. They also constitute part of the objectives of EU membership and of the transition. Successful political and economic transition will generate economic growth in the CEECs at a rate that should reduce the income gap between East and West in Europe (Rollo and Stern, 1992; Mayhew and Orlowski, forthcoming), and a major objective of the transition to EU membership should be to support the general transition process and to generate rather than impede economic growth in the CEECs.

6.2 The EU membership process

The EU initially offered the countries in transition in Central and Eastern Europe the Europe Agreements consisting of an industrial free trade area plus economic co-operation and restricted freedom of movement of capital and people. The first of these were signed in 1991 with Czechoslovakia, Hungary and Poland. Bulgaria and Romania, Slovenia, and then Estonia, Latvia and Lithuania followed. On the break up of Czechoslovakia, the Czech and Slovak Republics each were granted their own Europe Agreements. Future potential candidates for Europe Agreements include Croatia, Albania, Macedonia and perhaps, eventually, some other parts of former Yugoslavia (For details of the Europe Agreements, see Mayhew, 1998, chapters 2-4).

The EU was initially reluctant to envisage membership for transition economies. The reasons for this were never fully articulated. Their lack of economic development was clearly an issue as was their rudimentary economic structures as a result of the socialist division of labour under Comecon. Some member states also felt that expansion of the EU and not just to the East seemed likely to slow down the project of 'deepening' European integration – intensifying economic and political integration.

The Europe Agreements initially contained no commitment to membership, but the Copenhagen Summit Declaration of 1993 (European Council, 1993) accepted the objective of EU membership for the associated CEECs and the Europe Agreements became the *de facto* anteroom to EU membership. The Copenhagen Summit also generated four broad criteria for accession to the EU (see Chapter 5):

- the stability of institutions guaranteeing democracy, the rule of law, human rights and respect for and protection of minorities
- the existence of a functioning market economy
- the capacity to cope with competitive pressure and market forces within the Union
- the ability to take on the obligations of membership including adherence to the aims of political, economic and monetary union.

This was followed by a European Commission White Paper (European Commission, 1995) which set out in detail the EU directives and regulations which would need to be enacted and implemented to make EU membership a reality. Decisions about priorities and speed were explicitly left to the CEECs to make. The Cannes European Council conclusions (European Council, 1995) state that the White Paper does not anticipate or prejudge the accession negotiations and does not lay down further conditions for the negotiations, since adoption of the whole *acquis* (possibly subject to transitional periods) is required only on accession. But the key point, in the White Paper and more generally in the EU's approach to the issue of CEECs' membership, is that the single market requires that the *acquis* should be capable of implementation on day one of membership. Otherwise, the logic went, it would not be possible to implement the single market from that date. The extent to which that position can be justified is the focus of this chapter.

The CEECs with Europe Agreements (hereafter the CEEC-10) then applied for EU membership and the EU Commission prepared opinions on their respective cases for membership. Based on these opinions, published in autumn 1997 (European Commission, 1997), formal negotiations were opened under the British Presidency in 1998. Actual negotiations were opened with only five of the ten applicants – the Czech Republic, Estonia, Hungary, Poland and Slovenia. Of the others, doubts about the commitment to democracy under the Meciar government condemned the Slovak Republic to the slow lane, while economic issues (and to a degree human rights concerns in the Baltic States) led the Commission to conclude that the remainder were not yet ready for membership. However, it was left that, subject to annual review, the Commission could move countries up and down the readiness scale. Hence, in October 1998 the Commission in its first reviews (European Commission, 1998a) suggested that the pace of adaptation to EU norms in the Czech Republic and in Slovenia was slowing and it could endanger their chances of being among the first wave of new members. Equally, it made warm comments about Latvian progress and hence raised the possibility of it advancing to the ranks of the early members. Elections in the Slovak Republic have also begun to lift the political objections to membership.

In late 1998, it therefore seemed that the potential first wave of new members could number between five and seven. In the aftermath of the Kosovo conflict, UK Prime Minister Tony Blair suggested that special efforts should be made to begin accession negotiations to the EU for Bulgaria and Romania into the EU earlier than current progress suggests.[1]

So gradually a process conceived of as waves of new members began to look more like a yacht regatta in which some boats fall back and some cross the line together. This is unlike past enlargements where, Greece apart, separate negotiations were conducted with countries which then entered in a group. Now, potentially at least, countries could enter one at a time as they become ready.

The probability of such an outcome could be intensified by the other unique aspect of this enlargement which is the 'screening' process in which the Commission assesses chapter by chapter the readiness of each applicant to legislate and apply the single market *acquis*. In 1999, this process was approaching the end of the first stage and the applicant states seemed to have held together but the potential was there for some to advance and some to fall back. Only after the screening is finished do negotiations proper begin.

This is unlikely to happen before the end of 1999 and on a wildly optimistic timetable of one year for negotiations and two years for ratification by the European and national parliaments, the often-mentioned date of 2003 is just a possi-

---

1. Speeches in Romania, 4 May 1999, and Bulgaria, 17 May 1999, http://fco.gov.uk/news/speech.asp

bility for the first wave of new entrants. In reality 2006, when the next EU financial perspective runs out, is much more likely on past performance. Even the EFTA
applicants who had after all joined the European Economic Area and thus adopted the single market *acquis* before membership negotiations began (a *de facto*
screening process) took almost four years from beginning of negotiations to actual membership.

6.3 The *acquis* and transformation

In this section, we outline the key EU policies which impact on the transition
process. We focus on micro-economic policies. Macroeconomic stability is certainly part of the pre-accession partnership and EMU is part of the screening
process. EU membership will not automatically lead to EMU membership, so the
choice of exchange rate regime is to a degree independent of the state of the transition process.

6.3.1 The four freedoms

At the core of the single market is the policy objective of removing all barriers to
trade in goods and services and to the movement of capital and labour within the
EU, behind a single external trade policy. These four freedoms could be seen as
the irreducible core of the Union since they are accepted as a defining characteristic of the Union even by those who have doubts about other policy domains. It
is hard to give meaning to the idea of accession to the Union that did not involve
adoption of the single market and the four freedoms. Furthermore, adoption of
the single market provides a key test of transformation. Free movement of goods,
services and factors of production between the formerly communist states of Central and Eastern Europe and the largest market in the world is potentially an irrev-
ocable injection of competition and market discipline into the CEECs' economies.

On trade in goods, accession to the single market will provide a significant
improvement on the existing Europe Agreements between the EU and applicant
states. These are, at heart, free trade agreements with many remaining barriers –
notably rules of origin, contingent protection, and barriers to trade in agriculture
(see Rollo and Smith, 1993, and Mayhew, 1998, for an extended analysis). The
move to a customs union will remove many of the remaining barriers to trade,
above all that of rules of origin. Taken in conjunction with competition policy and
state aids policy (see below) the customs union will also destroy any case for contingent protection against the CEEC-10. The common external tariff will, for most
though not all applicants, reduce the level of tariffs against third countries (see
for example Maliszewska *et al.*, 1999, on the case of Poland). The Europe agreements already give duty free access for manufactures to the CEEC-10 but freedom
of movement of goods within the single market will make a significant contribution both to increasing competition in CEEC-10 markets and in CEEC-10 access to
EU markets with potential benefits for competitiveness, trade and growth.

On services, the changes are likely to be more significant than on goods. The degree of liberalisation associated with the Europe Agreements is rather limited. Rights of establishment are imperfect and restrictions on moving personnel remain in place – both important in delivering services exports – notably on the EU side (Winters, 1992). With full rights of access the CEEC-10 will be in a position to both benefit from increased access to EU markets and also from access to high quality service providers from the EU as competition in their home market increases. The latter will have important implication in areas such as telecoms, financial services and energy and construction services, all key inputs into activity across the economy and without which economic growth and transformation will be slower than otherwise and competitiveness will be reduced.

Flanking the freedom to trade in goods and services are a series of directives on the regulation of standards and of various services sectors most notably the financial sector. These provide for minimum prudential and consumer protection standards under home country control and supervision. This reduction in regulatory barriers via the process of mutual recognition and home country control suggests that goods and services markets in the applicant states will become much more open. Domestic regulations will become more predictable which should increase inward investment and give a boost to the competitiveness of local economies. Liberalisation of local services markets in particular will reduce costs for exporters of goods for whom services are key inputs.

Open services markets also depend on freedom of establishment to allow foreigners to deliver their products. This, in turn, requires both freedom of movement of capital and of labour. These freedoms, however, have wider implications for the transformation of formerly socialist economies. Open capital markets will speed up the flow of capital from abroad to various users, both for short-term and long-term commitments, which in turn should allow higher growth rates as investments which local savings and know-how are unable to support are triggered.

There is already considerable freedom of movement of capital among the applicant states. The three countries with currency boards – Bulgaria, Estonia and Lithuania – already have complete freedom of movement of capital. All of the other countries are keen to encourage long-term capital inflows, but all except the Czech Republic have varying levels of control on both long- and short-term investment flows. For example there are blocks on foreign ownership of land in Poland and Hungary. OECD members among the applicants are signatories to the OECD capital codes but these do not preclude exchange controls. On membership these barriers will need to disappear, though not necessarily on day one. Free movement of capital may give rise to political problems, notably on land ownership, which is sensitive across the region. There could also be macroeconomic management problems. Exchange rate regimes which are not either free floats or membership of EMU (or currency boards) will be more difficult to manage without capital controls. Membership of the new EU Exchange Rate Mechanism (ERM-II) as a precursor to

EMU membership will be difficult on narrow fluctuation margins without the buttressing of capital controls. Many commentators put the demise of the ERM-I in the early 1990s down to the abolition of capital controls in 1989.

More generally, freedom of movement of capital along with the application of the rest of the single market *acquis* and above all the access to European Court of Justice which EU membership offers should significantly increase the credibility of domestic regulation in the transition economies, which should increase the attractiveness of these countries to foreign investors (see Baldwin *et al.*, 1997, for an extended discussion). The potential for increasing growth rates is thus significant. These are necessary conditions if the applicant states are to enjoy their growth potential (Rollo and Stern, 1992) let alone reach the performance of Ireland over the last decade (OECD, 1999).

Freedom of movement of labour presents perhaps a different set of issues. First, the economic differences shown in Table 6.2 suggest that there is a potential for a significant flow of labour from the new member states to the EU-15. That certainly is the fear of politicians in neighbouring EU states. This outflow is not inevitable, however, and there has been much less economic migration from East to West in the last decade than some had expected. A dynamic economy at home plus the very real transaction costs of migration could stem such an outflow. If migration were to take place it has some potentially contradictory impacts on economic transformation. Most dangerous is that it encourages an outflow of the best-educated and trained people so reducing the potential productivity of the economy. This may be a particular problem where birth rates are low and populations are ageing. Ireland however shows that 150 years of continuous outward migration is not necessarily a bar to rapid development. In part this is because remittances from overseas workers can increase consumption and investment at home. Returning migrants bring capital and new ideas back from abroad which help to develop the home economy. But recent Irish development (OECD, 1999) has undoubtedly been helped by the high birth rate which meant that there was a new generation in high quality education available to work in the factories and businesses built by foreign capital.

There are dangers that integration into the EU economy could lead to an outflow of factors and a core-periphery pattern of development as discussed in the large recent literature on the 'new economic geography' inspired by Krugman (1991). Mobility of labour plays an important role in some models of economic geography and, as Ottaviano and Puga (1998) point out, will reinforce centripetal tendencies for the simple reason that if workers can move from a poorer periphery to a richer core, the core grows and the periphery becomes more peripheral. One has, however, to distinguish between inequality of distribution of economic activity and inequality of incomes between individuals. The difference between the EU and the US is instructive. The high degree of mobility of labour within the United States ensures that intra-regional or intra-state income inequalities are less than they are in the European Union. Puga (1998) points out that regional equality of income is greater in the USA than in Europe – only two small states in the US are below 75% of the US average of GNP, while almost 20% of the population of the EU lived in regions more than 75% below the EU GNP average in 1994. However, as detailed in Krugman (1991), regional specialisation of economic activity is much greater in the US than in the EU. Thus the effects of European integration on inequality might be different in the short run from the longer run. Increased integration, including increased mobility of labour, may well lead to increased concentration of some economic activities but a reduced dispersion of income. In the long run, the reduced income inequality may be welcomed; but in the short run the changing location of economic activity may create problems of adjustment, particularly in the CEECs.

Overall, the four freedoms offer the chance for the applicant states to accelerate the process of transformation to a market economy and potentially to raise growth rates. The main impacts will be on trade in agriculture and services, on capital movements and on labour. Freedom of capital movements will have implications for macroeconomic policy, potentially making exchange rate management more difficult. Freedom of movement of labour carries dangers of brain drain.

6.3.2 Competition policy

Competition policy is a vital area in ensuring that market disciplines apply across the production and distribution of goods and services. Domestic policies are already in place and functioning reasonably well (Fingleton *et al.*, 1996). In Poland and Hungary for example, the privatisation process has been at various points subject to competition policy disciplines.

The applicant states have, from the time of the Europe Agreements, been required to write their competition policy to be consistent with EU norms and in particular Articles 81 and 82 of the Treaty of Amsterdam.

Competition policy is an area of rivalry between the Commission and the member states. The norms are set out in the Treaty with the objective of preventing monopoly powers undermining the effectiveness of the liberalisation of the EU market. It is, however, the role of national competition policy authorities to deal with local monopolies, cartels and mergers; and of the Commission to deal with cross-border infractions, but even cross-border mergers have to be above a certain value to be the business of the EU mergers taskforce. It is important that competition policy rules are in place and are implemented as a guarantee that:

- inward investors are not unfairly excluded by local monopolies
- exporters are not able to cross subsidise exports from local monopoly profits
- consumers receive the full benefits of open markets.

These are however largely the function of local competition policy authorities subject to the oversight of the European Courts of Justice to ensure that the Treaty is enforced.

As far as transformation is concerned the external oversight is the key advantage of EU membership for competition policy. It means that there is a final and perhaps distant bulwark against regulatory capture of national competition policy.

The removal of anti-dumping policy is, as Messerlin (1994), Hoekman (1996), and Smith *et al.* (1996) have argued, the logical counterpart of the implementation by the CEECs of the EU's competition policy. The Commission, however, argues in the White Paper and elsewhere for full implementation of the single market programme before 'commercial defence instruments' can be withdrawn (European Commission, 1995a, paragraph 6.5).

6.3.3 State aids

Tables 6.2 and 6.3 provide data on the level of state aids in some Central European countries and in the EU. The statistics are not strictly comparable, as the Central European data cover the whole economy and the EU data refer only to manufacturing. Schaffer (1995), from whom the data in Table 6.3 are taken, reports that most subsidies go to non-manufacturing producers, with transport and mining being the major recipients of Polish state aid. However, he also cautions that direct government subsidies understate total state aid, in particular because of the extent of uncollected tax arrears, and he estimates the flow of tax arrears as being at approximately the same level as budgetary subsidies. All these qualifications notwithstanding, the two tables make the point that in broad terms, the level of state aids in the CEECs is of the same order of magnitude as in the EU.

As far as the functioning of the single market is concerned Article 87 of the Treaty of Amsterdam, which limits state aids, is potentially a key guarantee of openness. Anti-competitive behaviour by private agents is limited by the fact that predatory behaviour is subject to a profits constraint, and, unless there are high barriers to entry, by contestability constraints. But governments have potentially deeper pockets than firms and can sustain subsidy for a considerable time. The availability of state aids could therefore poison the single market and this is the case for discipline to be applied at the Union level.

Table 6.2: Government expenditure and subsidies in the Visegrád countries pre- and post-reform (as a % of GDP)

	1986	1992	1993
Czechoslovakia	25.4	5.0	..
Czech Republic	..	5.0	4.4
Slovak Republic	..	5.4	4.8
Hungary	25.4	5.8	4.8
Poland	16.3	3.3	2.5

Source: Schaffer (1995)

Table 6.3: National state aids to the manufacturing sector in the EU, 1990-1997. Annual averages as a % of value added in manufacturing

	1990-1992	1992-1994	1993-1995	1995-1997
Austria	..	..	..	1.5
Belgium	7.9	4.8	2.5	2.4
Denmark	1.9	2.8	2.7	3.0
Germany	3.5	4.8	4.4	3.1
Greece	12.5	10.5	5.2	5.6
Spain	2.1	1.7	2.1	3.0
Finland	..	..	..	1.6
France	2.7	3.3	2.1	2.0
Ireland	2.7	3.5	2.4	2.2
Italy	8.9	8.4	6.1	5.3
Luxembourg	3.5	2.9	2.2	2.3
Netherlands	2.5	2.1	1.1	1.2
Portugal	4.6	4.4	2.7	2.8
Sweden	..	..	..	1.0
United Kingdom	1.4	0.8	0.8	0.9
EU15	..	..	..	2.8
EU12	3.8	4.0	3.5	2.9

Source: Schaffer (1995)

These rules have a number of implications for transformation. First, they may limit the abilities of CEEC-10 governments to give adjustment aid to state-owned industries of newly privatised firms to ameliorate the impact on employment of restructuring – the German example may have something to offer here. This could be potentially politically sensitive in sectors such as coal or steel.

The record of the European Commission and the European Court of Justice in restraining state aids is spotty. It is really only in the 1990s that the policy has become a real constraint on the activities of government. And there are exceptions: most obviously regional aid and aids to Research and Development where these are cross-sectoral and non-discriminatory. Equally it has clearly been difficult to prevent subsidy races to attract inward investment both from other EU and non-EU investors. The use of government subsidy to regenerate the Eastern Länder has caused tensions between the Commission and the German government. The imperfect record of the EU in enforcing its own rules should underline the undesirability of asking CEECs to meet standards, in state aids or other policy areas, which the EU itself does not meet. Immediate application of these disciplines and competition policy is important for the implementation of the single market. They will also reduce the threat of other member states using countervailing duties or anti-dumping (though, as with competition policy, not by themselves sufficient – see paragraph 6.5 of the European Commission White Paper on enlarging the single market (European Commission, 1995)). But above all, the external constraints they impose will help contain local pressure groups pursuing subsidy or the creation of national champions, both of which may impede the transformation process.

6.3.4 The social and environmental *acquis*

The social and environmental areas of the *acquis* raise different questions from the issues already discussed. These are policies which are generally about the process of production of goods and services. Unlike regulation of product standards, regulation of process standards is not essential to the single market.

Further, to the extent that the effects of the standards are felt locally, the principle of subsidiarity suggests that they should be determined at the level of the member state or even lower (Bean *et al.*, 1998, Begg *et al.*, 1993). Communities should be able to chose their own trade-off between higher social and environmental standards on the one hand, and lower wages, higher unemployment, slower economic development on the other.

The justification of social and environmental dumping is sometimes made for harmonisation. The argument behind this is that such standards impose compliance costs on industry and hence those who do not apply the standards are getting a competitive advantage in the Single Market. The rhetoric of 'fairness' and 'level playing fields' is often brought to bear, with the clear message that protection of EU commercial interests is the priority.

In reality, differences in social and environmental standards are much less likely to distort the single market than state aids or differences in competition policy. Different levels of social protection may seem to confer a competitive advantage, but such an advantage will be eroded by adjustments in exchange rates or wages to restore trade or labour market equilibrium. To put the same point in reverse, if we impose a high level of social protection on a country, its workers will have to restore their competitiveness by accepting lower real wages. Any inter-sectoral impact will be of second-order magnitude.

By contrast, state aids are normally targeted on particular sectors, their sectoral impact will not be eliminated by economy-wide changes in wages or exchange rates, and since they are determined by political processes, their incidence may be hard to predict by private investors in other states.

Environmental standards are more likely to have intersectoral effects than social standards. Lax standards will favour pollution-creating industries. However, it is striking that the EU environmental standards that are likely to be most costly for the CEECs are those for drinking water and waste water, standards that have little impact on competitiveness. Furthermore, even if differential standards do have effects on sectoral competitiveness, that is no more 'unfair' or problematic for the single market than the effects on sectoral competitiveness of climatic differences between member states, *if* the differences in environmental standards reflect genuine differences in political and preferences and economic conditions between the different states, and are not deliberately chosen to give rise to sectoral advantage.

It is, however, a sensible objective of EU policy to prevent social and environmental policy differences being actively used as instruments of strategic trade and industrial policy particularly in negative-sum competition between member states for footloose foreign investment.

There may be a case for common standards on political grounds: the political cohesion of the Union requires a degree of commonality in the experience of all its citizens. There is something to be said for this as a long-term aspiration, but given the scope for inappropriate regulation to impose economic burdens on the CEECs, there would be something paradoxical about imposing such burdens, in the name of cohesion, on European citizens whose incomes are already far below the European average.

None of this is to argue that there is not a case for cross-border regulation where environmental effects spill across borders. But the case for cross-border regulation is independent of EU membership. If Austrian concerns about the safety of Slovak nuclear reactors are well-founded, they are essentially independent of whether the Slovak Republic is a member of the EU, and the best timetable for addressing these concerns is unlikely to coincide with the timetable for accession negotiations.

The discussion above of exchange rates exposes one important issue about the timing of the adoption of different EU policies. The macroeconomic effects of microeconomic regulation are obviously easier to adjust to by exchange rate changes than by changes in relative money wages, so it is sensible for the CEECs to adjust to EU social and environmental policy in advance of their fixing exchange rates with the euro or joining the monetary union.

In practical terms much of this discussion of principle may not matter. Communist governments professed to be in favour of environmental and social protection. Local regulations and standards are often more stringent than those demanded by EU regulation (see Mayhew and Orlowski, 1998). The question is rather one of the timetable for implementation, a point we return to below.

6.3.5 Agriculture

As we noted above, the opening of EU agricultural markets to the farmers of the applicant states is one of the major differences between trade access under the Europe Agreements and full EU membership. Currently the CEEC-10 have only very small tariff-free quotas on EU food markets. Membership of the EU implies adoption of the Common Agricultural Policy (CAP). If the EFTA enlargement is the model, the new members will at the point of accession have to adopt full EU support prices and market support mechanisms. Border barriers will disappear and agricultural free trade within the enlarged union will ensue.

The impact of this on agriculture in Central and Eastern Europe is far from clear. According to latest OECD figures, the total support including price support to agricultural producers expressed as a proportion of revenue in Hungary, Poland, Estonia, Latvia, Lithuania and the Czech and Slovak Republics is much lower than in the EU-15. The 'producer subsidy equivalent' (PSE) in these countries in 1997 averaged less than 20%, compared with over 40% in the EU-15. Yet agricultural prices are not necessarily so far apart. Gacs and Wyzan (1999, Table 6.1, p.74) provide a comparison of Hungarian and EU producer prices which shows Hungarian prices within the range of highest and lowest EU prices for all major commodities excluding beef. A comparison of Polish support prices in 1997 with EU support prices show wheat prices levels at or above EU prices.

Apart from price differences the other explanation for the divergence in support levels is the EU compensation payments introduced as part of the McSharry Reforms of 1992 and continued under the Agenda 2000 agricultural reforms. These direct subsidies aim to compensate EU farmers for cuts in support prices. The Agenda 2000 document (European Commission, 1998b) and the Berlin Summit Conclusions (European Council, 1999) confirmed that new member states should not be eligible for these compensation payments. The justification is that the applicants did not receive the high prices that were subsequently cut so have no need for compensation.

Two points arise. The first is that this will entail a two-level CAP with incumbents receiving one level of support and new members another on a permanent basis. Second, since CAP prices are set to fall further under Agenda 2000 and, as we have seen above, prices in at least one of the CEEC-10 are already at or above EU levels, it is possible that – contrary to expectation – after the Agenda 2000 price cuts (15% cereals, 20% beef, European Commission, 1998b) some CEEC farmers may face lower and not higher prices in the CAP on entry.

This raises a number of questions. Will some of the CEECs require nationally financed transitional subsidies to their producers to allow them to compete with low cost EU-15 imports? This is what followed the accession of Finland and Austria to the EU in 1995. Or will it increase the pressure on the EU to go back on its proposal to give no compensation payments to new members?

Finally it also raises the question of what will happen to consumer prices. For some countries, the price of at least some commodities may fall. Until now, and based on the OECD calculations of the Consumer Subsidy Equivalent (CSE), the expectation has been that adopting the CAP would increase food prices in the applicant states. The CSE measures the degree to which consumer prices of food are subsidised below world prices. It follows that the higher the CSE, the lower food prices. CSEs in the CEEC members of the OECD were some 20 percentage points above EU levels in 1997, suggesting that food prices will rise on accession. This would in turn threaten to push up real wages and hence reduce competitiveness. These negative impacts could offset to a greater or lesser extent the impact of budgetary transfers via the CAP and any higher agricultural exports as a result of access to EU-15 markets and subsidies on exports to the rest of the world.

6.3.6 Structural funds

As with agriculture, the key text here is Agenda 2000. After initial panic about the potential cost of applying unreformed structural funds to the CEEC-10 (see Baldwin, 1994) various approaches were proposed to ameliorate the impact of applying the unreformed structural funds on both the EU budget and applicant states (see Rollo, 1997, Mayhew, 1998). Initial estimates put the cost of applying the unreformed structural funds to the CEEC-10 at around 30 billion euro at 1995 prices or 15% of CEEC-10 GDP (Rollo 1997, Table 6.4, provides a summary table of estimates). This sum represented a doubling of the structural funds. Add to this even the more conservative estimates of the effect of applying the unreformed CAP to the CEEC-10 and figures of annual transfer of 20-50% of GDP could be generated (Rollo 1997, Table 6.4). These were clearly untenable and contrasted with the highest level of receipts from structural funds and CAP in the current EU, which is $7^{1}/2$% of GDP *per annum* to Greece.

These levels of transfers would have produced enormous macroeconomic adjustment problems if they were indeed possible. They would also put intolerable strains on bureaucratic infrastructure and local financial resources since the structural funds expenditure typically have to be matched by local funding. So other approaches were necessary.

Agenda 2000 proposed a limit of 4% of GDP on new member states receipts from the structural funds. This is a non-trivial number and will represent some 20 billion euro *per annum* (Mayhew, 1998) or around a fifth of total current investment in the CEECs and more after national contributions are included. This number should be added to private investment inflows of around $2^{1}/2$% of GDP in 1997 (EBRD, 1998 Table 4.2) which could rise once EU membership becomes a certainty (Baldwin *et al.*, 1997). The CAP could generate around another 1% of GDP *per annum* without compensation payments (three times that with them). Overall, therefore, new members might have to handle foreign exchange inflows in excess of $7^{1}/2$% of GDP *per annum* from EU transfers and capital markets.

At the micro level the structural funds will provide funds for investment. Communism left the applicants short of basic transport and other communication infrastructure as well as investment in environmental services. So money for public sector capital investment is welcome and if properly spent it should do much to improve the functioning of the economy and hence economic transformation. There are, however, three potential problems. First, the majority of the money will be available under the regional funds and as such, might be funnelled to the poorer and less dynamic regions within the individual economies which might result in a lower rate of return than if invested in the dynamic centres. Second, and linked, the need for national governments to release matching contributions from scarce public expenditure might shift the pattern of planned and locally funded investment away from national priorities and hence lower growth rates. Third, the structural funds are administration intensive and will put a significant burden on central and local government which may, in conjunction with the need to find matching funds, slow commitment and disbursement in the early years of membership at least.

The regional bias question is clearly less pressing for small countries since like Ireland they can perhaps be treated as a single region. So the Baltic States, Slovenia and perhaps the Slovak Republic, might be relatively unconstrained. But others will face some difficulties and Poland and Romania might face significant difficulties in adjusting their national priorities to the regional bias of the structural funds.

The structural funds represent a significant asset for the transformation project and in ideal circumstances the money would do most good dispersed as soon as possible, even before membership. This is recognised in Agenda 2000 which proposes both pre-accession annual transfers of 3.2 billion euro and a line of expenditure from structural funds and agriculture, building up from 4 billion euro on assumed accession in 2002 through to 14 billion euro by the end of the Financial Perspective in 2006. The blockages suggested above would slow this disbursement pattern further. Thus the fears of macroeconomic destabilisation are probably overdone in the early years of membership at least.

6.4 The *acquis*, open borders, and the case for transition periods

The analysis of the previous section shows that the *acquis* contains provisions some of which are integral to the four freedoms and the single market, but some of which are not. In discussing the timing of the CEECs' adoption of the different part of the *acquis* and the timing of EU accession, we should re-emphasise that the process should not be seen as a passive one of judging the extent to which the CEECs meet the standards of the EU, but rather as part of the process of cementing and developing the political and economic transformation of the CEECs. Thus as a matter of general strategy the urgent issues are those where adjustment to the EU's norms will provide economic disciplines, market access, and competition that will contribute to growth and efficiency; while adjustment to policies that are likely to be a burden on the CEECs' economies should be slow and should be accompanied by financial support from the EU.

Even in the core area of the free movement of goods and services there is an arguable case for post-accession transition periods in some policy areas. The economics of transition may require policies that differ from those of the EU. Financial deregulation may need to come late in the sequencing of economic reform, and free movement of capital may require confidence in the robustness of the financial structure and its regulation. EU rules on vertical restraints may be inappropriately demanding for economies that need rapid development of distribution networks. EU rules on state aids might need to be modified in the light of privatisation and restructuring needs, particularly in such difficult sectors as coal and steel. Such temporary departures from single market rules are not incompatible with the free circulation of goods in an enlarged single market, and in such cases, a timetable for the elimination of the underlying problems and for the full harmonisation of rules could form part of the post-accession transition.

The case for immediate application of the *acquis* is compelling in the context of measures which require physical controls at the border to enforce. Thus it would be impossible for example to have a slow approximation of agricultural prices as was the case in the first three enlargements. Britain, for example, took 5 years to harmonise agricultural prices. To administer this transition required a complex system of compensating border taxes and subsidies to bridge the gap between cheap British produce and expensive continental produce. With the abolition of customs barriers such 'accession compensatory amounts' are impossible to administer. The same would be true in the case of customs duties. An immediate move to the Common External Tariff is necessary if borders are to be abolished.

In the case of non-agricultural goods, trade with the EU is already adjusting under the Europe Agreements; and substantial parts of non-EU trade, for example with other CEEC countries, is the subject of preferential trade arrangements. Therefore only a modest proportion of the trade of the CEECs is affected by the external trade liberalisation that will for most CEECs characterise accession to the common commercial policy of the EU. Even for those countries whose external trade policy is more restrictive than that of the EU, the tariff reductions implied by EU membership are not huge. It is not surprising, therefore that Maliszewska *et al.* (1999) find that the accession of Poland to the EU's common external tariff is unlikely to give rise to difficult adjustment problems. External trade policy changes may add to the problems of sectors like coal and steel, but are unlikely to be the main source of adjustment difficulties in these sectors.

Where there are serious adjustment costs, given the unacceptability of using border barriers to cushion the impact, two approaches are possible – long adjustment periods, or financial assistance. The accession of Austria, Finland and Sweden provides an illustration of the latter. Their agricultural prices were all above CAP levels. The EU insisted that the prices should fall to CAP levels on day one of membership. The acceding member states however negotiated compensatory payments for their farmers based on the estimated fall in incomes. These subsidies were nationally financed and paid in such a way that they did not support production of specific products but rather supported farmers. In the jargon they were de-linked from direct production incentives. They were also time limited. In other words, they were transitional and financed by the taxpayer and not the consumer (as happened with delayed removal of border barriers in earlier enlargements).

The barriers against immediate free movement of persons in the Greek and Iberian enlargements illustrate this alternative; and are relevant not least because a similar rhetoric is developing in Germany and Austria about the political unacceptability of any large scale migration from the East. Thus there is a discussion to be had about how such adjustment can be managed on both sides of the negotiating table.

The difficult policy areas are the process regulation issues of social policy and environmental policy. The discussion in the previous section shows that one can question whether common social and environmental policies are a necessary and core part of the EU's arrangements. But the pressure for 'fairness' and for 'level playing fields' is strong. From the perspective of the eastern accession, the question in any case is not whether the *acquis* is too encompassing, but whether adjustment to these parts of the *acquis* can be the subject of particularly long transition periods.

The case for permitting long post-accession transition periods, especially with respect to environmental policy, is overwhelming. The communist legacy of environmental degradation faces the democratic governments in Central and Eastern Europe with huge costs, despite high legislated standards. The Commission itself puts these costs at over 100 billion euro.[2] These are costs which countries in transition, most of whom have not yet regained 1989 levels of GDP, cannot afford in the short run. To force too rapid an implementation could set economic development back another generation. The implementation of EU environmental policy is only one part of the environmental agenda in Central and Eastern Europe, and two decades seems a reasonable time frame for the implementation of that agenda.

The Treaty on European Union (Article 130s (5)) gives an explicit role to the Cohesion Fund in helping offset the costs of implementing strict environmental standards in the poorer EU member states. The logical response to the conjunction of unsustainable regulatory costs on the CEEC side and unsustainable budgetary costs on the side of the existing EU is to seek a solution in precisely the opposite direction – a long transition in which derogations from strict EU process standards are matched by non-application of fiscal transfers. How to achieve the working arrangements for this depends on how the EU more broadly addresses the issue of differentiation in an enlarged EU. The choice between more rapid adjustment to EU norms accompanied by generous financial assistance and slower adjustment with less assistance is a choice for the EU to make.

6.5 Conclusions

Accession is of necessity a drawn out and detailed process. The *acquis* is a large and complex regulatory framework. This short chapter has tried to draw attention to some of the external forces working on the process, and to some of canards which are often deployed in support of the proposition that enlargement cannot take place until every dot and comma of the *acquis* is legislated and applied in all

---

2. http://europa.int /comm/dg11/enlarg/compcos.htm

the applicant states and to a higher degree of compliance than is present in some member states who already enjoy the benefits of EU membership. Transition periods are consistent with the single market as are well-designed financial aids to ease the inevitable adjustment costs.

References

Baldwin, R. (1994), *Towards an Integrated Europe*, Centre for Economic Policy Research, London.

Baldwin, R., J. Francois, and R. Portes (1997), 'The costs and benefits of EU enlargement to the East', *Economic Policy*, No.24, pp.125-176.

Bean, C. *et al.* (1998), *Social Europe: One For All?*, Monitoring European Integration No.8, Centre for Economic Policy Research, London.

Begg, D. *et al.* (1993), *Making Sense of Subsidiarity: How Much Centralization for Europe?*, Monitoring European Integration No.4, Centre for Economic Policy Research, London.

European Bank for Reconstruction and Development (1998), *Transition Report 1998*, London.

European Commission (1995a), *White Paper: Preparation of the associated countries of Central and Eastern Europe for integration into the internal market of the Union*, COM(95) 163 final, 3 May 1995 and COM(95) 163 final/2, 10 May 1995.

European Commission (1995b), Fifth Report on State Aids, http://europa.eu.int/comm/dg03/aid/other.htm.

European Commission (1997), Opinions, http://europa.eu.int/comm/agenda 2000/index_en.html.

European Commission (1998a), Screening reports, http://europa.eu.int/comm/dg1a/enlarge/report/_11_98/index.html.

European Commission (1998b), Agenda2000, http://europa.eu.int/comm/agenda2000/index_en.html.

European Commission (1998c), Report on Agriculture in Central and Eastern Europe, http://europa.eu.int/comm/dg06/public/peco/fullreport.

European Commission (1998d), *European Economy*, No.65, Brussels.

European Commission (1999), Seventh Report on State Aids, http://europa.eu.int/comm/dg03/aid/other.htm.

European Council (1993), Conclusions of the Copenhagen European Council, Text accessible from link at http://europa.eu.int/comm/tfan/enl_en.html.

European Council (1995), *European Council of Cannes, Council conclusions on 'Preparation of the associated countries of Central and Eastern Europe for integration into the internal market of the European Union*, Europe Documents No.1943, 30 June 1995.

European Council (1999), Conclusions of the Berlin European Council, press release (25 March 1999) – No. sn 100/1/99rev(presse) http://ue.eu.int/newsroom/main.cfm.

Fingleton, J., E. Fox, D. Neven and P. Seabright (1996), *Competition Policy and the Transformation of Central Europe*, Centre for Economic Policy Research, London.

Gacs, J. and M. Wyzan (1999), *The Time Pattern of Costs and Benefits of EU Accession*, Interim Report IR-99-015/May, IIASA, Vienna.

GATT (1993), *Trade Policy Review: The European Communities, 1993*, GATT, Geneva.

Hoekman, B. (1996), *Trade and competition policy in the WTO system*, CEPR discussion paper, No.1501, Centre for Economic Policy Research, London.

Krugman, P. (1991), *Geography and Trade*, MIT Press, Cambridge, MA.

Maliszewska, M., J.J. Michalek and A. Smith (1999), *EU accession and Poland's external trade policy*, Discussion paper No.45, Faculty of Economic Sciences, University of Warsaw, Warsaw.

Mayhew, A. (1998), *Recreating Europe: The European Union's policy towards Central and Eastern Europe*, Cambridge University Press, Cambridge.

Mayhew, A. and W. Orlowski (forthcoming), *The impact of EU accession on enterprise adaptation and institutional development in the EU-Associated countries in Central and Eastern Europe*, EBRD Working Papers, European Bank for Reconstruction and Development, London.

Messerlin, P. (1994), 'Should anti-dumping rules be replaced by national or international competition rules?', *Aussenwirtschaft*, No.49, pp.351-374.

OECD (1999), *Economic Survey of Ireland*, Paris.

Ottaviano, G.I.P and D. Puga (1998), 'Agglomeration in the global economy: a survey of the 'new economic geography", *The World Economy*, No.21, pp.707-731.

Puga, D. (1998), 'Geography lessons', *European Economic Perspectives*, No.18, Centre for Economic Policy Research, London.

Rollo, J. (1997), 'Economic aspects of EU enlargement to the East', in: M. Maresceau (ed.), *Enlarging The European Union*, Longman, London, pp.252-275.

Rollo, J. and A. Smith (1993), 'The political economy of Eastern European trade with the European Community: why so sensitive?', *Economic Policy*, No.16, pp.140-181.

Rollo, J. and J. Stern (1992), 'Growth and trade prospects for Central and Eastern Europe', *World Economy*, No.15, pp.645-668.

Schaffer, M.E. (1995), *Government subsidies to enterprises in Central and Eastern Europe: budgetary subsidies and tax arrears*, CEPR Discussion paper, No.1144, Centre for Economic Policy Research, London.

Smith, A., P. Holmes, U. Sedelmeier, E. Smith, A. Young and H. Wallace (1996), *The European Union and Central and Eastern Europe: pre-accession strategies*, Working paper, No.15, Sussex European Institute, University of Sussex, Brighton.

Winters, L.A. (1992), 'The Europe agreements: with a little help from our friends', in: *The Association Process: Making it Work*, CEPR Occasional Paper, No.11, Centre for Economic Policy Research, London, pp.17-33.

Joining EMU

Arnout Wellink[1]

7.1 Introduction

In 1989, a single monetary policy in Europe seemed to be an option for a distant future. Indeed, European integration had lacked dynamism in the preceding years and seemed to regain its momentum only gradually. A mere ten years later, the internal market has been completed (1992) and the economic and monetary union (EMU) has started with eleven Member States (1999). Moreover, a number of Central and Eastern European countries (CEECs) have applied for membership of the European Union (EU). Formal negotiations on EU accession started in November 1998 and central bankers are involved in serious discussions about the possible implications of a future expansion of the Union. Perhaps, only Nostradamus could have foreseen this series of important developments that have happened over the last decade. At the risk of tempting fate, we will try and look ahead another ten years in this chapter.[2]

I will concentrate on the monetary relations between the candidate Member States and the euro area, restricting myself to the 'fast-track' countries, since they are the ones for which intensifying monetary relations is most relevant in the coming years. I will start with monetary relations in the run-up to EU membership. Then, I will step back for a moment to take a somewhat broader perspective in Section 7.3, where I discuss the macroeconomic preconditions for stable relations in the monetary field. Looking further ahead, the fourth section will go into monetary relations after EU membership. But I will first make some general remarks.

The European Council in Copenhagen (1993) agreed that the associated CEECs if they so desire will become EU members and that accession of a candidate Member State will take place as soon as this particular candidate fulfils the economic and political conditions. In this sense, EU accession is simply a matter of timing. The decision on the appropriate year for accession will, and should, to a large extent be based on political considerations. At the same time, it is important to

---

1. The author owes a debt of gratitude to Paul Cavelaars, whose contribution has been indispensable for the realisation of this chapter.
2. See Engering (1989) en Molle (1989) for similar efforts shortly after the tumbling of the Berlin wall.

keep in mind that the countries of Central and Eastern Europe should be given enough time to prepare themselves properly for joining the Single Market.

It should not be overlooked that there are important differences, not only between the so-called 'fast-track' countries and the other applicants, but also within both groups.3 Given their substantial differences, the candidate Member States should be dealt with on a case-by-case basis. Each country has several unique characteristics that will play a role in the accession process. There are, however, common elements as well.

The countries of Central and Eastern Europe are catching up quickly. One day they may become the most dynamic economies and societies in Europe. Nevertheless, at present some transitional provisions are likely to be necessary for the new Member States after joining the European Union. Without such provisions the expansion of the European Union may need to be postponed for many years, which is clearly undesirable. In the past, transitional provisions have also been applied to new entrants, including Spain, Portugal and Greece.

It is essential to strike a proper balance between the timing of accession and the application of the accession conditions. The *acquis communautaire*, the body of legislation which applies to all EU Member States, must remain the common denominator. Member States can decide to work more closely together in some areas, but they cannot detract from the *acquis*. Member States must satisfy certain requirements in the monetary and financial sphere. This is even true for Member States that have a derogation with respect to the monetary union. These requirements, relating to the free movement of capital, central bank independence and the ban on central bank lending to the government, among other things, are considered essential for the functioning of the single market. Transitional provisions may be required. Permanent exemptions or lengthy transitional periods, however, would be inappropriate as they could threaten the internal cohesion of the Union.

7.2 Monetary relations before EU membership

In assessing monetary relations between the applicant countries and the euro zone, an overview of current exchange rate arrangements of candidate Member States is a useful starting point. Table 7.1 lists the most important characteristics of the current exchange rate regimes.

As can be seen from Table 7.1 the 'fast-track' countries vary greatly in their approach towards the exchange rate. Estonia uses the most extreme form of exchange rate pegging, having implemented a currency board since 1992 (using the euro as of 1999). This effectively amounts to a complete surrender of mone-

---

3. The 'fast-track' countries identified by the European Commission in 1998 are Poland, Hungary, the Czech Republic, Slovenia, Estonia and Cyprus. The second group of associated countries consists of the Slovak Republic, Romania, Bulgaria, Latvia, Lithuania and Malta.

Table 7.1: Current exchange rate arrangements of 'fast-track' countries (1999)

Country	Monetary strategy	Exchange rate regime	Anchor currency	Bandwith
Estonia	currency board	fixed peg	euro	0%
Hungary	exchange rate targeting	crawling peg	basket (70% euro)	±2.25%
Poland	inflation targeting	crawling peg	basket (55% euro)	±15%
Slovenia	money targeting	managed float	–	–
Czech Republic	inflation targeting	managed float	–	–

– = not applicable
Source: IMF

tary autonomy. Hungary and Poland operate crawling pegs against a currency basket consisting of the euro and the US dollar. The Polish zloty and Hungarian forint are devalued against this basket at a constant rate of less than one per cent each month. The Czech Republic used to have a ±7.5% fluctuation band against a currency basket in which the D-mark had a weight of 65%, but was forced to abandon this policy in May 1997. Both Slovenia and the Czech Republic have floating currencies now.[4]

On the one hand, flexible rates have, generally speaking, the advantage that they quickly respond to policy changes, allowing the financial markets to exert a disciplinary function, whereas fixed rates may at least temporarily conceal underlying problems. On the other hand, flexible rates may lead to highly volatile exchange rate behaviour creating unnecessary uncertainty, potentially with adverse consequences for the economy. This is the traditional dilemma between fixed and flexible exchange rate regimes. In practice, many intermediate regimes exist in between these extremes. Crawling pegs (like the ones that are currently implemented in Hungary and Poland) lean somewhat more to the fixed regime, whereas managed floats (such as the systems in place in Slovenia and the Czech Republic) are relatively flexible exchange rate regimes.

Choice of an exchange rate regime

Transition economies are often faced with many challenges simultaneously. One is the need to implement structural reform and at the same time to achieve macro-economic stability. Practically speaking, it will be necessary to set priorities. It is important that output stabilisation and inflation reduction are implemented at an early stage, if only to win public support for the other necessary reform measures.

---

4. Given its relatively small economic size, Cyprus, which is one of the fast-track countries, will be left out of the analysis in the remainder of this chapter.

As soon as macroeconomic stabilisation has taken place, to some degree at least, governments can gradually shift their attention to structural reform. This means that different priorities will be set at different stages of transition. Given that each exchange rate regime has its strengths and weaknesses, different exchange rate regimes may be appropriate at different stages of transition. Put differently, there is no one-size-fits-all policy prescription. One may call this a pragmatic approach towards the exchange rate.

At an early stage of transition, a monetary policy that focuses on domestic variables may be less effective in stabilising actual and expected inflation, due either to the lack of timely and reliable money and banking statistics or to instability of money demand. In such circumstances, a fixed exchange rate can provide for a nominal anchor and thus help the credibility of a disinflation program (see IMF, 1997).

Further on during the transition process, priorities may shift towards structural reform.

In these circumstances, relatively high investments may be required for several years and the government may find it troublesome to maintain a (near-)balanced budget. In the absence of sufficient domestic private sector savings, such financing requirements will lead to external imbalances that make it difficult to maintain a credible fixed exchange rate peg without devaluations. In that case, a more flexible exchange rate regime may be preferable, as it provides more adjustment capability and since it may be more costly in political terms to adjust a pegged exchange rate than to allow movements in a flexible rate.

As the reform process progresses to a more advanced stage, transition countries may start to realise economic growth rates and productivity increases well above those of more established industrial countries, a situation which will tend to put upward pressure on the real exchange rate.[5] If the CEECs have achieved an inflation rate equal to the EU average at this stage, this phenomenon can lead to upward pressure on the nominal exchange rate as well. Such a situation calls for some degree of flexibility in the exchange rate somewhat further on in the transformation process. This would argue against participating in the monetary union too quickly after EU membership. We will come back to this issue later in this chapter.

---

5. This phenomenon is often referred to as the Balassa-Samuelson effect. It contends that increases in labour productivity in the tradables sector give rise to a real appreciation of the exchange rate. The productivity increase can lead to a real appreciation both via an appreciation of the nominal exchange rate and via higher wages in the entire economy, including the nontradables sector, which lead to a relative increase of the price level in the emerging economy compared to the level abroad (see Kopits, 1999, pp. 13-14 and Daviddi and Ilzkovitz, 1997, pp. 675-676).

Monetary strategies

Several of the 'fast-track' countries have relatively flexible exchange rate arrangements. This is the case for Slovenia and the Czech Republic and, to a lesser extent, for Poland. In the absence of a foreign nominal anchor, the desire to stabilise the general price level calls for a domestic anchor for inflation expectations. Monetary strategies which focus either directly on inflation or on an intermediate target like the money supply are a natural choice. As can be seen in Table 7.1, this is what Slovenia, the Czech Republic and Poland have done. Slovenia has adopted a strategy of money targeting, whereas the other two countries follow a direct inflation targeting strategy.

In principle, some tension may emerge between domestically-oriented strategies and exchange rate stability at some point in time. As the central bank has only one instrument, the interest rate level, it follows from Tinbergen's rule that it cannot pursue two goals simultaneously.[6] Practically speaking, however, a strategy which establishes low inflation expectations is likely to lead to a relatively stable exchange rate over the medium term as a side-effect.

Direct inflation targeting and money targeting may be somewhat more difficult to implement than exchange rate targeting. On a technical level, the successful adoption of inflation targeting requires that the central bank must be able to produce adequate inflation forecasts and that it must have a reasonable idea about the impact of changes in monetary instruments on inflation (magnitude, lags, and so on). Similarly, money targeting requires that some measure of money shows a relationship with the general price level which is sufficiently stable to give the central bank a reasonable degree of control. Both strategies require the availability of reliable statistics as a basis for policy.

As trade relations between the CEECs and the EU intensify, an implicit or explicit orientation of monetary policy towards the exchange rate against the euro seems appropriate. Currently, official reserves and foreign debts appear to be divided roughly equally between the euro and the dollar (see McCauley, 1997, pp.21-23). Some fifty to sixty per cent of international trade of the countries of Central and Eastern Europe is with the European Union and this percentage is likely to increase further as economic integration between the two regions continues (see Van Bergeijk and Oldersma, 1990). Therefore, it may be expected that the exchange rate against the euro will gradually be assigned increasing importance in the monetary policy considerations of the candidate Member States. In any case, the exchange rate regime will generally not be a completely free float. The foreign exchange markets of the CEECs are not very liquid, meaning that

---

6. This is not to say that central banks cannot temporarily succeed in achieving both goals at the same time. For instance, Spain and Finland formally maintained an inflation targeting strategy when they participated in the exchange rate mechanism of the European Monetary System for several years.

transactions that are small in absolute size can have a sizeable impact on the exchange rate. In addition, the economies of the CEECs are rather open in that international trade accounts for a relatively large share of national income. This implies that exchange rate fluctuations can have a significant impact on the economy, both on prices and output.

Pegging to the euro before membership?

Where pragmatism is called for in the monetary field, it does not make sense to establish all kind of institutional bells and whistles. Rather than participating in any formal exchange rate mechanism with the euro *before* EU membership, the countries in Central and Eastern Europe should focus on economic reform. All of the 'fast-track' countries have already gone through the first phase of stabilisation. For instance, they have managed to push inflation rates down to around 10% a year. The 'fast-track' countries are now in a second stage of transition, where further structural reform is needed. During such a period, monetary and exchange rate policies should provide for sufficient flexibility.

Before accession, any peg can only be a *unilateral* decision, as the commitment to conduct domestic policies that can sustain a certain exchange rate should come from the pegging country. Only after joining the European Union, could the new Member States – as indeed they are expected to – participate in the ERM-II, assuming that a credible peg against the euro can be established at that time.

Linking the currency to the euro cannot be a substitute for conducting stability-oriented macro-economic and structural policies. Rather, any formal link to the euro should be *preceded* by policy measures which make the envisaged currency link a credible one. Policy measures should focus on financial-monetary stability. This notion should be understood to include such measures as the inflation rate, the exchange rate, central bank independence, the current account and domestic and foreign debt.

7.3 Preconditions for stable monetary relations

The European Council in Copenhagen in June 1993 laid down the conditions for EU accession by the candidate Member States in Central and Eastern Europe (see Chapter 5). A judgement on these three groups of criteria – political, economic and the ability to take on the *acquis* – depends also on the capacity of a country's administrative and legal systems to put into effect the principles of democracy and the market economy and to apply and enforce the *acquis* in practice (see European Commission, 1997).

This section focuses on the macroeconomic preconditions for stable monetary relations, that is for working towards the ultimate goal of participating in the economic and monetary union of Europe.[7] These preconditions are much broader than the Maastricht criteria for economic convergence that have been established as necessary conditions for adoption of the single currency.[8]

Some of the macroeconomic preconditions follow directly from the principles of the single market that have already been laid down in the Treaty of Rome, such as free trade in goods and services and the free movement of capital. A related issue is the health and stability of the financial sector in the applicant countries, which is important both in order to be competitive in the single European market for financial services and in order to permit substantial cross-border capital flows without causing disturbances in the real economy. Other economic preconditions to be discussed in this section relate to the Maastricht requirements that all Member States had to adhere to as from the start of Stage Two of EMU on 1 January 1994, that is several years before the start of the single monetary policy. Requirements that are relevant in this context are central bank independence and the ban on central bank lending to the government. This section will discuss the 'fast-track' countries as a group and avoid judgements on individual applicants as much as possible, even though, as said, there are substantial differences in performance and any applicant country should be looked at on a case-by-case basis.

The income gap

We will take the income gap between the CEECs and the EU as a starting point. This is by no means a formal requirement for EU membership, but it could be a point of concern for politicians in the current Member States. The prosperity level in the candidate Member States is still substantially below that in the European Union. Average *per capita* income varies from one-sixth to almost one-half of the EU average for the 'fast-track' countries. This should be put in perspective. The income gap between the poorest of the 'fast-track' countries and the EU average is not much larger than the gap between Portugal and the EC average at the moment of the Portuguese entry into the Community in 1986.[9] *Per capita* income in the most prosperous of the 'fast-track' countries (Slovenia) is roughly equal to that of the poorest EU member (Portugal). Fischer, Sahay and Végh (1998) expect that for all current applicant countries taken together it will take, on average, about one generation to converge to the *per capita* level of the low-income European Union countries (Greece, Portugal and Spain).[10]

---

7. This ultimate goal follows directly from combining the above-mentioned presidency conclusions of the European Council in Copenhagen with Article 2 of the EC Treaty, which states that. "The Community shall have as its task, *by establishing a common market and an economic and monetary union* [..]".

8. See Article 109j of the EC Treaty.

9. Recall that Portugal had another thirteen years for reform and catching up before the start of monetary union on 1 January 1999.

10. This expectation is based on an average current income level of 4,900 dollars (PPP-based, 1995 data) and a 5-6% growth rate for all CEECs taken together (that is: including the slow-track countries) and a current income level of 11,690 dollars and a 2% growth rate for the three low-income EU members referred to in the main text.

Table 7.2: Income levels

Country	*Per capita* income in US dollars	as % of low-income EU
Slovenia	9,165	72%
Czech Republic	5,050	40%
Hungary	4,504	36%
Poland	3,704	29%
Estonia	3,211	25%
Low-income EU 1/	12,645	100%

1/ Average of Spain, Portugal and Greece. Data for 1997.

Source: IMF

Macroeconomic stability and international trade

A sustained convergence of macroeconomic fundamentals is a prerequisite for successful and stable monetary relations. Macroeconomic stability has improved greatly over the last couple of years. The five 'fast-track' countries have an average budget deficit of 2% of gross domestic product (GDP), an average debt-to-GDP ratio of 32%, an average inflation rate of 10% and an average current account deficit of 4% of GDP. See also Table 7.3.[11] But the differences between individual countries are substantial and the current situation is not free of risks. For instance, the transfer of social functions from state enterprises to the government budget could lead to an increase in the government deficit and debt during the transformation process (see Daviddi and Ilzkovitz, 1997).[12] Inflation risks now seem to be mainly related to uncertainty about the wage formation process, as there have already been substantial accomplishments in the abandonment of price controls. With regard to cyclical convergence, it seems that the EU and CEEC business cycles have come pretty much in line. In fact, Boone and Maurel (1998) find that the correlation between the German and the CEECs' industrial production and unemployment cycles is even higher than the correlation between those of Germany and the EU.

All associated countries have made considerable progress in the liberalisation of international trade. Europe Agreements have been concluded with each of the CEECs in the process of preparing for EU membership since 1991. The Agreements have led to a great deal of trade liberalisation on both sides, although some impor-

---

11. Cyprus has been excluded from the calculations because of its small size. The figures are unweighted averages for Estonia, Hungary, Poland, Slovenia and the Czech Republic.
12. Any public function or action involving government money should find expression in official figures for government debt. Postponing necessary reforms or excluding some government functions from official deficit and debt figures constitutes a greater risk. Reducing uncertainties with respect to official figures is likely to build up confidence and to attract rather than deter foreign investors, even if official figures show an increase in the government deficit.

Table 7.3: Selected economic indicators for five 'fast-track' economies

Country	Budget balance	Inflation rate	Current account balance
Estonia	-0.3	8.2	-8.6
Czech Republic	-2.1	10.7	-1.9
Slovenia	-1.0	6.5	0.0
Poland	-3.7	11.7	-5.2
Hungary	-4.6	14.4	-4.8

* The budget balance and the current account balance are expressed as a percentage of GDP.
* The inflation rate is the percentage change in year-end retail/consumer price level.
* Data are estimates for 1998.

Source: IMF

tant exceptions (notably in the agricultural sector) remain. The principle of asymmetry is central to the Agreements: the Union will reduce its tariffs more quickly than the candidate Member States. Nevertheless, the Europe Agreements lead to a situation where companies in the candidate Member States will face a higher level of competition some time before EU accession, which will help them to prepare for participating in the single market. The economic openness of the 'fast-track' countries is now on a level which is comparable to that of the European Union. The CEECs' average applied tariff is somewhat higher than EU tariffs on industrial goods, but much lower than EU rates on agricultural goods (see also Baldwin, Francois and Portes, 1997).[13] Trade liberalisation has led to substantial current account imbalances in some countries. Due regard should be paid to the possible employment consequences and to the sustainability of these imbalances, especially in the context of a fixed exchange rate regime.

Capital liberalisation

EU accession comes with the obligation to abolish restrictions on international capital flows. Apart from that, a gradual liberalisation of capital flows in the run-up to EU accession is desirable, as foreign direct investment and long-term portfolio investments can make important contributions to financing the transition process. Moreover, an inflow of capital from foreign companies can contribute to quick financial regulatory reform and stimulate legislation to improve the efficiency of the domestic capital market. The latter could be achieved by applying Western standards for both monitoring and ownership rights.

---

13. Tariffs are an incomplete measure, but offer at least some idea of the degree of protectionism.

Net capital flows to and from the CEECs have varied from excessively high capital inflows to sizeable net outflows over the past decade. Net inflows were modest in the early years after the tumbling of the Berlin Wall. At that time, the risk as perceived by investors was probably higher than it is now. In addition, existing foreign debt constrained the borrowing capacity of some CEECs. Since 1993, net capital flows to the region have risen substantially, and have become excessive on several occasions.[14] Later on, in the aftermath of the Russian financial crisis, most of the countries concerned have witnessed sizeable net capital ouflows.

There is no easy remedy for coping with such large capital flows. Sterilisation through central banks' open market operations has only short-lived effects. It prevents domestic interest rates from falling, thereby maintaining the incentive for capital inflows. Restrictions on capital flows are difficult to implement and have proven less than effective in times when investor confidence turns sour. Introducing controls to limit capital outflows in the middle of a crisis is doomed to fail. They may afford some temporary relief, but when people want to get their money out of the country, they will succeed in doing so in the end. What remains is long-term damage to investor confidence. Liberalising the capital account further is the more promising route. Adequate sequencing of short-term capital liberalisation may be required in order to gain time for adjusting the domestic financial sector to the competitive pressures that follow from capital liberalisation.

There has been considerable progress on capital liberalisation in the CEECs and it is expected that, under OECD rules, capital movements will be free of restrictions pretty soon. Therefore, most applicant countries are unlikely to require a transitional arrangement in the area of the capital account of the sort that was applied to Spain and Portugal when they entered the EU in 1986.

The financial sector

It is essential that the sequencing of capital liberalisation goes hand in hand with an improvement of supervision and a strengthening of the financial sector. The domestic banking sector needs to become sufficiently strong to buffer possible capital outflows and experienced enough to continue to make a sensible risk-return trade-off in its credit policy even under conditions of sizeable capital inflows. Similarly, well-developed domestic financial markets would improve the availability of credit for local companies, promoting economic growth. Therefore, financial sector reform should be high on the policy agenda in Eastern Europe.

The banking sector in the CEECs has much ground to make up with respect to EU banks, although there are of course important differences between countries and individual banks. In the communist past, many banks used to be part of, or

---

14. Net capital inflows in Hungary and the Czech Republic are reported to have reached a peak of about 15% of GDP in 1995 (Source: IMF; see also Manzocchi, 1998).

closely related to, the central bank. In addition, many of the borrowers used to be companies with close ties to the government. As a result, there were few incentives for risk control and return enhancement. Instead, some banks used to generate profits by exploiting certain privileges which no longer exist. See Sdralevich (1997) and Fischer, Sahay and Végh (1998) for a more detailed account.

What is necessary, is establishing a healthy banking sector. What has been done to some extent in some countries, but not all, is privatising state-controlled banks to accomplish this goal. This will provide bank managers with incentives to make proper risk-return assessments. Financial slack seems to have led to continuing soft budget constraints in several CEECs. Adequate bank supervision and financial markets oversight are required to ensure that sufficient weight will be given to risk control. This not only refers to making better decisions on new loans. Screening and monitoring prior to rolling-over existing loans is equally important (see Berglöf and Roland, 1997). Foreign ownership may help to transfer certain specific banking skills to the candidate Member States and may improve access to international capital markets, also in periods when foreign investors are less eager to pour money into these countries.

A bad-loan overhang in the banking sector can severely impede the functioning of the economy. This can be seen from the recent problems in Japan and other Asian countries, but also from the troubles in the Swedish banking sector several years before. Balance sheet restructuring in countries in Central and Eastern Europe may in some cases require intervention by the competent authorities. It may be necessary to let some banks fail. The authorities may be involved in facilitating bank mergers, in order to prevent such failures. It may also be necessary for governments to take over bad loans. This would enable some credit institutions to conduct business more effectively. In order to prevent moral hazard, the rescue of selected credit institutions can only take place under certain conditions, most likely including the laying-off of the decision-makers responsible for making these loans.

Attention should also be paid to the development of financial markets. More sophisticated domestic stock and bond markets will improve capital market access for domestic firms. This is important, as very few firms in the CEECs have access to the international capital markets. A more liquid foreign exchange market will make the real economy less vulnerable to speculative attacks, whether related to the country's own fundamentals or related to contagion effects of currency crises elsewhere (see Kopits, 1999, pp.36-37). This vulnerability is especially high in the context of a liberalised short-term capital account and a fixed exchange rate regime. This supports the earlier notion that candidate Member States should not be forced to join a uniform exchange rate agreement with the euro area at too early a stage.

Central bank independence and ban on monetary financing

Applicant countries should ensure an independent position of their central banks and prohibit any type of credit facilities of public authorities with the central bank. Moreover, the central banks have to pursue the objective of price stability. In Stage Three of EMU, which started on 1 January 1999, these requirements apply to all Member States, including those with a derogation.[15] Central bank independence and a formal ban on monetary financing help to anchor inflation expectations and thus contribute to the credibility of any anti-inflation or exchange rate commitment. Therefore, it would be attractive to implement the necessary measures in the applicant countries even before EU membership.

Central bank independence is legally in place in most CEECs, judged by the explicit mention of the independent status in the central bank law, the duration of the term of office of the central bank governor and the central bank's control over its own budget. Also in practice, central banks in many applicant countries are nowadays more free than before to determine their own policies without being overruled by instructions from their respective governments.

Monetary financing increases the money supply, as the government finances its expenses by borrowing new central bank money. This entails the risk of higher inflation and does not put a check on the government deficit. Borrowing from the central bank seemingly allows the government to conduct an expansionary fiscal policy without any adverse consequences, whereas borrowing in financial markets would confront the government with a higher risk premium in interest rates in reaction to its less responsible spending behaviour. Monetary financing is forbidden for EU Member States by the Maastricht Treaty, but has been formally banned in only a few applicant countries so far.

In their pursuit of price stability, central banks in transition economies can use the same concepts of price stability as those in more mature market economies. In practice, however, inflation in the CEECs is likely to be partly related to productivity increases that form part of the catching up process. Moreover, increases in the general price level may be more difficult to measure than in Western Europe as a result of more drastic relative price adjustments. These elements should be taken into account in the policy responses of central banks in the CEECs (see Daviddi and Ilzkovitz, 1997).

7.4 Monetary relations after EU accession

New entrants to the Union are expected to participate in the ERM-II. As the European Union moved to Stage Three of EMU on 1 January 1999, new entrants to the

---

15. These requirements follow from the Maastricht Treaty. Only the United Kingdom has negotiated an exception with respect to central bank independence.

Union will automatically receive a derogation status, just like the four current 'pre-ins': Denmark, Greece, Sweden and the United Kingdom. The derogation status implies that the new Member States will have to comply with the European Council Resolution on ERM-II, which states that "[..] Participation in the exchange rate mechanism will be voluntary for the Member States outside the euro area. Nevertheless, Member States with a derogation can be expected to join the mechanism [..]".[16]

The step to participating in the ERM-II needs to be taken in a credible and sustainable manner. Put differently, a currency joining ERM-II should not lead to risks for the mechanism as a whole. This notion implies that the central rate against the euro should be fixed at a rate close to market equilibrium for each newly participating currency. Determining an equilibrium rate for the currencies of the CEECs could be difficult if EU accession and ERM-II participation were to occur before the completion of the transformation process. In that case, the fixing of an appropriate central rate could be complicated by substantial relative price adjustments and by fluctuations in the actual exchange rate due to changing market expectations about government policies in the CEECs.

An exchange rate commitment must be supported by sustainable other policies. By the time new Member States start to participate in the ERM-II, they can be expected to have moderate nominal wage increases, (near-)balanced budget policies and a relatively sound banking system. In these circumstances, an ERM-II commitment will be credible and can inspire greater confidence among economic agents, including foreign investors. This is likely to lower interest rate premiums instantaneously, thus easing the debt-service burden.

Convergence towards ERM-II participation would depart from different starting points, calling for different paths of convergence. The ERM-II offers considerable flexibility in the form of a relatively wide fluctuation margin, timely realignments and the possibility of closer exchange rate links if appropriate. The ERM-II even allows for some variety of exchange rate arrangements within the mechanism, ranging from regular ERM-II pegs to progressively tighter arrangements (see also Berrigan and Carré, 1997). Whether a currency board would be possible within the ERM-II is a matter for discussion. In any case, keeping a currency board in place has several drawbacks. It would hamper the development of a foreign exchange market and, as it means having no full-fledged central bank, maintaining a currency board until the moment of participation in the monetary union would prevent commercial banks from becoming familiar with monetary instruments and procedures in a regular money market.

The ERM experience since 1993 suggests that the ERM-II bandwidth of 15% on either side of the central rate is wide enough to discourage speculators. This will

---

16. Resolution of the European Council on the establishment of an exchange rate mechanism in the third stage of economic and monetary union, attached to the Presidency Conclusions of the European Council in Amsterdam, 16-17 June 1997.

only work, however, as long as the central banks of the respective CEECs endeavour not to use the fluctuation margin completely. According to the Resolution on ERM-II, intervention at the margins will in principle be automatic and unlimited, with very short-term financing available. However, the ECB and the central banks of the other ERM-II participants could suspend interventions if these were to conflict with their primary objective. Ideally, new Member States should have acquired sufficient operational experience in managing a stable exchange rate regime before they begin to participate in ERM-II. The central bank must be prepared to engage in sterilised or non-sterilised intervention, if necessary (see Kopits, p.34).

In principle, EU membership will result in EMU membership once the criteria referred to in Article 109j of the EU Treaty, including the one on exchange rate stability, are satisfied.[17] Theoretically, this could be two years after EU membership, but caution is called for when it comes to EMU participation too quickly after EU accession. Recall that earlier accession processes were spread over a long period of time. In the case of the United Kingdom, Denmark and Ireland, it took twelve years between first application and accession to the European Union. For Greece this process lasted six years and for Portugal and Spain nine years.[18] After EU accession, it took another ten years in most cases to move towards full integration.

Let us conclude this section with an idea about the relations between the European System of Central Banks (ESCB) and the central banks of the candidate Member States. Although the candidate Member States obviously cannot take part in ESCB meetings before their accession to the European Union, it could be useful to invite the governors of the central banks of the 'fast-track' countries once a year to attend a special meeting of the General Council of the ECB. This would be similar to the current practice for the Council of Economics and Finance Ministers (Ecofin).

7.5 Concluding remarks

In this chapter we have discussed the monetary relations between the euro area and the countries of Central and Eastern Europe. The main points will be summarised below.

Like the other contributors to this book, we have tried to look ahead another

---

17. These criteria are well known by now. They refer to inflation, government deficit, government debt, the exchange rate and long-term interest rates. Strictly speaking, the criteria are necessary (though not sufficient) criteria for membership.
18. The EU enlargement in 1995 shows that events can move much more quickly than stated in the main text. Recall, however, that Austria, Finland and Sweden were members of the European Economic Area and had already adopted EU legislation as a result of their long association with the EU (see Van Brabant, 1996).

ten years in this chapter. The so-called 'fast-track' countries of Central and Eastern Europe will hopefully be ready to join the European Union within this ten-year period. However, a number of further reforms still need to be implemented. This is especially true with respect to financial markets and the banking sector. It seems an odd idea that CEECs could join EMU before some of the current non-participating Member States, given the fact that the UK and Denmark have been EU members for over 25 years and have much more advanced economies than the CEECs. At the same time, the Member States that decided not to join EMU from the start are themselves responsible for not being overtaken by the CEECs. Candidate Member States should be assessed on a case-by-case basis. Some transitional provisions are likely to be necessary, but the *acquis* must remain the common denominator.

With respect to the exchange rate arrangements of candidate Member States, a pragmatic approach will be required. Formal exchange rate arrangements are no substitute for economic reform. Different exchange rate regimes may be appropriate at different stages of transition. A fixed exchange rate can provide for a nominal anchor at an early stage, a more flexible exchange rate arrangement may be required to allow for sufficient flexibility during the transformation process. The exchange rate against the euro will gradually be assigned an increasingly important role in the monetary policy considerations of candidate Member States when the moment of accession approaches.

Any formal link to the euro should be preceded by policy measures which lend credibility to the intended currency link. Policy measures should first focus on financial-monetary stability (inflation, exchange rate, central bank independence, current account, domestic and foreign debt, other Treaty obligations). Subsequently, policy measures should include further liberalisation of the capital account and restructuring of the financial sector. Adequate sequencing will be required to enable the domestic financial sector to adjust.

In principle, EU membership will lead to EMU membership if the criteria are satisfied. New entrants are expected to participate in the ERM-II immediately upon becoming EU members. However, if applicant countries would be admitted into the EU sooner rather than later, completely fixing the exchange rates may not be desirable yet. For example, continuing productivity increases in the new Member States might lead to upward pressure on their currencies. This would argue for caution about EMU participation immediately after EU accession.

References

Alogoskoufis, G. and R. Portes (1997), 'The euro, the dollar and the international monetary system', in P.R. Masson, Th.H. Krueger and B.G. Turtelboom, *EMU and the international monetary system*, International Monetary Fund, Washington, D.C.

Baldwin, R.E., J.F. Francois and R. Portes (1997), 'The Costs and Benefits of Eastern Enlargement: The Impact on the EU and Central Europe', *Economic Policy*, April, pp.127-170.

Bakker, A.F.P. (1996), *The liberalisation of capital movements in Europe. The Monetary Committee and financial integration, 1958-1994*, Kluwer, Dordrecht.

Bank for International Settlements (1998), *Handbook on Central Banks of Central and Eastern Europe*, Basel.

Berglöf, E., and G. Roland (1997), 'Soft budget constraints and credit crunches in financial transition', *European Economic Review*, No.41, pp.807-817.

Berrigan, J. and H. Carré (1997), 'Exchange arrangements between the EU and countries in Eastern Europe, the Mediterranean and the CFA zone', in: P.R. Masson, Th.H. Krueger and B.G. Turtelboom, *EMU and the international monetary system*, International Monetary Fund, Washington, D.C.

Boone, L. and M. Maurel (1998), *Economic Convergence of the CEECs with the EU*, CEPR Discussion Paper, No.2018, Centre for Economic Policy Research, London.

Cavelaars, P. and G. van den Dool (1999, forthcoming), 'European monetary coopetation: from Rome to Maastricht', in: P.A.G. van Bergeijk, R.J. Berndsen and W.J. Jansen (eds.), *Economics of the euro area*, Edward Elgar, Cheltenham.

Christoffersen, P.F. and R.F. Wescott (1999), *Is Poland ready for inflation targeting?*, IMF Working Paper, Washington, D.C.

Daviddi, R. and F. Ilzkovitz (1997), 'The eastern enlargement of the European Union: Major challenges for macro-economic policies and institutions of the Central and East European Countries', *European Economic Review*, No.41, pp.671-680.

Eichengreen, B. (1999), 'Kicking the habit: moving from pegged rates to greater exchange rate stability', *The Economic Journal*, No.109, March, pp.C1-C14.

Engering, F.A. (1989), 'De wereldhandel in 2000' (World trade in 2000), *Economisch Statistische Berichten*, No.74, pp.1256-1257.

European Bank for Reconstruction and Development (1998), *Transition Report Update*, London.

European Commission (1997), *Agenda 2000 – Summary and conclusions of the opinions of Commission concerning the Applications for Membership to the European Union presented by the candidate Countries*, Strasbourg/Brussels.

Fischer, S., R. Sahay and C.A. Végh (1998), *How far is Eastern Europe from Brussels?*, IMF Working Paper, April 1998, Washington, D.C.

International Monetary Fund (1997), *World Economic Outlook, October 1997*, Washington, D.C.

Kopits, G. (1999), *Implications of EMU for exchange rate policy in Central and Eastern Europe*, IMF Working Paper, January 1999, International Monetary Fund, Washington, D.C.

Manzocchi, S. (1998), *The determinants of foreign financial inflows in Central and Eastern Europe and the implications of the EU Eastern enlargement*, CEPS working document, No.117, Centre for European Policy Studies, Brussels.

McCauley, R.N. (1997), *The euro and the dollar*, BIS working paper, No.50, Bank for International Settlements, Basel.

Molle, W.T.M. (1989), 'De Europese Gemeenschap in 2000' (The European Community in 2000), *Economisch Statistische Berichten*, No.74, pp.1271-1273.

Oesterreichische Nationalbank (1998), *Focus on transition*, several issues.

Sdralevich, C. (1997), 'Banks and Governance in Transition Economies', *Banco Nazionale del Lavoro Quarterly Review*, Special Issue, March 1997, pp.83-109.

Van Bergeijk, P.A.G. and H. Oldersma (1990), 'Détente, market-oriented reform and German unification: potential consequences for the world trade system', *Kyklos*, Vol.43, No.4, pp.599-609.

Van Brabant, J.M. (1996), 'Remaking Europe – the Accession of Transition Economies', *Economia Internazionale*, Vol.49, No.4, pp.507-532.

CHAPTER 8

Portugal's Accession to the European Union

Abel Mateus

8.1 Introduction

Portugal's accession to the European Union (EU) is certainly one of the most successful cases of the last two decades. Having applied to join the EU in March 1977, Portugal entered the European Community (EC) in January 1986, at the same time as Spain. This long gestation period was largely due to the lack of macroeconomic equilibrium of the late 1970s and the early 1980s, associated with public sector and current account deficits. The nationalisation of most of the economy that occurred after the 1974 Revolution and the brush with communism in 1975, as well as the incipient democratic process, originated major institutional changes. The EC was keen to aid the young Portuguese democracy, but could not accept as a full member a country in a state of flux. Anyway, the improvement in the terms of trade, and the strong recovery that followed, fuelled by the liberalisation of trade and the cut in the budget deficit led to a period of strong convergence between 1986 and 1991.

Since the signing of the Maastricht Treaty, the government decided to be one of the founding members of the euro. Thus, a programme of disinflation marked the period from 1991 to 1998. The country was able gradually to fulfil the convergence criteria and, in January 1999, entered the euro zone.

This chapter will review the two main periods of accession. Section 8.2 describes the pre-accession period, when the country experienced serious development and stability problems. Thus, by most standards, the country was bound for a rough start as a member of the EU. The negotiations, dealt with in Section 8.3, show a major concern with the structural problems of the country. Extending over a period of about seven years, they were finalised in synchronisation with Spain. Major sectors and policies were the subject of detailed negotiations, as the concern of the Portuguese authorities was the competitive position of the economy. The transitional period was quite long, and was completed only by 1993. However, the major impact occurred within a period of about three years.

The vigorous structural reforms pursued by the government in the second half of the 1980s and the very positive response of Portuguese business to a growth-oriented programme, supported by a large undervaluation of the currency that occurred as a result of the devaluation of the escudo in the context of the IMF stabilisation programmes of the pre-accession period, led to a strong recovery of the economy, as discussed in Section 8.4.

However, inflation was still high, and the public sector deficit continued to deteriorate. A largely accommodating exchange rate policy, based on a crawling peg, was abandoned in 1991 and in April 1992 the Portuguese escudo entered the ERM. The stabilisation programme adopted was exchange rate based and, in contrast with quite a number of Latin American cases, it succeeded. The inflation rate was brought down from about 14% to 2% between 1992 to 1998. Section 8.5 describes briefly the convergence process. We conclude with major lessons for other countries now preparing for accession.

8.2 The Pre-accession period: a country in a state of flux (1977-85)

Portugal was no newcomer to European integration when the country entered the EC in 1986. In spite of the dictatorship and the colonial regime that prevented earlier entry of the country, Portugal, aware as it was of the importance of the European integration movements, was a founding member of the European Free Trade Area (EFTA) in 1961. The trade liberalisation process that ensued, was one of the major reasons for the highly successful growth in the 1960s and early 1970s. Since most of Portugal's external trade was with EC countries, Portugal signed a Trade Agreement with the EC in 1972 that led to a substantial reduction in trade barriers.

The 1974 Revolution and the extensive adoption of socialist policies in 1975 caused profound institutional changes in the Portuguese economy. This internal shock was compounded by a large terms of trade loss. As a consequence, the country experienced major macroeconomic disequilibria: inflation, a government deficit and an external deficit, with a sudden increase in the domestic and external public debt. Convergence slowed down and the country had to adopt two major stabilisation programmes, with the support of the IMF.

The first oil shock strongly affected the Portuguese economy. The deterioration in the terms of trade by 18% caused a GDP loss of about 4.7% by 1977. In conjunction with the loss of the colonial markets and a reduction in export markets due to the appreciation of the escudo, these external shocks totalled about 8% of GDP. The 1974 Revolution was followed by an increase of about 28% in real unit labour costs in 1974-75, as wage growth rates exploded. The credit expansion and the widening of the public deficit exacerbated the external and internal shocks. As a result, the large exchange reserves that had been built-up in previous decades were depleted in two years and the current account deficit reached 8% of GDP in 1977, as shown in Figure 8.1.

The exhaustion of foreign exchange and the rapid build-up of the external debt led to the request by the government for an IMF stand-by loan to support a stabilisation programme. The programme was inevitable, since a large loan put together by the USA and European countries to 'support the young Portuguese

Figure 8.1: Twin deficits as a percentage of GDP

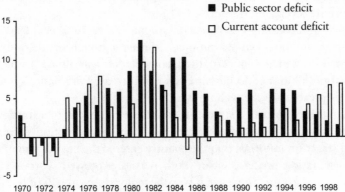

- Public sector deficit
- □ Current account deficit

democracy' was made conditional on the agreement on an IMF programme. The first programme was based on devaluation followed by a crawling peg regime, interest rate increases and quantitative restrictions to credit. Despite a sudden improvement in the current account deficit, the public sector deficit continued to deteriorate. Besides, to skim around credit targets, public enterprises were encouraged to borrow abroad, which led to the continuation of the build-up of external debt (250% of exports of goods and services in 1982). A second crisis occurred after the second oil shock. Including payment arrears, the budget deficit reached about 18.5% of GDP.

The second stabilisation programme of 1982-84 included several measures to improve the budget deficit, a further increase in interest rates and devaluation, together with a ban on public enterprises borrowing abroad. Inflation picked up strongly, and reached record levels in 1983-84, as Figure 8.2 shows.

Figure 8.2: Inflation rate
(Percentages)

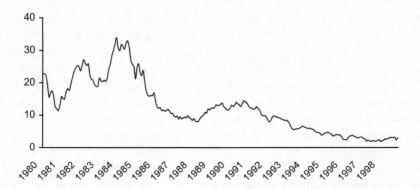

The current account deficit decreased dramatically in 1984-85, due in part to the stabilisation programme and also to the improvement in the terms of trade associated with the reversal in oil prices.

However, the economy was plagued with major structural problems. Most of the industries and financial institutions had been nationalised, the public sector deficit remained a major concern, the labour market was almost paralysed with a dismissal prohibition, and labour costs had increased dramatically due to the premature spreading of the welfare state.

It was in this context of a state of flux in the economy, with a fragile political and social situation – governments had a relatively short duration – and the need for major structural reforms, that the country entered the EU. We will next examine the negotiation process, where both parties expressed worries about the impact of the accession. However, it was the major political will of both the Portuguese governments and the EU that propelled the process to a successful conclusion.

8.3 The negotiations

Portugal requested accession to the EC in a letter from Prime Minister Mario Soares, on 28 March 1977, and the European Council gave a favourable answer on 6 June 1978. Negotiations started on 17 October 1978, and were organised at two levels. There would be at least three annual meetings between the Commission and Portuguese ministers and two quarterly working sessions with deputies. Negotiations lasted for about seven years, from 1978 to 1985. The agreement of accession between Portugal and the EC was finally signed on 10 June 1985. Portugal became a member of the EC on 1 January 1986. Table 8.1 gives more details concerning the timetable of negotiations.

The Portuguese government set up a Commission for European Integration (CEI), with representatives from those ministries directly concerned (Industry, Trade, Agriculture, Public Works, Planning, Employment, Social Affairs, Finance, Foreign Affairs, Justice and the Autonomous Regions). This commission remained for most of the time a department of the Ministry of Finance and Planning. Headed by a vice-minister, it included 15 high-ranking officials who conducted most of the work between the Portuguese government and the Commission. Also, a body of technical support staff was established, known as the SIE (*Secretariado para a Integração Europeia*). An important role was also performed by the Portuguese Mission to the European Communities, that liaised with the Commission, and was composed essentially of five highly qualified members. There was also a Cabinet for the European Integration composed of the main ministers that met periodically to resolve major questions of policy.

The negotiations between Portugal and the EC ran in parallel with the negotiations between Spain and the EC and to a lesser extent between Greece and the EC. The parallelism of the negotiations resulted in periods of lull and periods of

Table 8.1: Timetable of negotiations

Date		Major step in the negotiations
1977	28 March	Portugal presents a request to enter the European Communities
1978	20 April	The Commission sends a document about the problems of enlargement to the European Council
	19 May	The Commission decides favourably on the Portuguese request
	6 June	The European Council decides favourably on the Portuguese request
	17 October	Formal opening of negotiations between the Commission and Portugal
	1 and 21 December	First working session of deputies about organisational issues
1980	12 March	The Commission adopts a common position on social policies to be applied to Portugal and Spain: freedom of labour movements within EC of Portuguese and Spanish workers within a phased transition of 7 to 10 years
	27 July	Agreement on social policies
	3 December	Agreement on a package of financial aid by the EC for pre-accession programmes
1982	12 February	Agreement on regional policies, capital movements and transportation
	28 September	Agreement on fiscal issues and the steel and coal community
1983	25 January	Agreements on foreign direct investment and the right of establishment
	27 June	Agreements on the harmonisation of legal systems, environmental and consumer protection issues
	18 July	Start of major negotiations on agriculture
	3 October	Agreements on the industrial sector and external relations
	22 October	Agreements on agriculture and social issues
1984	27 November	Agreements on agricultural industries
	18 December	Agreements on fishing and critical agricultural sectors
1985	29 January	Agreements on critical agricultural (wine) and industrial sectors (automobiles), elimination of quantitative restrictions by Portugal
	28 and 29 March	Protocols relative to agriculture, fishing, social affairs, institutional aspects and financial relations with major agreements on these issues
	June	Portugal signs the Treaty of the EC
1986	1 January	Portugal becomes a member of the EC

Source: *Ministério das Finanças e do Plano* (1985)

speedy work, in order to synchronise major agreements between all the parties concerned. It is interesting to note, for instance, that in the ministerial meeting of 18 July 1983, the Portuguese delegation protested against the slow pace of the negotiations.

We can distinguish two phases in the process of negotiation: the first phase, that started on 17 October 1978 and ended with the Belgian Presidency of 1982, was based on the strategy of 'packages': agreements were first reached on common positions. Issues of disagreement were isolated and looked at subsequently. The second phase concentrated on a few protocols: agriculture and fishing, financial relations and the issue of labour movements and social security for Portuguese workers in EC countries.

The agenda was basically set up according to the different community policies: economic and financial relations, customs union, external relations, right of establishment, transportation, agricultural and regional policies, *etc*.

We will now describe the major agreements reached on the Portuguese transition. The aim of the government in these negotiations was to obtain derogation in almost all the areas of community policy applicable to Portuguese policies and liberalisation.

- As a consequence of the trade liberalisation process of the 1960s, when Portugal was a member of the EFTA, tariffs had been lowered significantly. According to a study for 1978, the unweighted average of the effective rates of protection, based on the tariff structure, was 22% for trade between Portugal and the EC and 23.6% for the rest of the world. The main problem came from a surtax of 20% on 29% of imports, and 30% on most of the other 'non-essential' imports, introduced in 1976. A further lowering of tariffs for manufactured products took place during a period of eight years, according to the following timetable (Table 8.2).

Table 8.2: Lowering of tariffs for manufactured products, 1985-1993 (1985 = 100%)

1985	100%
1986	90%
1987	80%
1988	65%
1989	50%
1990	40%
1991	30%
1992	15%
1993	0%

All quantitative restrictions on imports, except on automobiles (which had a transitional period until the end of 1987), and including controls on import licences, had to be eliminated from the start. All trade monopolies had to cease by the date of entry. The common external tariff was phased in with the same system of the lowering of internal tariffs, as shown above.

The CEECs should not take this as an example of trade liberalisation. Most of the Portuguese economists would agree that it was a rather long and gradual process and that it delayed adjustment in most of the industrial sectors.

Textile exports from Portugal to the EC were subject to administrative controls for three to four years. Negotiations in the context of the Multifibre Agreement subsequently accorded a more liberal position to third countries. The absurdity of this situation was resolved and administrative control was repealed before the expiry date.

Since Portugal was a member of EFTA, entry to the EC would automatically terminate all free trade agreements with that organisation. Special external trade relations between Portugal and third countries were substituted by the Generalised System of Preferences of the Community with developing countries, but derogation was obtained for certain products from a restricted number of countries.

- The liberalisation of the current account had to be completed by December 1990. Foreign exchange allowances for Portuguese citizens travelling abroad were increased every year. The same occurred for private transfers that represented an income outflow, as well as with the real estate investments. The free establishment of banking activities was conditional until the end of 1993.

- The liberalisation of the capital account was to be completed by December 1992, including inward foreign direct investment (December 1990), and outward foreign direct investment (December 1992).

- The Single Act, signed in 1987, but in which Portugal participated already as an observer, excluded for the most part the cases of Portugal and Spain, because negotiations were underway. The Single Act was directed at lowering further the quantitative and administrative restrictions on the movement of goods, capital and labour. In particular, the liberalisation of capital movements was to be undertaken until the end of 1995, and Portugal decided to anticipate it to the end of 1992. The EU passport for financial institutions was established in 1992, and procurement of goods and services was opened to all EU firms also in the same year.

- Portugal would participate in the European Monetary Co-operation Fund with a quota of 145 million ECU (debt) and 290 million ECU (credit) in the short term and in the long term credit a quota of 260 million ECU. The Portuguese escudo became part of the ECU basket in 1989.

- Fiscal reform was undertaken. A value-added tax was introduced in the course of three years that substituted a general transaction tax and several consumption taxes, with a limit of 15,000 ECU for SMEs, and a zero-rate for basic consumption goods and agricultural inputs. A surtax on imports had to be abolished on the date of the accession. Such fiscal reform is central to the sustainability of public finances. Without it, reducing the public sector deficit is impossible. This is perhaps the single most important policy area in the CEECs, since it is central to improving the efficiency of economic policies and of the tax administration.

- Subsidies to inputs, monopolies for imports of cereals and food subsidies characterised Portuguese agricultural policy. These were incompatible with the Common Agricultural Policy (CAP). Portuguese negotiators were particularly sensitive to the agricultural sector and food industries, in view of the low productivity of the sector, *vis-à-vis* the EU average. They were able to negotiate two transitional systems: a classical transition for sugar, canned fruits and vegetables, amongst others, and a phased transition covering the most important products (milk, beef, fresh fruits and vegetables, cereals, eggs, poultry and wine). Under the phased transition, there were two transitional periods of five years. The first transitional period lasted until 31 December 1992, and could be extended for a second period until the end of 1995.

If agricultural prices were above the EU prices, then Portuguese prices would be taken as a reference, and it would be expected that the approximation to the EU prices would take place over a period of seven years. If the Portuguese prices were below EU prices, the support prices would have to be adjusted by 1/7, 1/6, *etc.*, every year. However, for several of the most important products (cereals, wine, milk and beef) the accession agreements established two phases. The first phase lasted for about three years, in which Portugal could maintain the same policies, with gradual changes. Major changes were postponed until the second phase, with had a duration of up to seven years. During this phase, the mechanisms of the CAP would be more vigorously introduced. As an incentive, agricultural aid instruments for supporting changes in productive structures would be channelled at above the EU average for the Portuguese farmers.

In transactions between Portugal and the Community, compensatory amounts were to be collected by importing states (when prices were lower in the exporting country) or accorded by the exporting state (when prices were lower in the importing country). In case of no financial aid for a given product, the EC would start to introduce aid at 1/7 of the community level, and so on. Import restrictions could be maintained only for certain products from third countries, and were gradually reduced over a five year period

The negotiations for agricultural policies will certainly be one of the most difficult issues for the CEECs, given the larger share of agriculture in terms of both GDP and employment. Today, the CAP is recognised by a number of European economists, including the author of this chapter, as being one of the most wasteful and incoherent of all community policies. Today's CAP is rather different from the early 1980s and has been slowly adapted in order to be sustainable with the CEECs accession. However, the Portuguese experience shows that it can be a major hindrance to the full favourable impact of the EU integration. The impact on consumer welfare should be assessed carefully, and structural policies should be put in place to improve labour and land productivity even before accession takes place. Postponing adjustment with subsidies to producers is a complete waste of resources.

- Portugal had to terminate discriminatory aid accorded by the state to companies and consisting of reductions or exemptions from duties for certain products. This rather long track record of state intervention and subsidisation was – and to some extent still is – central to the Portuguese economic and social policy. In this regard, the CEECs do have a historical experience with deeper roots. It is still felt today in the Portuguese society that the transition to a free market economy is one of the most difficult processes.
- Labour movements from the Southern European countries to North-Western Europe were particularly strong during the 1950s and 1960s, up until the first oil shock. The more developed countries in the EU were concerned that easing entry conditions would strengthen those flows, at a time when unemployment in those countries was on the rise. Another concern was that giving the same social security benefits to immigrant workers would substantially increase the state burden. At the beginning of negotiations the Commission estimated that there were 479,000 Portuguese workers in the EU, of whom 80% were in France, and 336,000 Spanish workers, mainly in Germany and France. The Commission proposed a common policy for both countries, with a transitional period of seven years (10 years in the case of Luxembourg) in three phases in order to introduce free labour movements. Within the transitional period immigration was still subject to previous authorisation, and emigrant family members had a waiting period until they could get a job. Social security benefits in the first phase were granted according to the status of family residence.
- The financial protocol included a stand-by loan of 1 billion ECU for supporting the Portuguese balance of payments, but that was never used. However, the prospect of accession undoubtedly created a strong impetus for stabilisation in the early 1980s.

  It is important that, from the perspective of the regional and social fund, the whole Portuguese territory was considered an underdeveloped and critical region, receiving the highest aid from those funds.
- Finally, other areas of major concern for the Portuguese authorities were trade and capital flows between Portugal and its neighbour Spain, that had never been subject to a liberalisation programme. In fact, most economists predicted, based on gravitational (see Chapter 4) and other trade theories, that those flows would be experiencing the highest growth. In general, the same agreements reached with the other countries of the Community were applicable to Spain. Nevertheless, Portugal could apply additional restrictions to imports of steel and paper pulp, and Spain to textiles, paper pulp, cork and petroleum products.

  This experience shows that there are substantial synergies that could be exploited by adjacent countries wishing to join the bloc. The impact of trade creation and the welfare improvement that can spring from trade among countries with adjacent borders can be considerable.

An interesting question was raised by the fact that the Portuguese market was more open to the EC than the Spanish market, and that Portuguese products were accorded more privileges in the EC market for an initial transition period. Special origin rules had to be devised to prevent 'trade deflection' and a minimum of national value added had to be incorporated in Portuguese products in order to be classified as being of Portuguese origin.

The same problem can occur with CEECs joining when they have major trade flows remaining with third countries. This is a point that needs to be dealt with quite carefully.

- A final important area was the adoption of secondary legislation, that is, all the changes that had to be made to render Portuguese law compatible with Community law and to incorporate the new legislation. The Ministry of Justice led most of this work. Thus, a major effort needs to be done in implementing institutional changes in CEECs in order to strengthen their law and their judicial systems.

Most of the observers are of the opinion that the negotiations took too long and that the EU procrastinated on a number of fronts. It is now obvious that the EU did not want Portugal to accede before Spain. But there were two other major reasons. First, as we have seen, the Portuguese economy experienced major macroeconomic desequilibria up to 1985, with a serious balance-of-payments deficit. Second, the political situation was still in a state of flux, with very weak governments up to 1985, when Cavaco Silva became Prime Minister.

The process of negotiations for Portugal's accession shows that such negotiations are inherently complicated and may take a long time, although today's *acquis communautaire* is more precise and clear-cut. Notwithstanding, most of the Portuguese negotiators concede today that requests for derogations were too many and unnecessarily broad.

The transitional period was also rather long, postponing some of the crucial reforms that needed to be made,[1] and delaying the beneficial impact on economic growth, as the subsequent discussion will make clear.

---

1. The political process was also to blame. Because of the opposition from the socialists, it was only in 1989 that it was possible to privatise without any restrictions.

8.4 The economy in the aftermath of the accession (1986-91)

After 1986, the economy experienced a strong recovery, with GDP growing at 7.2% in the 1987-1990 period. As a consequence, convergence to the EU accelerated (see Figure 8.3). The terms of trade improved by 24% in 1984-85, and the current account of the balance of payments went from a deficit to a substantial surplus, also aided by a real devaluation of 26% between the peak of 1975 and 1985, which restored the level of competitiveness to that of the 1960s. The degree of openness of the economy increased from 29% in 1985 to 44% of GDP in 1991, the largest acceleration in the country's history.

Two major factors were behind this performance. First, macroeconomic stabilisation of the economy was undertaken throughout the period. The government deficit decreased from 8% in 1982 to 3% in 1989, and monetary policy was tightened (the growth rate of M3 went from five points below overall credit to five points above). Second, structural reforms were undertaken within the economy. The opening of economic activity to private entrepreneurship started in 1983 for banking, insurance, cement and fertilisers. However, it was only in 1988 that the possibility was opened for privatising up to 49% of nationalised firms. The privatisation process was launched in 1989, and the principle of a market economy was introduced in the Constitution in 1989. Afterwards, the intensity of the privatisation process was second only to that of the UK. Meanwhile public enterprises had been increasing their efficiency and their deficit was reduced from almost 6% of GDP in 1983 to less than 1% in 1990.

Figure 8.3: Portugal's income gap to the EU
Portuguese GDP *per capita* in PPP as % of EU GDP *per capita* in PPP

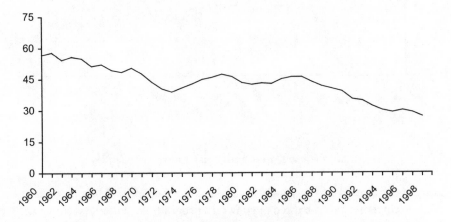

The VAT and the unification of income tax launched fiscal reform, under the agreement of accession, with the replacement of a complex system of transaction and consumption taxes. The reform significantly improved the revenue raising capability, increased efficiency and reduced tax evasion.

The Revolution had completely forbidden the dismissal of individual workers, and raised indirect labour costs significantly. The reforms adopted in 1988 introduced short-term labour contracts that were extensively used afterwards. In most firms, the wage scale returned to pre-revolution levels, and remuneration schemes became more productivity-incentive compatible.

The financial sector was extensively modernised. The privatisation process gave priority to banks and insurance companies. By 1993 most of the capital in the sector was already in private hands. Credit controls were replaced by market-based indirect instruments in 1990-91, and an overall reform of the regulatory framework took place in 1992, based on EU legislation.

The fast growth of the economy and of the speed of the reforms led to a decrease in the unemployment rate, as Figure 8.4 documents. However, the increase in public consumption and the high wage increases were already leading to an overheating of the economy by 1992. By then a new programme, of nominal convergence, was taking shape.

Figure 8.4: Unemployment rate
(Percentages)

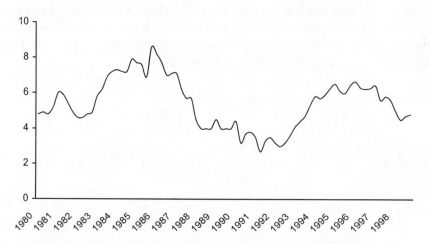

8.5 Gearing-up to monetary union (1992-98)

After the approval of the Union Treaty and the European Monetary Union in Maastricht, Portugal embarked in 1992 on a programme of nominal convergence, in order to be able to enter the euro area. This programme had by-partisan support, even when the socialists took control of the government in late 1995.

Despite the progress made in terms of structural adjustment, there were worrying signs of an overheated economy. Inflation was running at about 14% in

May 1990, on a yearly basis, and the budget deficit had deteriorated to 5.9% in 1991, largely due to an increase in public sector wages.

The implementation of a disinflation programme started with the pegging of the escudo to a shadow basket in 1989, mimicking the ECU. As a consequence, there was a significant real appreciation of about 20% between 1989 and 1992. However, the appreciation was largely cushioned by the over-devaluation of the early 1980s. Interest rates were substantially raised in 1991-92 and liquidity control was tightened. There were massive capital inflows, despite the capital controls 'à la Chile' (copied from Spain) implemented since 1991.

The government thought that the economy was suffering all the costs of shadowing the ERM without any benefits. Thus, in April 1992 the escudo entered the ERM, despite the opposition of the central bank. Another conflict between the central bank and the Ministry of Finance ensued, due to high interest rates and capital controls. The Minister argued that interest rates should be lowered to stem the inflow of capital, and that capital controls should be abolished. However, the central bank was of the opinion that interest rates had to remain high for some time in order to lower aggregate demand, and that capital controls would help to keep the escudo within the target zone. In August 1992, the conflict had finally come to an end, with a success for the liberalisation school. The central bank announced that all capital controls would be abolished and that complete freedom in capital movement would be enacted before the end of the year.

Figure 8.5: Differential in inflation rates (Portugal-European Union)

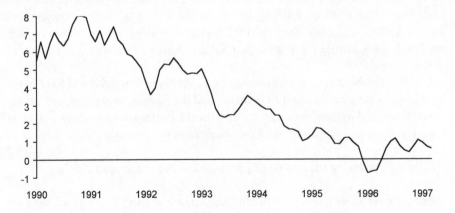

Although inflation and short-term interest rates were slowly coming down, the economy was hit by the 1992-93 recession in Europe. With the abolition of borders that occurred at the end of 1992 (Single Act) and the introduction of the new VAT system, there was a large budget deficit in 1993 that jeopardised the convergence policy. The convergence programme was also affected by the major turbulence that hit the ERM. The escudo had to be devalued, after the adjustment in the peseta on three occasions, and calm only came after the enlargement of the bands in the summer of 1993. As Figures 8.5 and 8.6 show, the gradual reduction in the budget deficit and the differential in interest rates finally paid off. By 1995 most of the convergence criteria were already pointing to a significant improvement.

Figure 8.6: Long-term interest rates
(Percentages)

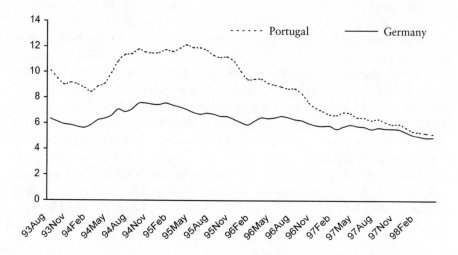

However, it was only in the second half of 1996, after the Stability Pact had been agreed upon and the probability of the formation of a single currency area increased, that long-term interest differentials narrowed substantially. In fact, until mid-1996, Portugal was given just a slight chance of becoming a member of the euro area.

Quite a number of economists recognise today that Portugal could have benefited from lower interest rate differentials, had the budget correction been implemented earlier. Anyhow, the sacrifice ratio for the Portuguese economy was quite low, when compared with most of the adjustment programmes.

8.6 Assessing the impact of participation in the European Union

There were very few estimates regarding the impact of entry to the EU on the Portuguese economy. To our knowledge there were no studies made to guide negotiations other than price comparisons and sector trade and production data. The first macro-assessment was undertaken in a study sponsored by the Commission. This study used a general equilibrium model, HERMIN, to estimate the likely impact of the Single Market Act and the Community Support Framework, that in the case of Portugal is similar to the impact of the EC accession. The study identifies four types of effects of trade liberalisation: (a) static effects of traditional trade theory – resources flow from low to higher efficiency sectors, and consumption possibility sets expand; (b) location effects – relocation of multinationals and foreign direct investment (FDI); (c) dependency effects – with a higher degree of integration, economic growth in core economies has a higher multiplier effect on peripheral economies; and (d) dynamic effects – associated with economies of scale and a higher level of competition.

Table 8.3 reproduces the results of the simulations. The total impact of accession to the EU, due to trade liberalisation, including FDI flows, increases GDP by approximately 11.5% during a 15-year period, amounting to about 0.7 percentage points *per annum*. Considering that presently the long-term growth rate has been estimated at 3.5%, this amounts to 20% of the yearly growth rate. Portugal has experienced the highest impact, followed by Ireland and Spain with 9%. Greece has experienced an almost zero impact. The most important impacts on the Portuguese case are the transfer of resources from the non-tradable to the tradable sectors with a higher level of efficiency, and the impact of the increase in the export of manufactured goods. These effects are intensified by FDI inflows. The accession would reduce the unemployment rate by about 7.7 percentage points, *ceteris paribus*.

Table 8.3: Simulation results of the impact of Portugal's accession to the EU

	Trade liberalisation effects with increased FDI inflows		Effect of Structural Funds		Combined effect	
	GDP	Unemployment	GDP	Unemployment	GDP	Unemployment
Portugal						
1995	3.9	−1,9	10.6	−6,4	10.4	−7.9
2010	11.5	−7.7	11.6	−5.5	14.7	−11.5
Spain						
1995	4.8	−1.2	2.2	−0.4	0.9	−0.6
2010	9.2	−2.0	2.1	0.1	1.4	0.4
Greece						
1995	−1.3	2.0	6.9	−3.8	4.7	−2.7
2010	0.1	1.6	7.4	−2.1	5.9	−2.9
Ireland						
1995	5.0	−1.4	2.7	−0.4	6.6	−2.0
2010	9.2	−1.2	3.4	0.3	10.5	−1.0

Source: European Commission (1997)

Another important benefit derives from the official transfers from the Community budget. Although net transfers from the EU have amounted to about 2.3% in the 1993-97 period, structural funds negotiated under the Delors I totalled about 3% of GDP (1989-93) and under Delors II 4% of GDP (1994-1999), on a yearly basis. This was the highest percentage among the countries with an income *per capita* below the EU average. According to Table 8.3, and assuming high infra-structure externalities[2], the impact of the structural funds was to increase GDP by about 11.6% over a period of 15 years, against 7.4% for Greece, 3.4% for Ire-land and 2.1% for Spain. The yearly impact on GDP of 0.77 percentage points for Portugal is different from the estimate of 0.50 of Gaspar and Pereira (1991), using an endogenous growth model.

The combined impact of trade liberalisation and structural funds, according to Table 8.3, amounts to an increase in GDP of about 15% over a period of 15 years for Portugal, compared with 10.5% for Ireland, 5.9% for Greece, and 1.4% for Spain, which is a much larger country[3].

8.7 Conclusions

Several lessons can be learned from the Portuguese case. First, it seems clear that stabilisation should be a pre-condition for accession. In fact, it is very difficult for economic agents to confront the challenge of integration with persistent macro-economic disequilibria. Profits of enterprises, producing tradeables, depend strongly on exchange rate levels. Clearly, an overvalued exchange rate will give a wrong signal to firms as how profitable they are. As wages usually boom ensuing the accession, it might be advisable to enter with a slightly undervalued exchange rate.

The second lesson is that structural reforms and structural adjustments should be pursued at the same time as trade liberalisation in order to maximise the wel-fare impact and maintain the political momentum for reform. As the case of Por-tugal shows, it is important to undertake fiscal and public administration reform, to privatise and liberalise price mechanisms, and to improve infrastructures, with particular attention being paid to human capital during the transition period, before and after the accession. As the previous calculations show, the Portuguese experience after joining the EC has been thoroughly positive. The trade liberali-sation and FDI effects were positive and large as well as the impact of structural funds.

Third, public administration should be prepared earlier in the transition process to prepare, control and monitor public investment projects and to con-trol EC transfers to the private sector. There is always a major temptation for inter-est groups to extract benefits from this process, and corruption is a major prob-lem that needs to be tackled from the start.

Fourth, liberalisation should be undertaken sooner than later. In fact, as the Portuguese case shows, there is always opposition from interest groups resisting

---

2. Estimating the impact of human capital and public infrastructure on increasing total factor productivity incorporates externalities.
3. The lower impact for Spain is due to the smaller elasticities for the impact of externalities estimated and to the fact that community transfers are a much lower percentage of GDP.

liberalisation, with the spectre of foreign competition destroying the productive structure. However, it is not possible to modernise and improve efficiency, with benefits accruing to consumers, without reducing trade barriers.

Fifth, a larger degree of gradualism in dismantling trade barriers should be accorded only after very thorough scrutiny, and should usually be discarded in preference to an across the board treatment. In general, as the Portuguese case shows, particular attention should be given to agriculture, in view of the social aspects and the vulnerability of rural populations.

Sixth, a country with an open market-oriented economy will benefit most from trade liberalisation, so market mechanisms and entrepreneurial capability are required to reap the benefits of the new investment and business opportunities. Financial sector capacity building is extremely important to facilitate the process of intermediation.

Seventh, the transition process triggers major structural changes: sectoral and regional restructuring, labour migration, growth of competitive firms and declining of non-competitive ones. Thus, a strong economic and political leadership, with a clear understanding of the benefits and costs, sometimes with the winners buying out the losers – or at least a social safety net to lower hardship – needs to be in place.

Finally, trade and service account liberalisation should precede the liberalisation of capital flows and financial liberalisation in order to avoid financial crises.

References

Álvares, Pedro (1999), *The enlargement of the European Union and the experience of Portugal's accession negotiations*, Instituto Nacional Administração, Lisbon.

Economic Commission (1997), *The Single Market Review*, Vol.2, Brussels.

Gaspar, Victor and M. Pereira (1991), *A Dynamic General Equilibrium Analysis of EC Structural Funds*, mimeo.

Mateus, A.M. (1998), *Economia Portuguesa* (The Portuguese Economy), Verbo, Lisbon.

Ministério das Finanças e do Plano (1985), *Síntese da Negociação*, Secretariado para a Integração Europeia, Lisbon.

Enlargement of the European Union: A Polish Perspective

Dariusz Rosati

9.1 Introduction

Poland has always been an inseparable part of Western civilisation, even though her frontier location and turbulent history occasionally made this affinity subject to other influences. It was therefore more than natural that after restoring full independence in 1989, Polish political elites immediately opted for a policy of return to Europe. Since then, much ground has been covered, and Poland is now one of the leading candidates to join the European Union as a full member within the next few years. At the same time, however, the process of integration has not been free from friction and delay, and a number of practical and political problems still remain to be solved.

In 1998, the process of European integration entered a new stage. After several years of preparations and discussions, and conforming to earlier political decisions, the European Union opened negotiations with five Central and Eastern European countries (CEECs) on their full accession to the Union. Long awaited eastern enlargement is thus becoming a reality.

The historic significance of this fact is undisputed. For the first time in its 40-year history, the Union is reaching beyond the traditional boundaries of Western Europe to integrate the countries of the Central and Eastern part of the continent which, between the end of the World War II and 1989 was under Soviet domination. Together with NATO enlargement, the eastward extension of the EU is going to be a decisive step in eliminating the remnants of the post-war division of the continent and establishing much broader foundations for economic and political cooperation among the European nations.

The process is welcomed by those CEECs that, since the 1989 political breakthrough, have made clear that they wish to join the EU as full members. The decision by the EU to open membership negotiations with a group of the more advanced CEECs helped to dispel uncertainties and doubts over the prospects for the enlargement process, frequently expressed in the Eastern part of the continent where political elites and the public at large have sometimes been frustrated by the slow pace of enlargement and inconclusive declarations of EU representatives. Now the key questions over the accession do not seem to be anymore 'whether' or 'if', but rather 'when' and 'how'.

The purpose of this chapter is to make a résumé of Poland's road to the European Union, to assess the current status of integration, and to discuss problems and issues on the way to full accession. The key observation is that, while the accession is certain to bring about important net benefits to both sides, the overall political climate around the integration process has deteriorated significantly over the last few years owing to grossly exaggerated fears and concerns about some negative implications of the accession. A stronger political commitment is needed, together with a broad and comprehensive information campaign on the potential costs and benefits of accession to both sides in order to make steady progress in integration and to maintain the necessary popular support for accession.

9.2 A short history of the accession process: 1989-1999

Poland formally established diplomatic relations with the EU only in late 1988, when both the increasing pressure for economic and political reforms at home and the rapid progress of *perestrojka* in the Soviet Union, pushed the government towards a more independent and open foreign policy *vis-à-vis* Western countries. However, it was the political breakthrough in 1989 that opened up possibilities for establishing much closer contacts with the then European Community. The first agreement on trade and cooperation was signed in October 1989, significantly improving the access of Polish firms to EU markets. At the same time, in view of the serious economic crisis in Poland, the Community extended ad-hoc economic and humanitarian aid and granted Poland extensive import preferences under the GSP framework. But there were no official talks on accession at that time.

The membership issue appeared on the agenda in 1990, when Poland started negotiations on the association agreement with the Community. The political climate on both sides was then very favourable: Western governments were still euphoric about the political changes taking place in Eastern Europe, and were standing ready with generous support for the democratic and market reforms in Poland and other ex-communist countries, while the Polish people were equally enthusiastic about the prospects of rapidly improving living standards through trade and economic integration with Western countries. The Association Agreement was signed in December 1991 and its trade part (The Interim Agreement) was implemented as of 1 March 1992. The remaining parts of the Agreement, later renamed the Europe Agreement, came into force on 1 February 1994.

The main objective of the Europe Agreement was to stimulate trade and other economic relations between Poland and the European Union, as well as to ensure the gradual convergence of Poland's economic, political and legal systems towards Western European standards. The ultimate goal, as specified in the Europe Agreement, was to bring Poland into the EU as a full member. However, since neither specific steps nor a binding timetable for accession were decided upon, the process was left open-ended.

The membership objective was later officially confirmed during the EU summit meeting in Copenhagen in 1993, when it was stated that Central and Eastern European transition countries might join the EU if they so wished, provided they met certain political and economic criteria (see Chapter 5). However, as the criteria were not very specific, it was not possible to establish a clear perspective for membership.

The reluctance of the EU to make specific commitments on the future accession of Poland (and other CEECs) reflected the rapidly changing sentiments on the part of Western countries with respect to the prospects of future eastern enlargement of the EU. There were growing concerns about the possible negative implications of accession for Western economies, such as the need to extend protective subsidies to Eastern European agriculture and the disruptive impact on the labour market of the potential migration of a low-wage workforce from the East. On the other hand, the EU itself was more and more focused on important internal reforms, with the enlargement issue pushed somewhat aside as a second priority. As a result, in subsequent summits between 1993 and 1996 the EU countries were not in a hurry to fix any concrete dates for enlargement.

An important step forward was made in 1997, when the European Commission issued the opinions on the level of preparedness of individual candidate countries (the so-called *avis*), with the recommendation to begin accession negotiations with five Central European countries, including Poland. The accession talks started in the spring of 1998 with a detailed examination of Polish laws and their consistency with the *acquis communautaire* (the so-called screening process), and the beginning of the negotiations proper have been planned for October 1999.

At present, the official goal of the Polish government is to wrap up the negotiations possibly within next $1^1/_2$-2 years and to make Poland ready to join the EU on 1 January 2003. The Polish authorities quietly abandoned their earlier and much publicised target date of 2000, as a result of a more realistic assessment of the necessary adjustments to be made, and in recognition of growing political resistance to rapid accession on both sides. Even this later date was initially received with a heavy dose of scepticism by the Commission, and only more recent reactions by some EU leaders give grounds for cautious optimism.[1] On the other hand, the pro-European rhetoric of the Polish government has been maintained in rather general terms and has not always been followed by actual policy decisions. This has been underlined by frequent controversies within the government on the speed and scope of the adjustment process.

---

1. For example, see the declaration of the French Prime Minister L. Jospin after his recent visit to Poland in July.

9.3 Benefits and costs of EU eastern enlargement

The decision to expand the EU has been motivated by the important political and economic benefits to be gained from enlargement. These benefits are expected to accrue both to the new member countries and to the incumbent EU countries. However, with few exceptions, the literature of EU enlargement has mostly concentrated on the costs of enlargement, particularly for EU countries (*e.g.*, see Courchène *et al.*, 1993; Baldwin, 1994). One important exception to this pattern has been a study by Baldwin, Francois and Portes (1997). It is necessary to restore the balance in this discussion and to demonstrate that the benefits of EU enlargement will largely exceed the costs. From the Polish perspective, this is important because ignoring the benefits and focusing excessively on the costs of enlargement has clearly affected the attitude of EU countries towards the enlargement, raising much more scepticism and doubt than only few years ago.

9.3.1 Political benefits

Political reasons for enlargement stem from the fact, that the European Union – and indeed the whole underlying idea of European integration – has always been a politically motivated project from the beginning. The political benefits of economic integration, including now EU enlargement, can be classified into four categories: international security, internal stability, support for democracy and reforms, and geo-strategic advantages.

The first political aim of integration is to enhance international security. Close economic and political cooperation between nations, firms and individuals is meant to work in favour of security and peace. Economic integration speeds up economic development and helps to reduce disparities in wealth and income levels, which could sometimes lead to international conflicts. By establishing international networks of production and trade contacts which bring benefits to all involved, integration helps to develop broadly-based popular support for international cooperation and open borders, thus reducing the potential for alternative ways of protecting national interests, such as aggression and armed conflict. The security aspect is particularly important in the case of Central and Eastern Europe, where state borders have changed frequently in the past and long-established traditions of ethnic and national hostilities may still be present. For Poland, this is a particularly sensitive issue in the light of dramatic experiences from World War II and the Soviet era. But the problem of security obviously has a much wider significance: both lessons of history and sheer logic indicate clearly that Western Europe cannot be fully secure unless peace is firmly established throughout the whole continent, including the CEECs.

Similar considerations and expectations have now played a role in the case of Eastern Europe which has a long history of wars and armed conflicts, stirred either by rivalries between external powers or by home-grown nationalist tendencies and ethnic tensions. The idea of offering prospects of prosperity to Eastern Europe through cooperation and integration with the West has been seen as a powerful safeguard against instability.

The second political goal of integration is to contribute to internal stability in the CEECs. This is being achieved not only through reinforcing the Western European concepts of the rule of law and democratic institutions, but first of all through improved prospects for faster welfare growth for all social groups. This again is particularly important in the case of transforming economies, where social discontent caused by depressed standards of living inherited from communism might lead to continued instability. One of the threats to internal stability in the early stage of transformation may be social frustration, caused by the collapse of the traditional egalitarian welfare state and rapidly growing diversification of incomes and wealth. This frustration may be further strengthened by the impact of the gap in living standards between transition economies and their Western neighbours. Prospects of rapid improvement in the level of material well-being offered by the integration perspective are thus essential for avoiding excessive frustration and for maintaining domestic social and political stability.

The third political aspect that should be emphasised is that the accession to the EU could also be considered as an instrument for strengthening reform policies and buttressing democracy in the CEECs. Populism, nationalism and authoritarian tendencies can effectively be held in check if a country belongs to international organizations and thus has to conform to internationally recognized standards and norms of democracy and the rule of law. On the foreign policy front, reinforced commitment to democracy is important, given that the regained or newly established independence of former Soviet satellite countries might open up old territorial disputes and revive old ethnic animosities. Clearly, democracy prefers to live in peace; extending European institutions to Eastern countries is thus seen as one of the safeguards for stability and predictability.

Finally, Central and Eastern Europe is a geographic area of strategic importance, located between Western Europe and Euro-Asiatic Russia. Unless its geopolitical status is clearly established, it might eventually become an area contested politically and economically by external powers – an 'arena' for conflicts. However, if it becomes an integral and undisputed part of the expanding EU, it may play a very constructive role as a 'bridge' linking the expanded EU with Russia and other CIS countries. The 'arena *versus* bridge' dichotomy has been an important factor behind pro-European tendencies strongly present in CEECs' foreign policies.

Political benefits, as vitally important as they certainly are, are however very difficult to measure in pecuniary terms. After all, how can the value of non-realized conflicts be estimated? This is probably one of the reasons that they have never been given enough attention in routine discussions on the costs and benefits of EU enlargement, and they have typically been mentioned only *en passant*, dominated by more prosaic and more immediate considerations, such as budgetary costs or migration pressures. Another reason might be that these political benefits seem now so obvious, natural and uncontroversial that they do not appear to command much attention. In fact, they are considered as if they had already been fully assimilated and had become irreversible, thus not requiring further efforts.

This would be a dangerous and unjustified complacency. Public opinion in Poland is particularly sensitive to political and security considerations, and for good reasons, given the country's history. There is no reason to assume that the current 'window of opportunity' may actually last forever, unless it is solidly buttressed by necessary long-term institutional and political arrangements. The EU enlargement, together with NATO enlargement, provides for such an arrangement. This is why the political considerations provide crucial arguments in favour of enlargement and must not be ignored or belittled in current debates.

9.3.2 Expansion of trade: theoretical considerations

Economic arguments for eastern enlargement are derived primarily from the theory of integration (Baldwin, 1994; Baldwin and Venables, 1995; Molle, 1995). Integration refers to the elimination of barriers to trade and factor movements as well as unification of institutional arrangements, and may lead eventually to the creation of one integrated economic system. As a general proposition, the theory of economic integration tells us that expanding markets and removing barriers to trade and resource flows increases economic efficiency, both in the static and in the dynamic sense, and thus contributes to economic growth. The theory tells us also that there are two broad categories of economic benefits to be obtained from EU enlargement: a) gains from free trade in goods and services, and b) gains from the free flow of resources.

Free trade allows for more efficient specialisation among countries and better response to consumers' needs. In the longer run, it improves efficiency through increased competitive pressure, economies of scale and better technological opportunities. These long-term benefits are considered to be more important than the short-term ones. EU enlargement means, *inter alia*, the removal of all trade barriers between EU-15 and the new members.

Considering the effects of free trade in goods it should be noted, however, that the EU is not a free trade arrangement (FTA); it is a customs union (CU). One important implication is that establishing a CU – in contrast to a free trade area – implies adopting a common external tariff. This may lead to welfare losses in one or several member countries, if their initial situation is one of free trade rather than of protectionism. This is, however, a rather remote possibility in the context of EU enlargement, because the bulk of trade between CEECs and EU is in manufactured products, where the applicant CEECs have had relatively high levels of tariff protection (except Estonia and the Czech Republic), generally higher than that of the EU-15. The average MFN tariff applied in the EU is now about 3%, while in the applicant CEEC it is between $6^{1}/_{2}$ and 7% for all industrial goods, with much higher tariff differentials for goods such as transport equipment, machinery or wood products (Baldwin *et al.*, 1997; Drabek, 1998).

Only in agri-food products and fish is the EU's MFN tariff higher that that of CEECS (16% *versus* 2% for agri-food products, and 11% *versus* 8% for fish). Extending the common tariff to CEECs would thus lead to expansion of industrial imports to CEECs and some reduction-cum-diversion of imports of agri-food products. This may entail some additional costs in terms of higher domestic prices and may require compensation for non-EU exporters (mainly the United States) under GATT/WTO rules.

Static effects are insufficient to make a comprehensive assessment of the CU. Firms, people and governments do not remain idle, but try to adjust to changing conditions. It is commonly argued that one of the most important long-term benefits is the positive impact of increased competitive pressures on technical efficiency. Firms, confronted with more foreign competition which they cannot contain through political action, reduce costs, apply new technologies, rationalise employment, or increase marketing efforts. These adjustments shift the supply curve downward in the long run, producing efficiency gains. The problem with these gains is that they are very difficult to measure. In principle, they could be assessed by the changes in unit production costs, but these would also reflect economies of scale and some other factors. This is probably one of the reasons that empirical research studies on the efficiency gains arising from the CU rarely produce conclusive results.

The second important long-term benefit is in the economies of scale, arising from the expansion of sales to a larger market. These are easier to quantify than the more elusive efficiency gains and, provided certain assumptions are made, can be measured by the changes in unit production costs, typically calculated on a sector basis. However, some specific benefits are internal to the firm – they include the effects of firm's growth and of the learning-by-doing process. Even though these gains are rather difficult to measure directly, their importance is undisputed.

International production networking (IPN) is one of the popular strategies employed by multinational firms to lower costs and improve competitiveness (Zysman and Schwartz, 1998). As in the previous cases, the economic gains from networking may be reflected in the fall in unit production costs, but unless special breakdown techniques are used, it is always very difficult to attribute an observed change in production costs to a specific set of factors. Generally, the long-term effects of the CU are almost certain to be positive, and they are considered much more important than the short-term effects.

9.3.3 Trade between Poland and the European Union

Expansion of mutual trade has been spectacular: the share of the EU in Poland's total trade turnover increased from 34% in 1988 to 55% in 1992 and to 67% in 1998 (average for exports and imports). From this perspective, the Polish economy seems to be as closely integrated with the EU as the economies of the present member countries, where the share of intra-EU trade is broadly similar. However, this would certainly be a false conclusion. First, trade between Poland and the EU is unbalanced, with a large and growing deficit on the Polish side.[2] Second, the structure of mutual trade is distinctively different: while intra-industry trade, linked to expanding international production networking, dominates within the EU, intra-industry trade with Poland is still underdeveloped, not only when compared with the trade of EU countries, but also with some other CEECs, such as Hungary.

Table 9.1: Trade between Poland and the European Union, 1991-1998
(In millions of US dollars)

	1992	1993	1994	1995	1996	1997	1998
Exports	7,644	8,973	10,823	16,030	16,168	16,490	19,275
Imports	8,585	10,724	12,405	18,801	23,760	27,007	30,620
Trade Balance	-941	-1,751	-1,582	-2,771	-7,592	-10,517	-11,345

Source: Calculated from Polish statistics, Central Statistical Office

Table 9.1 shows the growing deficit in Poland's trade with the EU. In 1998, the registered trade deficit exceeded 11 billion dollars, or more than 7% of GDP. While part of this gap mirrors the corresponding inflows of foreign direct investment (FDI) in kind, an increasing proportion reflects structural weaknesses in Polish export sectors, such as the excessive reliance placed on unprocessed and semi-processed goods (steel, other metal products and chemicals) and the low competitiveness of many manufactures. However, it also reflects excessive subsidisation of EU agricultural exports as well as pervasive protection (explicit or contingent) of EU markets with respect to some 'sensitive' exports from Poland, such as steel products, textiles and foodstuffs. The huge trade gap raises serious concern among Polish politicians and the general public. There is a widespread opinion

---

2. Unregistered border trade is not included because the composition of that aggregate is unknown. The figures reported in the balance of payments statistics are net purchases of foreign exchange by banks, from various sources, including not only proceeds from border trade, but also from private tourism and remittances. Moreover, at least half of those amounts are due to purchases by CIS residents. Generally, the inclusion of unregistered trade transactions would not change the picture of trade with the EU much.

that the gains from trade are not equally distributed, with the EU gaining much more, partly because of unfair trade practices applied by the EU. This opinion was reinforced last year when Polish exporters of foodstuffs to Russia lost most of the Russian market as they were unable to compete against the heavily subsidised (or simply free) deliveries of foodstuffs coming from the EU. If such practices continue, the growing deficit in trade with the EU may have far-reaching political implications in Poland.

An equally important problem concerns the structure of Polish exports. As is well known, intra-industry trade is less sensitive to fluctuations in market conditions and tends to grow faster than other segments of trade. However, the share of intra-industry trade in Poland's trade with the EU is still lower than the EU average. Table 9.2 shows the changes in the indices of intra-industry trade for six CEECs between 1991 and 1995.

Table 9.2: EU and CEECs: indices of intra-industry trade, in %, 1988-1995[1]

Country	1991	1992	1993	1994	1995
Bulgaria	24.25	27.42	30.00	31.63	24.95
Czech Republic 2/	37.45	41.96	47.48	50.18	47.53
Hungary	43.81	45.13	44.58	44.34	37.56
Poland	29.65	33.41	33.11	33.42	29.39
Romania	22.44	19.49	20.56	23.04	16.76
Slovak Republic 2/	37.45	41.96	31.17	35.15	29.55

1/ manufacturing trade only (3-digit SITC 5, 6, 7, 8 minus 68, revision 3);
2/ Czechoslovakia for 1991-1992.

Source: Rosati (1998a) and own calculations of the author

It is clear from Table 9.2 that Poland lags behind the Czech Republic and Hungary in terms of actual integration through development of intra-industry links, and that not much progress has been made since 1991, at least for 3-digit SITC classification. This picture may suggest that the expansion of trade with the EU has been mostly concentrated in traditional, low-tech sectors.

9.3.4 Capital inflows

The second category of economic benefits is concerned with gains from free flows of resources, in particular capital inflows. New EU members are certain to gain from increased inflows of capital, in particular in the form of FDI. These inflows have already been substantial in the case of some more advanced transition countries, but they can be expected to expand further once the CEECs concerned become full members. This is because integration expands the size of the market, replacing separate national markets by one regional market. Moreover, the reduced investment risk (resulting from political and economic integration) and institutional-cum-policy convergence leads to lower transaction costs in member countries, which in turn results in higher rates of return.

More generally, FDI are driven to a foreign country by three main motives (Dunning, 1993): a) to supply the local market (market-oriented FDI), b) to reduce production costs (cost-oriented FDI), and c) to acquire special assets (asset-oriented FDI). Market-oriented FDI has been flowing into CEECs already for some time; actually, according to numerous surveys, the willingness to cover the largely untapped Eastern markets has been the most frequently cited motivation for making FDI in CEECs so far. This consideration is likely to favour larger CEECs or those with higher purchasing power – which again means preferences for Poland, Hungary and the Czech Republic. The examples of market-oriented FDI in Poland include investments made by many international firms, ranging from Volkswagen and PepsiCo to McDonald's and insurance companies.

Cost-oriented (or efficiency-oriented) FDI tend to exploit the advantage of inexpensive and relatively well-trained labour in CEECs, although the advantage can be offset by other cost items such as underdeveloped infrastructure or administrative barriers. These FDIs frequently form part of international production networks (IPN) established by MNCs in their efforts to increase competitiveness on a regional and global scale. Cost-oriented FDIs come typically at a later stage, when economic conditions in the host country are considered stable and predictable. An example of such an FDI in Poland is of the extent to which Fiat operations are carried out.

The third type of FDI occurs less frequently in CEECs, as it normally aims at the acquisition of a unique type of a resource or asset (*e.g.* some mineral resources, industrial patents and unique technical skills, see Zimny, 1998). This category of FDI has been dominant in Russia (oil and gas industry), but there are also some examples in CEECs (*e.g.* ABB in Poland).

How will the EU enlargement affect the FDI flows into CEECs in general and into Poland in particular? The first impact of EU enlargement (together with that of NATO enlargement) will be the reduced political risk in new member countries. The political risk – *i.e.* the risk of such events as political instability, nationalisation, conflict with neighbours and external aggression – is considered important by foreign investors (various country-risk analysts, such as Euromoney or Institutional Investor, assign typically the weight of 25% to the political risk within the overall risk, the same weight as they assign to the overall economic performance of a given country). The fact that CEEC-5 have attracted much more FDI than other CEECs seems to suggest not only that the market has assigned lower risk levels to CEEC-5, but that it has probably anticipated their future EU membership and that the impact of membership on political risk has already been partly absorbed.[3] The significance of the political risk seems also to have been confirmed recently in the case of Romania: the change of government in late 1996 and the adoption of a much more reform and European-oriented policies (including faster privatisation) most probably contributed to the massive, five-fold jump in FDI levels in 1997.

The second impact of EU enlargement is the reduced economic cost of FDI resulting from the harmonisation of laws and convergence of structural and economic policies in CEECs. The cost of establishing a foreign firm by a MNC will be lower if the regulatory framework in the target country is the same as in the home country, including product standards, rules of contract enforcement, guarantees and dispute settlement mechanisms. Such an environment will be considered as 'friendly' and will require less effort to start production. This benefit is particularly important for FDI originating in the EU countries. Harmonisation of laws and policy convergence will also substantially reduce the economic risks associated with FDI, such as the risk of a sudden change of economic regime, the exchange rate risk or currency convertibility risk.

The third impact of EU enlargement is that on the size of the market. The removal of trade barriers will integrate national markets of CEECs with those of the EU into a larger regional market. This will induce a further reallocation of production activities within the new, expanded economic area. In this process, some new FDI may come to new member countries, but also a reverse is possible: some FDI which had come to CEECs because of import barriers may now decide to discontinue production and replace it with direct exports. This is, however, rather unlikely, given other locational advantages of CEECs. The impact of the expanded market, on the other hand, is likely to have a positive effect on inflows of FDI from outside the EU, mainly from the USA and Japan, because intra-regional trade will become more attractive than extra-regional trade (Gacs and Wyzan, 1998).

Theoretical considerations suggest, therefore, that EU enlargement will have a strong and positive impact on FDI inflows to new member countries, although it is rather difficult to predict the actual magnitude of future FDI inflows. Some inference can be drawn from the experience of earlier enlargements. Zimny (1998) shows that EU accession was associated with a substantial increase in FDI inflows, both in value terms and as a proportion of the total inflows to EU and OECD, in the United Kingdom, Ireland, Austria and Sweden. Moreover, the very perspective of accession seems to have attracted increased amounts of FDI to Portugal, Spain, Austria and Finland – as shown by the absolute and relative figures for the period of 3-1 years before accession. The only two exceptions to this pattern – for quite different reasons – are Denmark and Greece, with the latter country expe-

---

3. The only example of NATO's influence on FDI is Spain's accession in 1982 and it does not show any significant impact on FDI. However, the political situation in Spain before and after NATO accession has not changed very much and the level of political risk has been low and stable (Rojec, 1998). The geo-strategic situation of CEECs is quite different, and they are still considered to be more exposed to the risks of political reversals in their internal policies as well as being more vulnerable to pressures from Russia. In this case, NATO membership may have a stronger positive impact on political risk than in Spain.

riencing serious political instability at the time of and after the accession.4

The cases of Ireland and Portugal on the one hand and of Greece on the other are particularly instructive. They demonstrate that EU accession is a necessary but by no means a sufficient condition for attracting increased inflows of FDI. What counts is political stability, overall economic performance and sound domestic and international policies. If these conditions are met, FDI are likely to come on a large scale.

These observations are confirmed by the results obtained by other authors. Baldwin *et al.* (1997) have made the most serious attempt so far to estimate the costs and benefits of EU enlargement. They have used a macroeconomic simulation model, including 9 regions and 13 sectors, to estimate real income effects (GDP effects) of the elimination of tariffs between EU and CEECs and the adoption of the common EU tariff. They also included a rough estimate of the reduction in transaction costs (removal of frontier controls, adoption of common standards, etc.), assumed to be 10% of all trade costs. Under the 'conservative scenario', *i.e.* excluding the impact of reduced risk on capital inflows, the estimated GDP gains for seven CEECs (CEEC-5 plus Bulgaria, Romania and the Slovak Republic and minus Estonia) were 2.5 billion ECUs in 1992, or some 1.5% of GDP. However, under the 'optimistic scenario', *i.e.* accounting for the impact on capital inflows of a fall of 15% in risk premium (or 45 basis points of the spread on dollar-denominated fixed-rate issues), the estimated gains are much higher, amounting to 30.1 billion ECUs in 1992, or 18.8% of GDP. One of the conclusions of the study was therefore that the new member countries can expect very large inflows of FDI just before and after accession, because of greatly reduced political and economic risks.

Such high figures for capital inflows and GDP gains are doubtful, because they assume a very high absorption capacity of CEECs. Also, the earlier EU enlargements have not been associated with such massive GDP increases in new member countries. Nevertheless, even if the optimistic scenario is probably unrealistic, a large-scale positive impact is rather undisputed. This is confirmed by statistics on FDI inflows. The inflows of FDI to CEECs have increased substantially since 1991, although to a varying extent in individual countries (see Chapter 4). On average, at least two thirds of capital inflows come from EU countries.

Although substantial, actual FDI inflows are much below the levels that the study by Baldwin *et al.* would suggest. Only in Hungary in 1994 and in Estonia in 1998 did FDI reach the level of about 10% of GDP; in other countries this proportion was generally much lower, varying in 1998 from less than 1% of GDP in

---

4. The level of political and economic risk in Denmark was probably low even before the accession, which may partly explain the weak reaction of FDI flows. Another explanation could be that both in Denmark and Greece there was a strong opposition to EU membership before and after accession, which could have increased uncertainty about the future relations of both countries with the EU.

Slovenia to some 5% of GDP in the Czech Republic and Romania. The massive inflow of FDI to Poland in 1998 – the largest ever registered – was equivalent only to 3.3% of GDP – far less than the estimates predicted by the 'optimistic scenario'.[5]

9.3.5 Free movement of labour

High mobility of manpower should complement free movement of capital in order to maximise gains from efficient allocation of resources across the economically integrated area. However, this is not yet the case. Unlike capital mobility, however, the movement of labour between the EU and the applicant countries is severely restricted, and is likely to remain so for the foreseeable future. Western countries are clearly afraid that any liberalisation would induce large flows of the low-wage workforce from CEECs. While these fears are understandable, they seem to be largely unfounded in the light of a number of statistical and analytical studies (*e.g.*, see Borjas, 1994 and Cogneau *et al.*, 1998). In addition, the experience of German unification, and the visa-free regime granted to more advanced CEECs, demonstrate that the potential for mass migration is negligible.[6]

Poland is clearly interested in removing all barriers to labour mobility once it joins the EU. This is not only necessary to assure an optimum allocation of resources across the enlarged Union, but also to establish a proper balance in reciprocal liberalisation: free access for generally more competitive EU producers to the Polish market should be matched by opening up labour markets on the other side as well. Obviously, mass migration should be avoided; in case such a danger arises, temporary, well-addressed restrictions could be introduced, *e.g.* in the form of regional quotas. However, it would be unwise to impose restrictions in advance, in anticipation of a threat that may never actually materialise. This would have very negative economic and political implications.

9.3.6 Structural assistance programmes

One clear benefit from EU enlargement for new members is that they will have become eligible for the whole range of structural assistance programmes, involving large transfers of resources from the EU to CEECs. However, the overall magnitude and structure of these transfers has been determined only recently.

In some early studies, the amount of structural funds allocated to new members from Central and Eastern Europe was estimated to be set at a level broadly

---

5. Obviously, other categories of capital inflows may also contribute to economic growth (*e.g.* purchases of stock of domestic companies or venture capital). However, in many cases inflows of portfolio capital may be destabilising for the economy, especially when they are driven by high interest rate differentials and speculative considerations.

6. While generally correct, this conjecture may not be valid for some specific regions such as the Vienna region in Austria. In such cases, however, regional policy instruments should be used rather than EU-wide restrictions.

comparable to that for Greece and Portugal, *i.e.* at about 200 ECUs *per capita* up to 1993, and up to 400 ECUs *per capita* after the Edinburgh summit meeting decided to double that amount (Courchene *et al.*, 1993). These forecasts have quickly proved to be far too optimistic (or pessimistic – from the EU viewpoint). At the Amsterdam summit in 1996, a new financial strategy for the EU was proposed in the form of the New Financial Framework that set broad guidelines for the financial and budgetary aspects of eastern enlargement. Nevertheless, it took almost three years of tough and sometimes bitter bargaining before the guidelines were formally approved at the EU summit meeting in Berlin in March 1999. The so-called Financial Perspective for 2000-2006, adopted at the summit meeting, classifies all assistance programmes under four headings: structural assistance programmes[7], assistance to agriculture within the Common Agricultural Policy (CAP), support for domestic policies, and administration.

The key underlying assumptions are that six new members will first join the EU in 2002, that there will be a limit on financial transfers to new members equal to 4% of their GDP, and that the amounts earmarked for enlargement will not be used for other purposes ('ring-fencing' of expenditures). The following table shows the amounts of planned transfers between 2000 and 2006.

Table 9.3: Pre-accession aid and funds for new members in the EU budget for 2000-2006, (appropriations for commitments, in millions of 1999 euros)

Item	2000	2001	2002	2003	2004	2005	2006
Pre-accession aid	3,120	3,120	3,120	3,120	3,120	3,120	3,120
of which:							
agriculture	520						
Structural funds	1,040						
PHARE	1,560						
Total available							
for new members	-	-	6,450	9,030	11,610	14,200	16,780
of which:							
Agriculture	-	-	1,600	2,030	2,450	2,930	3,400
Structural funds	-	-	3,750	5,830	7,920	10,000	12,080
Domestic policies	-	-	730	760	790	820	850
Administration	-	-	370	410	450	450	450
Net transfer for new members	-	-	4,140	6,710	8,890	11,440	14,220
(net of contributions							
of new members)							

Source: Presidency conclusions – Berlin European Council, 24-25 March 1999, D/99/1; Financial Times, 26-27 March, 1999, p.2

---

7. Structural Funds include five separate programmes: FEOGA (agriculture), European Social Fund, European Fund for Regional Development, the Cohesion Fund and the Financial Instrument for Fishery, which are spent on six specific 'development objectives'.

The 4% limit would suggest that the maximum amount of EU transfers to Poland in 2003 (assuming 5% GDP *per capita* growth per annum between 1999 and 2003) would be about 170 euros *per capita* (240 euros in the Czech Republic and 400 euros in Slovenia). But the amount of funds allocated in the budget suggests a much smaller figure – the total transfer of 6,710 euros in 2003 is equivalent to an arithmetic average *per capita* for five CEECs of around 110 euros. The actual amounts may be even lower because of the limited absorptive capacities of CEECs. The experience of the EU shows that only 70% of available structural funds are effectively spent because of problems with raising the 'matching funds' by the recipient countries. Assuming the same disbursement ratio of 0.7 for the new members and an equal *per capita* distribution, the likely amount of structural funds actually flowing to Poland in 2003 would be only about 75 euros *per capita*, later increasing to some 160 euros *per capita* in 2006. This would suggest a much lower level of transfers than in the case of previous enlargements.

The second component of structural assistance is the Common Agricultural Policy (CAP). Some early estimates of the expected financial transfers under the CAP gave very high figures – ranging from 31 billion to 37 billion euros *per annum* for four Visegrad countries – casting doubts on the feasibility of the plans to extend this form of structural support to new members from CEECs (see Tyers, 1994; Anderson and Tyers, 1995; Baldwin, 1994). These high figures were subsequently revised downward, taking into account the reduction in the CAP budget obtained through the McSharry reform in 1995. More recent studies gave estimates of 9-15 billion ECUs for Visegrad-4, with Baldwin *et al.* (1997) suggesting a 'consensus' estimate of 10 billion ECUs.

In the light of the Financial Perspective for 2000-2006, even those downsized estimates turned out to be largely exaggerated. The total of CAP funds available for the whole EU will grow to 43.9 billion euros in 2002, and will fall gradually afterwards to 41.66 billion euros in 2006 – a result of observing the rule that CAP spending must not rise faster than 74% of the EU's GDP growth. In line with the significant tightening of CAP spending, agricultural assistance to new members has also been planned to be much more limited, raising from 1.6 billion euros in 2002 to 3.4 billion euros in 2006. Even assuming that Poland will take at least 60% of this amount, this level of assistance represents less than 40% of CAP average spending per hectare in incumbent members, such as Germany.

9.3.7 Financial costs

It is sometimes argued that the costs of EU enlargement for CEECs will include the need to restructure certain sectors (agriculture, heavy industry) and to adopt rather demanding EU standards in areas such as environmental protection, nuclear safety, transport and public security. True, these are all very costly reforms, also entailing important social and political implications. Nevertheless, these reforms will have to be carried out, sooner or later, and irrespective of EU accession – they are plainly inevitable if the process of improving living standards in CEECs and the catching up with Western Europe is to be sustained. The EU accession may influence the timing of these reforms, but it will also surely help to finance them with some extra funds coming from the EU. Some other costs, linked to open borders and free flows of resources, may include an outflow of highly qualified specialists to Western countries.

One standard and fairly specific cost of accession is the obligatory contribution to the EU budget. At present, the member country contributions amount on average to some 0.3% of their GDP, but individual contributions vary, partly in reflection of GDP *per capita* levels. For CEECs, these contributions will certainly be less than their receipts under the structural assistance programmes. Using a model of voting power in the EU, Baldwin *et al.* (1997) estimated the equation regressing the levels of *per capita* contributions to the levels of *per capita* GDP.[8] Applying the same equation to estimate the expected budgetary contributions of the new members and assuming 5% growth rates between 1996 and 2002, Rosati (1998b) estimated the total amount of the CEEC-5 contribution to the EU budget at 3 billion euros, with Poland accounting for roughly half of this figure.

These estimates have proved to be broadly correct. The Financial Perspective for 2000-2006 assumes the total contribution from the CEEC-5 in 2003 to be 2.32 billion euros, rising to 2.57 billion euros in 2006. This amount would be almost three times smaller than the payments they are supposed to receive via structural funds and CAP transfers, as indicated in the last line of Table 9.3. The figures show that the balance of financial transfers is highly positive for new members.

9.3.8 The expected balance of financial benefits and costs for Poland

Assuming broadly equal *per capita* distribution of structural transfers among new members and a 70% disbursement ratio, Poland is expected to receive structural transfers of 4.04 billion euros in 2003, rising to 7.46 billion euros in 2006. Assuming the following 50% share in budgetary contributions from the CEEC-5, the amount of net transfers would be lower, rising from 3.35 billion euros in 2003 to 6.86 billion euros in 2006. These figures represent *per capita* transfers of 86 euros and 176 euros respectively, or 1.9% and 3 1/2% of Poland's expected GDP in 2003 and 2006 (see Table 9.4).

The figures given in Table 9.4 suggest that both in *per capita* terms and as a proportion of GDP the expected net transfers will be much lower than transfers obtained by Greece, Spain, Portugal and Ireland after they had joined the EU. Given that earlier estimates may have raised unrealistically high expectations, the actual transfers are likely to be regarded by new member countries as insufficient

---

8. The equation is of the following form (variables expressed in 1993 ECU): Contribution *per capita* = -9.6 + 0.012 (GDP *per capita*), R(square) = 0.86

Table 9.4: Hypothetical net balance of financial transfers in 2003-2006:
The case of Poland (millions of 1999 euros)

Item	2003	2004	2005	2006
Transfers	4,507	5,716	6,933	8,144
Structural funds	2,526	3,432	4,333	5,235
CAP	1,257	1,517	1,814	2,105
other transfers	724	768	786	805
Budgetary contribution	1,160	1,360	1,380	1,285
Net transfers	3,347	4,356	5,553	6,859
per capita	86	117	142	176
as a % of GDP	1.9	2.4	2.9	3.5

Source: Own calculations of the author

and, in comparison with earlier enlargements, also unfair. This consideration may be one of the reasons behind the steadily falling support for EU membership in many CEECs, including Poland.

9.4 From Euro-euphoria to Euro-scepticism: the rise and fall of popular support for EU accession in Poland

Immediately after the political breakthrough in 1989 the pro-European orientation in Poland's foreign policy gained wide popular backing. In fact, the two strategic objectives – NATO membership and EU membership – enjoyed the support of all the major political groups in Poland. This unequivocal support, which peaked in 1994-1997 has been an important factor behind the rapid progress in gradually approaching the two institutions.

However, since 1997 popular support for EU membership has weakened quite considerably. This is illustrated by the results of the public opinion surveys conducted by CBOS, a major public opinion polling organisation – see Table 9.5. The results of the last survey in May 1999 are particularly disturbing: they show that the percentage of people supporting the accession has fallen by almost one third since 1996, while the percentage of people being against tripled.

Table 9.5: Support for Poland's accession to the European Union:
Results of public opinion surveys, 1994-1999, in %

Question	June 1994	May 1995	May 1996	April 1997	May 1998	December 1998	May 1999
In favour	77	72	80	72	66	64	55
Against	6	9	7	11	19	19	26
Undecided	17	19	13	18	15	17	19

Source: CBOS (1999), p.2

Another important tendency, evident from the surveys, is that more and more people are in favour of gradual rather than rapid accession (see Table 9.6). This is yet another symptom of growing wariness and even mistrust towards the EU.

Table 9.6: How fast should Poland join the EU?
Results of public opinion surveys, 1997-1999, in %

Question	April 1997	August 1997	December 1998	May 1999
Poland should aim at entering the EU as soon as possible	40	39	34	26
Poland should first modernise the economy and join the EU later	48	43	50	58
Undecided	12	19	16	16

Source: CBOS (1999), p.4

There is a host of different reasons behind the declining support for EU accession in Poland. First, once the modalities of accession become more widely known and discussed, including the need to restructure certain areas of the economy, the intuitive support for integration with affluent Europe has given way to more sober and particular calculations that in many cases do not give immediately positive outcomes. Second, the government has failed so far to present a coherent integration strategy, with all benefits and costs identified and properly discussed. This leaves room for the populist demagoguery practised by some political parties, partly because their particular group interests seem to be endangered by accession, and partly because of sheer ignorance. Those populist arguments have, however, received quite substantial resonance in public opinion, especially among farmers and industrial workers employed in traditional heavy industry sectors. Third, open borders and free inflow of goods and services from the EU have demonstrated that economic integration does not only mean more opportunities and wider consumer choices, but also tougher competition. This has led to standard calls for protection against competitive imports from many segments of the economy, and has eventually been translated into increased reluctance with respect to accession.

However, there are also reasons on the side of the EU. Protectionist trade practices, especially in agricultural trade, have clearly undermined the credibility of the EU in the eyes of the Polish farmer. In addition, many politicians in Poland have found it difficult to reconcile the constant pressure by the EU to liberalise and deregulate the Polish economy with flagrant cases of protectionism and heavy-handed interventionism. The cases of doubtful practice in areas such as the access of Polish enterprises to EU markets in the construction sector and of exports of 'sensitive' products, have also played an important role in creating an image – in the eyes of many – of the EU as a protectionist and bureaucratic organisation, guided by selfish considerations. Finally, internal disputes and arguments among EU members and within the EU itself, including the recent dismissal of the EU Commission, have also contributed to a fall of popular support for rapid integration.

9.5 The current status of accession negotiations between Poland and the EU

The 'screening' stage of accession negotiations started in April 1998 and is expected to be completed by September 1999. Its purpose is to review Polish legislation from the point of view of consistency with the whole body of EU laws and regulations – the so-called 'acquis communautaire'. The screening process is performed in 36 separate areas, and in each area the Polish side is expected to come up with one of the three alternative declarations:
- There are no issues for further negotiations, which means that European laws have already been adopted in full;
- There are some issues of a technical or temporary nature which will be solved by the time of accession;
- There are important problems that have to be discussed and negotiated, with a possibility of applying for a derogation or a transition period.

Until the end of June 1999, Poland has submitted negotiating positions in 18 areas: science and research, education and youth, cultural and audiovisual policy, telecommunication and information technology, common foreign and security policy, industrial policy, small and medium enterprises, statistics, customs union, external relations, protection of consumers and health standards, company laws, economic and monetary union, competition policy, free movement of goods, fisheries, energy and employment and social policy. Out of these, negotiations have been temporarily closed in seven areas, considered as problem-free: science and research, education and youth, small and medium enterprises, telecommunication and information technology[9], industrial policy, and protection of consumers and health standards.

A preliminary assessment of the negotiating positions submitted in the remaining areas suggests that the most difficult problems are likely to arise in the following areas: competition policy, free movement of goods, agriculture and free movement of labour. As far as competition policy is concerned, the Polish side has applied for derogations with respect to state aid extended to enterprises undergoing restructuring, enterprises in the area of environmental protection, and enterprises registered in special economic zones. The latter derogation may be rather difficult to obtain. In the area of free movement of goods, the Polish side

---

9. Poland initially asked for a transition period in opening access to certain restricted frequencies in GSM telecommunication, but later this application was withdrawn.

has reserved to itself the right to ask for a derogation with respect to price controls for pharmaceuticals.

In the two most problematic areas – agriculture and the free movement of labour – Poland has not yet submitted the negotiating positions. In the former, the thorny issue is the level of financial support for Polish farmers, while the latter concerns the extent to which Polish workers will be allowed to migrate freely to EU countries from the moment of accession. These two issues are likely to absorb much time and effort during negotiations; they will probably end with a compromise that would most likely swap some concessions in the two areas.

9.6 Concluding remarks

The progress in integrating Poland with the European Union has been substantial. Within less than a decade, trade flows have been radically reoriented and massive flows of FDI have linked large segments of the Polish economy with Western markets. However, the process is far from complete and important challenges lie ahead, foremost among them being the rapidly eroding popular support for accession in Poland, as well as growing concerns on the EU side about the negative financial and economic implications of enlargement for member countries. The adoption of the Financial Perspective for 2000-2006 is an important and welcome step in removing uncertainty surrounding the enlargement process; but at the same time the financial framework it provides for the eastern enlargement is much more modest and restricted than in the case of previous enlargements.

At this particular juncture there is a need for the Polish authorities to undertake a concerted and determined political effort aimed at maintaining the momentum of the integration process and securing broad public support for the enlargement. Specific benefits and costs of enlargement should be clearly identified, assessed and submitted for public debate. It should be made clear that the enlargement would bring important net benefits both to Poland and to the EU. In the areas and sectors that are likely to be adversely affected by the enlargement (metallurgy, coal mining and some rural areas), special programmes for the alleviation of economic and social costs of enlargement should be elaborated and implemented.

On the EU side, more imagination and a longer-term perspective is needed to properly and fully judge the implications of the enlargement process. The historic significance of enlargement is far too important to be subordinated to purely technocratic considerations. The enlargement, once completed, will be a great success for all Europeans, and it should be seen as such, not as a sacrifice or as a nuisance. Only then can united Europe live in peace, friendship and prosperity.

References

Anderson, K. and R. Tyers (1995), 'Implications of the EC Expansion for European Agriculture Policies, Trade and Welfare', in: R. Baldwin, P. Haaparanta and J. Kiander, eds., *Expanding Membership of the European Union*, Cambridge, University Press, Cambridge.

Baldwin, R.E. (1994), *Towards an Integrated Europe*, CEPR, London.

Baldwin, R.E, J.F. Francois and R. Portes (1997), 'The Costs and Benefits of Eastern Enlargement: The Impact on the EU and Central Europe', *Economic Policy*, No.24, pp.127-170.

Borjas, G.J. (1994), 'The Economics of Immigration', *Journal of Economic Literature*, Vol.32, pp.1667-1717.

CBOS (1999), 'Polacy, Czesi i Wegrzy o integracji z Unia Europejska. Komunikat z badan', *Centrum Badania Opinii Spolecznej*, Warszawa.

Cogneau, D., J-Ch. Dumont and E.M. Mouhoud (1998), *Regional Integration, Migration, Growth and Direct Investment. A Reading of the Economic Literature*, paper presented at OECD Conference, Lisbon, December 1998, OECD, Paris, DEELSA/ELSA/MI (98)5.

Courchene, T., C. Goodhart, A. Majocchi, W. Moesen, T. Prud'homme, F. Schneider, S. Smith, B. Spahn and C. Walsh (1993), 'Stable Money – Sound Finances', *European Economy*, No. 53, European Commission, DG II, Brussels.

Drabek, Z. (1998), *Common External Tariff of the European Union and the Structural Adjustment in Central and Eastern Europe: Notes*, WTO, Geneva, (mimeo).

Dunning, J.H. (1993), *Multinational Enterprises and the Global Economy*, Addison-Wesley, London.

Gacs, J. and M. Wyzan (1998), *The European Union and the Rest of the World: Complements or Substitutes for Central and Eastern Europe? Interim Report*, IIASA, Vienna.

Molle, W. (1994), *The Economics of European Integration. Theory, Practice, Policy*, Dartmouth Publ. Co. Ltd.

Rojec, M. (1998), *Foreign Direct Investment How Much* NATO *and* EU *Membership Enhance Investments by Non-*EU *Investors?*, Lubljana, (unpublished).

Rosati, D.K. (1998a), 'Emerging trade patterns of transition countries. Some observations from the analysis of unit values', MOCT-MOST, No.8, pp.51-67.

Rosati, D.K. (1998b), 'Economic Disparities in Central and Eastern Europe and the Impact of EU Enlargement', paper prepared for UNECE and CEI, Geneva, (mimeo).

Tyers, R. (1994), *Economic Reform in Europe and the Former Soviet Union: Implications for International Food Markets*, Research Report No.99, International Food Policy Research Institute, Washington, D.C.

Zimny, Z. (1998), *Integracja a zagraniczne inwestycje bezposrednie: doswiadczenia Unii Europejskiej i wnioski dla Polski*, (Integration and foreign direct investment: EU's experiences and implications for Poland), UNCTAD, Geneva, (mimeo).

Zysman, J. and A. Schwartz (1998), Enlarging Europe: The Industrial Foundations of a New Political Reality, in: J. Zysman and A. Schwartz (eds.), *Enlarging Europe: The Industrial Foundations of a New Political Reality*, A BRIE/Kreisky Forum Project, University of California, Berkeley, pp.1-27.

CHAPTER 10

Enlargement of the European Union: A Hungarian Perspective

András Inotai

10.1 Introduction

After decade-long informal contacts with the Commission, Hungary became the first transforming country to sign a trade and co-operation agreement with the European Community (EC) in 1988, immediately after the Luxembourg Declaration between the EC and the already defunct Council of Mutual Economic Assistance (CMEA). Hungary's main approach to the EC, its growing trade partner since the mid-1970s, was to be as professional as possible concerning concrete trade policy issues and as cautious as necessary in political and diplomatic terms. The country did not enter a blind alley like Romania did, signing an agreement with the EC just to annoy the Soviet Union while not having an economic, legal and institutional structure capable of actually making use of such a special treaty. In turn, Hungary expected that its long-awaited and fully deserved special relationship with the EC, as materialised in September 1988, would constitute a landmark in bilateral relations, at least in the medium term. However, history intervened, and Hungary had to accept a relatively rapid 'downgrading' of its position, as, within a rather short time, practically all CEECs concluded agreements with much the same or very similar contents. The PHARE programme, scheduled initially just for Hungary and Poland in May 1989, became a multi-country basket; trade and co-operation agreements were quickly signed with other CEECs, and the first Association Agreements were concluded with four Central European countries, to be followed later on by six other applicants from the region.

Notwithstanding this 'institutional homogenisation', Hungary's micro-level achievements could not be 'standardised'. The completely mistaken assessment of the first years of transformation, based on the macroeconomic performance criteria used for developed industrial economies, which were completely unable to characterise the transformation process, temporarily pushed Hungary into the background. During recent years, however, both the sustainability of the transformation process, and a successful adjustment to the economic, legal and institutional requirements of the European Union (EU), have fundamentally upgraded the micro-level factors.

10.2 From association to negotiations on full membership

The signing of the Association Agreement for a period of ten years in December 1991, and its implementation, which started early in 1992 (and became fully-effective after ratification by the EU member countries early in 1994), created the necessary external anchor for successful transformation and modernisation for Hungary in three areas. First, it provided a framework of economic stability, essential for transformation in small and open (vulnerable) economies. Second, it opened up large segments of the EU market to Hungarian goods, excluding agricultural products (and, temporarily, some sensitive commodities). Third, it brought financial support, although this was extremely modest in comparison with the huge burdens of economic modernisation and catching-up that was envisaged.

From the very beginning Hungary, together with Poland and ex-Czechoslovakia, gave fundamental consideration to the Association Agreement as a stepping stone towards full membership. Therefore, these three countries urged the EU to define the basic criteria of membership. The Copenhagen accession criteria were the ambiguous, but still necessary, result. They created new and previously never stipulated conditions for membership. The criteria opened the way for the enlargement process and ensured that no future summit meeting could ignore this issue from its agenda.

The next key step was the decision made at the Madrid summit (December 1995) which gave the green light to official preparations for starting negotiations on accession (opinions and country reports on negotiation capabilities). Fortunately, it coincided with two basic Hungarian developments. First, the new government that took position in the summer of 1994 had to manage the macroeconomic imbalance inherited from the first democratically elected government by introducing an austerity package. This package was already in the process of implementation and promised to produce the first results at the moment when the start of the negotiations could be programmed. Second, a restructuring of the EU-related decision-making structure, a long-delayed issue, had to be faced. Immediately after the outcome of the Madrid summit, the government created a four-pillar structure in order to prepare the country efficiently for the start of fully-fledged negotiations. While the previously established inter-ministerial working group dealing with technical and legal issues of adjustment remained in place, the management of EU-related issues became firmly located in the Ministry of Foreign Affairs, by creating an EU-Integration Secretariat. Two new bodies emerged: the Integration Cabinet, headed by the Prime Minister and with the participation of key ministers responsible for EU issues, and an independent Strategic Task Force (STF) consisting of 19 working groups and a network of about 500 experts (the director of the STF was also a member of the Integration Cabinet).

As part of the strategic approach to Hungary's accession to the EU, a timetable for the period between 1996 and 2002 was designed. Negotiations were planned to start at the beginning of 1998, and be concluded by the end of 2000 and resulting, in case of a quick ratification process, in full membership by 2002. This time-frame is still valid for Hungary's EU-accession strategy.

For various reasons, Hungary has opposed all proposals for regional co-operation, which might jeopardise its full membership of the EU (Central European customs and payments union, membership in EFTA or in the Single Market, partial membership covering political and security co-operation but excluding economic integration). From the very beginning, it was clear that the status of association and of full EU membership would differ considerably. First, only full membership enables the liberalisation of trade in agricultural goods. Second, access to sizeable financial transfers, a major modernisation resource, can only be achieved through full membership. Third, the implementation of the 'four freedoms', including that of labour, although after a longer transitional period, cannot be reached within the framework of association. Fourth, in order to participate in the decision-making process of the EU, Hungary has to be a full member. While it remains outside the EU, it has to accept all of its decisions without having the possibility to influence them.

The Agenda 2000 of the Commission and the subsequent decision by the European Council in December 1997 in Luxembourg have classified Hungary into the group of first-wave candidates, with which negotiations were started in April 1998. Both in the country reports attached to Agenda 2000 and in the first progress reports published in November 1998, Hungary got the best notes from the Commission. Based on the three basic Copenhagen criteria (politics, economics, legal and institutional development), Hungary was classified as the most serious candidate for full membership during the first 'eastern' enlargement of the Union. In this assessment, the results of several decades of Hungary's political, economic and social development were recognised. The gradual opening up of politics, and more importantly, that of the society, as well as important micro-economic progress characterised by the chosen way of privatisation, produced an unprecedentedly favourable starting position for the official negotiations, just before the parliamentary elections in May 1998. The situation was further enhanced by the role played by foreign direct investment, institutional modernisation, and the bold implementation of a programme to regain macroeconomic stability in order to bring microeconomic maturity in harmony with macroeconomic requirements. Evidently, the level of Hungary's maturity for membership in the EU remained uneven, but it was in all areas as high as, or higher than, in any other applicant country.

In the legal context, adjustment to the *acquis communautaire* started at the moment of ratification of the Association Agreement. The government(s) produced clear timetables, supported later by the Cannes White Book. More importantly, the imposition of EU directives, standards and guidelines was not a one-way, top-down process. The growing importance of foreign companies, mainly that of subsidiaries of EU-located firms, as well as externally oriented Hungarian companies, quickly familiarised the business society with EU rules. This process, albeit sometimes unconsciously, initiated a bottom-up process of legal harmoni-sation. As a result, the legal absorption capacity, one of the basic conditions for successful membership, can be evaluated as sufficiently strong in comparison with other applicant countries. Nevertheless, there are still several areas not covered by EU legislation or gaps between laws approved by the Parliament, but not yet enforced.

Economic adjustment is the key success story of Hungary. Trade has funda-mentally been reoriented towards the EU. In 1998, 73% of Hungarian exports were marketed in EU countries and 65% of imports originated from the Union. Geographic shifts in trade patterns have been accompanied by sizeable market gains. In 1998, about 2% of the EU's total extra-regional exports and imports were with Hungary (compared with 0.6-0.7% in 1989). Even more important have been the structural changes. Once a mainly 'agricultural country', in less than a decade, Hungary became the leading Central and Eastern European exporter of machinery and equipment to the EU. With machinery exports of 8.35 billion euros in 1998, Hungary accounted for one-third of the total machinery exports of the ten associated countries, or 30% more than the corresponding fig-ure for the Czech Republic and almost double the amount of Polish machinery exports to the EU (see Inotai, 1998). The structural upgrading is even more notice-able in the German market, the main buyer of Central and Eastern European products (see Chapter 4). In 1998, two-thirds of Hungary's exports to Germany consisted of 'technology-intensive' goods (machinery, electronics, computers, pre-cision instruments, pharmaceuticals and transport equipment), in comparison with less than 50% for the Czech Republic and Slovenia and just about 25% for Poland. In addition, unit prices for Hungarian exports of final manufactured goods to Germany amounted to 13,525 D-mark per ton, while the same figures were 10,053 D-mark for Slovenia, 5,857 D-mark for the Czech Republic and 3,960 D-mark for Poland. More surprisingly, even the equivalent Austrian unit price remained below the Hungarian one, *viz.* 12,812 D-mark (Inotai, 1999, forthcoming).

In terms of EU-orientation, export patterns, the degree of intra-industry trade and partly also the volume of trade, Hungary has already become largely inte-grated into the micro-structures of the EU.[1] In contrast with other less developed countries which joined the EU in the eighties, Hungary opted for another, but probably more fortunate way to integrate: it envisaged real integration first, to be

---

1. To take the German example, in 1998 Hungary exported more goods to Germany than five EU member countries (Denmark, Finland, Greece, Ireland and Portugal). Its exports of trans-port equipment were 64% higher than the aggregate exports from all five countries together, and its machinery exports equalled those of Ireland and Denmark together. In addition, Hun-gary proved to be the main exporter of electrotechnical goods in the above comparison (Ino-tai 1999, forthcoming).

followed by institutional integration later. The Mediterranean countries, on the contrary, first reached institutional integration and, only under this umbrella and to quite different degrees across countries, real integration followed later.

Hungary's successful micro-level integration mainly resulted from a relatively open society that existed well before the political landscape had changed so dramatically, from the legal and institutional framework of a market economy which started to be established earlier than in neighbouring transforming countries and, to a large extent, from the way of privatisation. Consequently, foreign direct investment became the leading agent of transformation and EU-integration, not only converting the Hungarian economy into a competitive international location for production but, also, increasingly into an area for selected services and research and development activities.

Despite the progress achieved and Hungary's favourable placing among other candidate countries, there is still much to be done in the institutional field. The quality of public administration has to be improved constantly. Even a well-prepared administration would be seriously challenged by adjustment to the EU. This is even more the case in Hungary, where, immediately after the political change, well-trained experts were attracted by lucrative jobs abroad, in international organisations, multinational companies and by new entrepreneurial activities in Hungary. Moreover, the last three democratic elections always resulted in new coalition governments that, unfortunately, could not separate short-term ideological and political interests from the requirements of a well-functioning public administration. Thus, each time, ideology-driven efforts have negatively affected the elite of public administration and, consequently, reduced its general level of knowledge and threatened to disrupt the necessary institutional continuity in preparing for full membership in the EU.

10.3 Negotiations on accession in progress

Based on its political, economic and institutional progress, Hungary's application for full membership, submitted on 1 April 1994, was positively assessed by the Commission in the first country reports attached to Agenda 2000 in July 1997. The European Council decided to start negotiations with six countries, including Hungary, in the spring of 1998. These negotiations are carried out at two levels. First, the screening process, consisting of a multilateral and a bilateral part, was initiated in April 1998 and was successfully completed early in July 1999. Simultaneously, effective negotiations could start on the issues already screened during the Austrian EU Presidency in November 1998. A second round of negotiations took place in June 1999, under the German Presidency. Altogether 15 of the 31 chapters have been opened and eight of them have been successfully closed.[2]

2. In principle, and due to the evolutionary character of EU legislation but also because of changing interests of the negotiating partners, all chapters remain open until the whole process of negotiations is finished. Hungary, like Slovenia and the Czech Republic, could temporarily close eight chapters, while Poland and Estonia have closed seven chapters and Cyprus ten.

Negotiations on selected subjects have to be preceded by national position papers. Hungary has already submitted most of these documents and intends to provide all remaining papers during the Finnish Presidency. Together with other first-round candidates, it expects that in the second half of 1999, another eight chapters can be discussed and the chapters left open during the German Presidency can be temporarily closed. In this way, in an optimistic scenario, negotiations may be finished by the end of 2000 and the ratification process may start (or even be completed) in 2001. This optimistic approach, however, assumes that the coming rounds of negotiations on increasingly difficult and complex topics, will not experience a noticeable slowdown. Therefore, a very clear and EU-conform Hungarian standpoint in critical areas is required. In addition, global and European political and economic developments have to be supportive to quick enlargement. Finally, also the EU has to get prepared to accept new members.[3]

The progress made until now fits well into the Hungarian timetable of being ready for accession as of 1 January 2002. Evidently, this date is not carved in stone and, to a very large extent, it depends on the decisions to be taken by the EU and the member countries, rather than on decisions made by Hungary. Nevertheless, the setting of a clear timetable is indispensable for Hungary. First, it exerts the necessary discipline on the public administration, on business and on all actors that are likely to be affected by accession. Without a clear, and for the internal preparation compulsory, date, preparation would not be successful and, more importantly, would suffer substantial delay.[4] Second, a date is always necessary when temporary derogations have to be defined. During the screening process, and more importantly in the position papers, Hungary had to classify its process of preparing for membership into three parts: that part of the *acquis communautaire* which has already been adopted and enforced; that part which will be implemented before accession, and a final part where temporary derogations may be requested. In order to separate part two from part three, with implications both for the successful preparation and for negotiation strategy, a date 'for internal use' is extremely important.

The negotiations on accession are, at least on the surface, dominated by a large number of 'boring' technical details. However, a candidate country like Hungary, with an extremely low degree of leverage, should not be lost in technicalities. Suc-

---

3. One of the three big obstacles to enlargement was eliminated in the Berlin summit in March 1999, when the financial framework of the EU was accepted for the period 2000 to 2006. There are justifiable hopes that a 'mini' inter-governmental conference on accession-related institutional issues will start early in 2000 and be successfully completed well before the first enlargement could materialise. At present, the reform of the common agricultural policy seems to be more problematic. Here, the outcome of the next round of international trade negotiations is likely to influence the position of the EU more than the potential implications of enlargement.
4. For a comparison, the Single Market or the Economic and Monetary Union could hardly have been implemented without a clear agenda, including the year of completion, a relatively long time before the goals were more or less achieved. There is no doubt that the setting of a date has an obvious mobilising impact.

cessful membership, both for Hungarians and for the present member countries, needs a consequent evaluation of some strategic issues.

First, in Hungary, both politicians and the broad society, have to recognise that negotiations with Brussels are different from traditional diplomatic or economic bargaining. Clearly, the negotiations, reflecting the interests of both partners, will not result in a new treaty reflecting well-balanced compromises. Accession fundamentally implies that the country that wants to join an existing organisation has to adopt all the rules of the game developed in this organisation over decades. The scope and validity of EU treaties cannot be changed, at least not from the outside.[5] Only a relatively small number of temporary exceptions is feasible.

Second, the smaller the bargaining power of an applicant is, the more imperative it is to design a comprehensive overall strategy of accession. Although the main priority is accession, the security, political, economic and social dimensions have to be broader and consider potential global, regional and local opportunities and threats alike. There is a danger that, in absence of such a strategy, accession will become the only (and not the main) priority which, over time, could clash with other developments. As a result, the lack of a comprehensive approach is likely to lead to avoidable clashes of interests, is likely to postpone the date of accession, and is likely to increase the costs (and decrease the benefits) of membership.

Third, a strategy not only has to take the present day possibilities and constraints into account but should also focus on those of the future. No doubt that at the moment of Hungary's accession both the EU and Hungary will be different than they are today. In fact, Hungary will not join the EU of today but an EU that will exist in a few years time. This requires the drafting of some credible scenarios, with adequate Hungarian adjustments and responses that are mainly determined by future needs and opportunities, rather than by short-term and short-sighted bureaucratic considerations.

Fourth, the interdisciplinary approach has to be strengthened substantially. Accession to the EU should not be a legal process exclusively. Although the legal framework has to be adopted, its implications affect practically all areas of Hungary's everyday life and development. More importantly, the EU is much more than a legal entity. Security, political, economic, social, psychological and other factors have to be assessed carefully. Also, interdisciplinarity would already need to be taken into account in selecting the derogation requests (see the next section). Particular importance will be attached to such an approach in the final stage of negotiations, when all open issues have to be mutually weighted, and solutions will have the character of a package deal.

Fifth, the utmost care has to be given to the definition of 'national interests'. On the one hand, as far as possible, expropriation by particular pressure groups or

---

5. An eventual enrichment of the *acquis* represents an exception (see the higher environmental standards of Sweden, Finland and Austria that have to be taken on by present member countries as well).

political demagogy should be avoided. On the other hand, it has to be observed very clearly that 'national interests' are a relative concept (one issue may be of 'national interest' in comparison to another one but may loose this status when compared to an even more important topic). Moreover, this concept is not a static but a dynamic one and changes over time. Finally, in negotiations with the EU, the best protection of 'national interests' is high-quality preparation and credible arguments always complemented by 'special values' that could contribute to the enrichment of the present EU. Interests and values (Hungarian contributions) should form a well-balanced package during the whole process of the accession negotiations.

10.4 Key forthcoming issues

According to most experts, the negotiations on accession are likely to enter their decisive stage in 2000. This assessment is partly based on the fact that the crucial topics, both for the EU and for Hungary, will appear on the agenda in the second half of 1999. Partly because the multi-level impact of the EU will be increasingly felt in the Hungarian economy and society as the country enters into the last stage of implementation of the Association Agreement[6] and partly because the country will be experiencing the EU's resistance to some or several derogation requests formulated in the position papers.

The key issues can be divided into two main groups: those to be negotiated in Brussels and those contributing to the best possible preparation of Hungary for the future part of negotiations and for successful accession.

Problem areas for negotiation

It is already clear that the most problematic fields for negotiation will include agriculture, environment, labour, structural funds, EMU and the Schengen arrangements.

In the last decade, Hungarian agriculture experienced several setbacks, due to external impacts and to domestic problems. Even so, agriculture can remain or become a competitive sector based on unique climatic and soil conditions, expertise and growing internationalisation. In statistical terms, it already fits into the EU at least in the same way as Greece, Ireland or Portugal do, since less than 7% of GDP is produced by agriculture and about 8% of the active population is employed in this sector.[7] However, Hungarian agriculture is not yet fully prepared for membership. To be sure, uncertainties about the future of the common agri-

---

6. Based on the principle of temporary asynchrony, Hungary will have to liberalise its imports from the EU completely by 2001 in order to establish free trade for manufactured goods. Also, other liberalisation steps (movement of services and capital, areas of the *acquis* contained in the Association Agreement) fall into the last two years of implementing the Association Agreement.

cultural policy (CAP) do not make the elaboration and implementation of a Hungarian agricultural strategy any easier. Nevertheless, if Hungary wants to participate in the CAP from the very beginning of its membership in the EU, it has to remove the obstacles to the rapid development of a competitive agricultural sector. The main obstacles, mainly based on outdated ideology but difficult to remove because of the present party composition of the government, are the lack of capital to modernise the sector and the substantially constrained market to sell and buy agricultural land. The longer it takes to eliminate these barriers, the more difficult the negotiations in Brussels will be, and the more harmful the consequences will be for the future of Hungarian agriculture in the EU.[8]

In the last few years, Hungary's environmental standards have improved substantially in several sectors. In addition, as a result of the previous pattern of development and of successful privatisation and restructuring, the extent of polluting industrial production is much lower in Hungary than in most other applicant countries. Also, the positive side of the rather ambiguous development in agriculture is the elimination of many environmentally damaging activities. Nevertheless, the present situation lags far behind the corresponding EU rules. Rapid adjustment to the EU raises two problems. First, the costs to comply fully with EU environmental standards would seriously burden the central budget. Second, international competitiveness of some companies, including EU-rooted ones working in Hungary, might be impaired. Therefore, progress in environmental adjustment depends to a large extent on the financial resources available from the pre-accession fund, and, later on, from the structural (and maybe cohesion) funds.

In contrast with environmental adjustment, it is the EU which is expected to request a temporary derogation concerning the free flow of labour. According to many surveys, Hungary's migration potential is and will remain limited, provided enlargement takes place quickly and broad economic and social progress materialises. It is not quick enlargement that may increase the migration potential but just the opposite, the delaying or postponing of accession. In recent years, Hungary has been one of the main beneficiaries of labour market rigidities in Western Europe. Since capital works in a global framework, while manpower is seriously restricted to national (and regional) levels, international capital started to join Hungarian labour. This is a far better combination of production factors than if Hungarian guest workers were to go to the available capital in the present EU countries. Consequently, Hungary should not delay negotiations by insisting on the free flow of labour as a precondition for membership. As this request can not be fulfilled by the EU in the foreseeable future, it would only delay joining the EU,

---

7. Generalisations with respect to all applicant countries are not only far from the reality but also extremely detrimental.
8. While apparently 'protecting Hungarian interests', the government practically supports those EU agricultural lobbies that are not interested in or just fear a competitive Hungarian agricultural sector.

without any tangible benefit for Hungary.9

An important step in shaping the future of the EU's structural funds was made during the Berlin summit. Money, both for the pre-accession fund (3.12 billion euros per year for a seven year period) and for future members (a yearly increasing sum starting in 2002) has been singled out from the general EU budget. Beside its clear political message that the first enlargement to the East may take place as soon as 2002, in accordance with the Hungarian self-made target date, Hungary as a member of the first wave new countries, is expected to benefit from the structural funds as soon as possible. The amount Hungary will be entitled to depends on the number of new members joining with Hungary at the same time and on the institutional absorption capacity of the country at the moment of membership. However, the volume and modalities of the Hungarian contribution to the EU budget (another phasing-in period, similar to the phasing-in of structural funds) is to be negotiated.

Hungary's membership of the EMU is unlikely to raise urgent issues during the negotiations. It is generally accepted that, in the spirit of the Copenhagen criteria, new countries will have to share the basic political and economic objectives of the EU, without participating in all community areas from the first moment of membership on. After some years, of course, Hungary will have to become a member of the EMU. This step, however, will be preceded by membership in the ERM-II, at the moment of joining the EU, which will amount to an obligatory preparatory period of two years at least before EMU membership may materialise. At present, Hungary, as do most other first-wave applicant countries, already complies with the fiscal criteria of Maastricht but, in need of further structural reforms, still needs some years to bring down inflation (and long-term interest rates) to the Maastricht level. Predictions related to membership in the EMU are also subject to the future of the EMU itself.

Finally, the adjustment to the Schengen criteria represents a major, and to some extent a special Hungarian, challenge. Considering the sizeable Hungarian minority (altogether around 3 million) in some of the neighbouring countries, some Hungarian politicians and experts are inclined to ask for special conditions to maintain and strengthen contacts with Hungarians outside Hungary, once the country becomes member of the EU. In contrast, the acceptance of the full scope of Schengen seems to be a fundamental precondition for membership of the EU. However, Hungary's preparation for the Schengen rules has to be split into two main tasks. Stricter border controls and more transparency in justice and home affairs should be implemented continuously, while the visa policy has to be changed at the moment of membership, provided the EU will still have the same visa policy as practised today. The predominant challenge of Schengen is twofold,

---

9. This issue may be differently interpreted by the individual applicant countries and may represent another essential difference characterising the current economic situation and the negotiation priorities even among the first-wave candidates.

and neither part should be seen in connection with some short-sighted opinions and attitudes in Hungary.

More specifically, the future Schengen borders have to be defined in case the Slovak Republic will not be among the first-wave of new entrants. Both for political, financial and technical reasons, it would be convenient to draw the new Schengen-conform external borders of the Union along the eastern borders of Poland, Hungary, and evidently, of the Slovak Republic. In this case, Poland's, the Czech Republic's and Hungary's long borders with the Slovak Republic would not be external borders of the Union. It would save a huge amount of money, strengthen political cooperation in East Central Europe and, most probably, grant partial membership to the Slovak Republic in the Schengen *acquis*, before joining other areas of the EU.

On the other hand, Schengen has been designed to enhance security and stability for member countries. To be sure, Hungary's joining of the Schengen *acquis* would generate additional security for all members of the group, including Hungary. However, the new external borders of the Union, all represented by Schengen countries, may create a temporary or lasting division between the enlarged EU and its neighbouring non-members. As a consequence, it may generate additional conflicts and instability. Thus, a careful analysis is needed to assess security gains against potential security losses and to develop a system that promises the highest net gain for the stability of the whole continent. Depending on the future of the European political and security situation, this area may be one of the few fields, where the new countries, including Hungary, may be in a position to enrich (modify) the present *acquis*. Once again, it has to be emphasised that the starting point of such an approach is the future of European stability and not any consideration regarding Hungarian minorities in the neighbouring countries. It is another issue, whether, and if yes, how, the Hungarian minorities may or may not be a beneficiary of such a development.

Urgent domestic tasks

Both Commission country reports of July 1997 and November 1998 have indicated that Hungary is among the best-prepared countries or even the most-prepared country for future membership. This statement provides a favourable starting (and interim) position for Hungary in the process of official negotiations on accession. Also, the Commission and Hungary share the common view that applicant countries and their readiness for membership have to be assessed on a country-by-country basis, according to the merits and deficiencies of each candidate.

In the coming period, it is not unlikely that, due to the increasingly obvious differentiation in national adjustment capacities (and the different impact of internal pressure groups), the 5+1 group currently negotiating for accession, will be further classified into at least two groups. Provided it happens, it is Hungary's overriding interest to remain in the front of the first group.

This would, however, require a much more pronounced and unambiguous

Hungarian integration strategy. In fact, at this moment, the image of Hungary seems to benefit from three developments. First, the fully-fledged results of a painful austerity policy have become manifest, although with some delay. Second, the indisputable priority given to European integration by the previous government (between 1994 and 1998) still holds preparations on steam. Third, as a result of the increasing problems arising in other applicant countries, the distance between Hungary and other first-wave candidates is growing.

This partly real, partly deceptive, picture must not, however, divert attention from the urgent tasks ahead of the country. As Hungary enters into the 'hard core' of negotiations, more comprehensive communication is needed at home. While the preparatory stage for starting negotiations was a predominantly diplomatic and legal task, an all-embracing dialogue with different groups of the society is on the agenda of the present stage of negotiations. According to the experience of countries that previously joined the EU, the successful 'mix' of external and domestic work is about ten to ninety. In other words, even the best-prepared official negotiations at the highest professional level are unable to replace the obligatory homework for a relatively smooth adjustment to the EU. The relevance of this task is emphasised by the fact that the costs and benefits of accession do not appear at the same time with the same strength. Costs usually become manifest in the preparatory stage (and later, during the first years of accession), while benefits need more time to be perceived by larger business and social groups and by the general public.

Without reviewing the full range of domestic tasks, four elements have to be priority issues for the government. In all areas, most of the activities still have to be started. In some cases, even much 'mental' preparation has to be carried out.

First, a clear selection mechanism for qualifying different derogation requests has to be put in place. It is only natural that different interest groups formulate, and try to include, their special desires into the Government's package of possible derogations. However, if the government lacks clear selection criteria, all or almost all derogation needs may be put on the agenda for negotiations, with extremely harmful consequences for the time and the conditions of accession. In general, the more derogation requests are presented, the longer negotiations may last and the stronger the concerns of the Commission and of the member countries may be about the EU-maturity of the given country (or sector). In addition, a higher number of derogation requests may induce the EU (and the member countries) to ask for similar derogations that may hurt Hungarian business and development interests more than its own derogations may protect them. Moreover, it is evident that a number of derogation needs will not be acknowledged by the EU. In some cases they are against some of the basic community-level achievements, the hard core of the *acquis*, where even temporary exceptions are unlikely (for instance in the fields of commercial policy, competition policy, state subsidies, single market, most probably also Schengen; in general, the first pillar legislation). In other instances they have been defined in order to avoid or postpone painful adjustment processes that result from growing global competition and from the logic of socio-economic transformation. In other words, they have to be faced with or without accession.[10] The overriding government approach should be that no derogation is worth of delaying accession. Any delay would result in tangible economic, financial and, under certain circumstances, also security, losses, the extent of which would be several times greater than the most serious potential damage any forceful and premature adjustment may generate. Therefore, the government has to introduce economic and social policies to mitigate the potential damage in all those areas in which derogation requirements have to be abandoned. Moreover, companies in need of costly adjustment should be helped to create longer-term restructuring plans to be financed (partly) through the pre-accession resources and later from structural funds.

Second, a restructuring of the central budget towards EU priorities is urgently needed. This includes a clear preference for sectors and activities that have to be adjusted to EU requirements. It must also comprise investments and modernisation support for all areas that should remain or may become competitive once Hungary joins the EU. In turn, activities, mainly in non-competitive agriculture, that are sentenced to death with or without membership, should not be given economic support (some social support may be provided, which, however, is a completely different category). Most importantly, the central budget must create the necessary co-financial capacity in order to make use of the EU funds to which Hungary will be entitled. By prolonging the previous distribution pattern of the annual budget and by not defying deeply-rooted (and, in many cases, ideology-based) vested interests centred around different ministries and other authorities, it will hardly be possible to ensure the sufficient co-financing capacity of the Hungarian economy. To create this capacity, one does not need to 'print new money', but one needs to use the available resources much more efficiently. Financial resources assigned to different ministries should unambiguously support accession to the EU and not the preservation of outdated structures.

Third, and in the context of the above-mentioned reform of the central budget, the co-operative behaviour among different ministries, sectoral decision-making bodies and government agencies has to be strengthened considerably. To some extent, this task is one of changing mentality and of education. Partly, however, this can be achieved through new patterns of having access to money. If EU-related budgetary resources have to be applied for by different ministries, they will have to learn how to work together, instead of blocking eachother's efforts. Since most of the activities that can be financed from the pre-accession fund (and, later on, from the structural fund) require the co-operation of authorities in different

---

10. Similar behaviour can be observed in the EU as well. Fears for an 'eastern' enlargement are, in many cases, overlapped by global or domestic challenges and are erroneously attributed to the coming enlargement (competition of goods and some services, most of the concerns connected with labour market strains, *etc.*).

sectors and levels, a central budget that generates more co-operative attitudes would be a most welcome instrument to increase the EU conformity of the Hungarian actors.

Fourth, Hungary has to do everything it can in order to keep the enlargement process open. This behaviour must not be limited to the period of negotiations.[11] The most important reason for an unchanged attitude after accession is not the 'special relationship' between Hungary as an EU-country and the Hungarian minorities living outside the EU. The government has to be fully aware not only of the historic opportunities presented by accession to the EU, but, to the same extent, of its historic responsibilities for the whole region of Central and Eastern Europe in general, and the non-EU neighbouring countries, in particular. Only if regional stability can be sustained and strengthened and promising business opportunities can be exploited will normal relations with the minorities be guaranteed. Any other sequence starting with the 'solution' of minority problems would only undermine regional stability. Increasing regional instability will also worsen minority problems, let alone divert the attention of international business from the region.

10.5 Political support, public opinion

Recently, Hungary's international standing has been upgraded substantially. Although this achievement is based on many years of consequent work by more than one government (and its opposition), the 'hard-core' evidence is manifested in membership in NATO and Hungary's role in the war against Serbia. As a result, in the post-Kosovo regional setting, Hungary's role as a regional stability and security anchor has been widely recognized. This is a good starting point to achieve the second main goal of Euro-Atlantic integration, namely membership of the EU.

During the whole of the last decade, Hungary's political elite, whether a factor in government or sitting in the banks of opposition, has been characterised by a unanimous support for accession to the EU. Although a different emphasis on some relevant issues concerning the preparation for joining the EU can be identified across the main political parties, there is no disagreement on the necessity and desirability of accession.[12]

Until now, public opinion has also indicated a fundamentally positive view on accession. This was partly due to the justified hopes for higher growth, more job opportunities, higher living standards and an accelerated catching up process

---

11. In this respect, Hungary must avoid the obvious mistake Austria made after becoming a member of the EU. While during the negotiations, 'eastern' contacts of Austria were sold in Brussels as a major Austrian asset, once the country became member, it converted itself into one of the most hesitant supporters of further enlargement.

12. Several experts made the observation that the present government seems a bit less enthusiastic about quick accession. Moreover, while the previous government had quick accession as a priority, the present one may have different (and not necessarily mutually supporting) priorities at the same time.

based on having access to the financial resources of the EU (mainly in overall socio-economic modernisation, regional development, support to depressed economic areas, *etc.*). On the other hand, it was not possible to prepare a credible cost-benefit survey with clear quantitative consequences for potential winners and losers in the process of Hungary's accession. Similar to other countries which joined the EU earlier, the higher educated, more mobile, foreign language-speaking and younger people with international contacts were identified as the most important winners, while the unskilled, less mobile, rural, elderly population, without international experience and knowledge of foreign language(s) were classified as potential losers. A more differentiated picture is expected to emerge as a result of more concrete impacts of preparing for membership and of the coming additional adjustment burdens deriving from the outcome of negotiations on accession. Even so, a considerable part of the society will only experience impacts of membership with a substantial delay. As has been shown in Sweden, Finland and Austria, those linked to the domestic, or even more to the local market and activities, or working in the non-tradeable sector, are much less directly influenced by the consequences of membership.

Obvious winners hardly need any convincing arguments from the government, while obvious losers can hardly be convinced of the benefits of accession. In the latter case, only those arguments which demonstrate that losers would be even greater losers without accession, and that the next generation of the current losers may already become a beneficiary of Hungary's new status in Europe will carry much weight. Much more attention has to be given to some other and more problematic issues.

First, most of the business community has to be supportive of accession. This, however, needs a constant dialogue (and not a one-sided, ad hoc information campaign by the government). If the business world observes that its interests have not been defended by the Hungarian negotiators, whatever the reasons for such a development may be, it may easily become hostile to accession. While it is obvious that a large number of short-term business interests will have to be sacrificed, the perception may be different if this happens in a constant dialogue with the business people involved and with a common search for alternative ways of preserving old or shaping new interests. If the government just ignores the business partners, the rather modest negotiating position of Hungary may be weakened, since the other side does not have to consider at least part of the relevant domestic pressure the Hungarian negotiating team has to face.

Second, in its communication policy, the government has to avoid creating any kind of illusions or easy promises that cannot be fulfilled immediately or even some time after accession. In this context primarily, the overheated expectations of some less developed regions have to be moderated. Even if depressed regions should receive a sizeable amount of EU support, it is certainly not guaranteed that they would be able to absorb it better than more developed areas. Moreover, even if efficient absorption of external resources can be granted, favourable economic and social consequences will only be felt after a certain time lag. Additionally, better performance depends on a number of other factors (level of education, cooperation capability of local authorities, professional mobility, development of neighbouring regions, *etc.*).

Third, with accession to the EU, both its problematic areas and beneficial aspects should remain isolated from political populism and demagogy. First of all, it is the task of the government and of the mass media to influence outdated views and to educate those who would like to reap the fruits of membership but at the same time insist on non-EU-conforming activities and solutions. In this respect, part of the agricultural population, mostly located in the less developed eastern and southern part of the country, has to be 'enlightened'. This, however seems to be not only a professional but also a political task, since the backbone of support for the smaller coalition partner can be found in these regions.

Fourth, it will hardly be possible to avoid the reproduction of double losers. Those who proved to be the losers of the transformation process (unskilled or semi-skilled workers, employees with no prospect of finding another job, rural areas, *etc.*) have an above-average inclination to become the losers in the accession to the EU as well. The more the emergence of a double-loser-status can be prevented, the better the prospects are for not only support for accession but also for making use of the potential benefits of membership.

Finally, it has to be stressed that with the advance of negotiations, the Parliament's competence to control the negotiating team has to be extended. Democratic control over the activities of the negotiators was one key issue of preparation for membership in Austria, Finland and Sweden. The aim is not only to prevent the negotiators of a small country from getting too much (temporarily) power and misuse it in certain cases. More importantly, all political parties and the general public have to be convinced that Hungary's process of joining the EU is developing in a democratic way. The interested public has every right to know what is at stake in Brussels, and what can or cannot be achieved. To deprive the general public of this experience would be extremely harmful and counterproductive, not only during the first years of membership but also in the overall process of democratisation.

References

Inotai, A. (1998), *The Main Features and Current Trends in the European Union's Trade Relations with Hungary and the Ten Associated Countries 1989-1997*, Institute for World Economics of the Hungarian Academy of Sciences and National Committee for Technological Development, Budapest.

Inotai, A. (1999), *Hungary's export performance to Germany in regional, European and global comparison*, Institute for World Economics and National Board of Technological Development, Budapest (forthcoming).

Part III

Russia and Ukraine

Russia: A Lost Decade?

Daniel Gros

"The economic system of Russia has undergone such rapid changes that it is impossible to obtain a precise and accurate account of it.... Almost everything one can say about the country is true and false at the same time.
[...] If one is to make any generalisation in present conditions, it must be this – that at a low level of efficiency the system does function and possesses elements of permanence".

J.M. Keynes (1925)

11.1 Introduction

The verdict on 'ten years of transition' in Russia seems clear: a lost decade.[1] A comparison with Poland is instructive. At the end of the 1980s, Poland was in such a deep crisis that widespread famine was feared and many in the West had given up hope. By contrast the Soviet Union, while also visibly under strains, was still functioning and had a very strong natural resources base. Ten years later the perspective is completely different: Poland is growing vigorously, whereas the Soviet Union is only a distant memory and after a currency crisis in 1998 the economy of Russia almost collapsed under the weight of its foreign debt. The comparison with Poland illustrates the difference a decade can make in terms of real income. If one sets the GDP of Poland and Russia for 1988 at 100, Poland will have reached almost 120 by the end of the millennium. A cumulative increase of 20% over ten years might not look like much, but it is quite an achievement compared with Russia, which recorded a fall in income of almost 50%. This means that the Polish reform delivered more than double the real income in the space of a decade.

How did Russia get in such a mess? At the outset the position of the Soviet Union, and in particular that of the Russian republic, looked much stronger as it had vast resources of oil, gas and other minerals and could count on a very large

---

1. The term *'decada perdida'* was applied in Latin America to the 1980s, but the worst performance there was that of Argentina with a fall in GDP *per capita* of 'only' 20% between 1980 and 1990.

military/industrial complex. The fundamental answer must be that the similarity in the official reform rhetoric over the last ten years masked a quite different reality.

Evaluating Russia is not straightforward. The dictum put forward by Keynes continues to be valid today. Over the last ten years, judgements on the effectiveness of the Russian reforms by international institutions, academics and the press ranged across the entire spectrum from very optimistic to extremely pessimistic. The best example of Russia-'mania' is probably Layard and Parker (1996) with the title: "The coming Russian Boom". The boom had a rather short life, but predictions of descent into hyper-inflationary chaos and disintegration proved equally off the mark. It is thus not easy to provide an overall judgement of the reforms in Russia as already anticipated by Keynes 70 years ago. Hence, this Chapter does not pretend to provide a comprehensive overview of developments in Russia over the last decade. Instead, it concentrates on the most salient features of the reform process in Russia, often comparing them to what happened in Central Europe in order to find some general features that can help in understanding how the Russian economy works in general and hence where it will be going in the future.

After describing the developments that led to the reform process in 1992, Section 11.3 analyses the circumstances of the 'big bang' price liberalisation of January 1992. The main conclusion here is that the very large size of the jump in prices, which was politically costly for the reformers, could have been anticipated. Moreover, the benefits of price liberalisation were not apparent as quickly as in other reforming economies because local and regional price controls persisted for some time and there was no immediate reaction from the supply side because of the desolate state of the agricultural sector.

External liberalisation, discussed in Section 11.4, was another area where it should have been possible to achieve results quickly. A closer look shows, however, that substantial distortions remained, at least until the end of 1993. Their budgetary effects contributed, perhaps decisively, to the delay of stabilisation for a number of years as discussed in Section 11.5.

Stabilisation was finally achieved, but it was built on weak foundations. The speculative attack of August 1998 proved so damaging because the huge capital flight had left the government with a foreign debt it could not service unless it received fresh capital continuously.

The common thread that emerges from this analysis is the large discrepancy between appearances and reality. Official programmes also often seem to have little to do with the actions of the Russian government. Combined with the virtual absence of market institutions and enforcement mechanisms for private sector contracts, one can begin to see why the reform process has had only partial success so far.

Before presenting its conclusions, the chapter touches briefly on the unavoidable question of 'who lost Russia?'. If the real question is why stabilisation was not achieved in 1992-93 despite large official aid flows, the answer has two parts:

Russia is to blame because given the massive subsidies on imports, most of the aid that was actually delivered, namely trade credits, actually had a negative impact. Thus more of that sort of aid would have made matters worse. However, even given the (wrong) policies pursued by Russia, the right sort of aid, namely direct subsidies on the budget, could have increased the chances of achieving stabilisation. It takes two to tango (meaning, in this case, to produce a failure): more aid for the reformers would have been desirable, but if the reformers had been smarter in using the aid that was available, they could have achieved stabilisation at a much earlier date.

The reader should be warned from the outset that any accurate analysis of the Russian economy is made extremely difficult by the absence of reliable statistical data. Prices (foreign exchange rates, commodity prices, *etc.*) can be measured without great difficulties and are regularly recorded in the Russian business press. However, serious problems arise in the case of variables that require calculations and adjustments or are based on data from many different sources. The problems are most severe on the external side. The estimates for Russian imports based on customs data and those based on national accounts differ by as much as 50%. The corresponding estimates of the trade surplus for example, in 1996, were therefore also very different: 38 billion *versus* 17 billion dollars.

11.2 Setting the stage

11.2.1 Preliminaries

This section provides a brief description of the political developments that led to the late start of the reform process in 1992. It is not widely appreciated that the partial reforms initiated before 1992 were important because they set the stage for what happened later.

The Russian state in its present form is young, since it emerged only in December of 1991 from the ruins of the Soviet Union. The beginning of the reforms in January 1992 thus coincided with the creation of a new state. The main reason that fundamental reforms started so late was that Mikhail Gorbachev persisted in his belief that socialism was superior to capitalism. As long as Gorbachev was the head of the Soviet Union (as First Party Secretary of the CPSU and later as President of the Soviet Union), no real reforms were possible.

The movement towards reforms acquired momentum only when Boris Yeltsin, then President of the RSFSR (Russian Soviet Federated Socialist Republic), acquired more effective power than the Union government under Gorbachev by standing up publicly to the attempted putsch in August of 1991. Immediately after the failed putsch, it still seemed that it would be possible to keep the Soviet Union together at least as an economic and monetary union. That would have implied that reforms would have to take place at the Union level. In the last three months of 1991, however, the Union government rapidly lost most of its influence and the republics became the only real power centres. Moreover, most republics were not willing to contemplate radical reforms, whereas the leadership of the Russian republic, which had inherited most of the reformist elements of the Union government, was determined to act as quickly as possible. Nevertheless, the Russian government did not really have the legal and political means to proceed on its own as long as the Soviet Union continued to exist. The creation of the Commonwealth of Independent States (CIS) and the dissolution of the Soviet Union in December of 1991 finally gave Russia the possibility to start real reforms.

When the Gaidar government came to power in Russia at the end of 1991, it proposed to implement a package of radical reform and stabilisation measures. The intention then was certainly to effect a 'big bang' in Russia, even if these words might not have been used. Two years later, the leading reformers (Deputy Prime Minister Yegor Gaidar and Finance Minister Boris Fyodorov) left the government and explained to the Western press that Russia's problem was not that it had undergone shock therapy, but that, on the contrary, there had been no shock at all (and by implication, no therapy). What went wrong? Before addressing this question it is useful to take into account the background of numerous reform plans developed while the Soviet Union was decaying.

11.2.2 Background: failed reform plans in the last years of the Soviet Union

January 1992 certainly opened with a 'big bang' in the form of 300% price rises in the first days of that month. This indicated that a very serious imbalance had been accumulated during the previous regime. In order to understand why it had come to that point, it is useful to consider briefly the last years of the Soviet period.

The 'big bang' that was supposed to take place in Russia in January 1992 came after a long period during which a number of competing reform plans had been discussed, but nothing much had been done. Indeed, reform projects enjoyed a long tradition in the Soviet economy. The system of central planning never worked satisfactorily, even to the standards of its creators, and was therefore overhauled from time to time – since World War II, in 1957, 1965, and 1975. On top of that, the currency was changed in 1947 and 1961. None of these reforms, however, was supposed to change the nature of the system. Similarly, the various partial (and mini-) reforms attempted between 1985 and 1989 were also directed at increasing the efficiency of the existing system of central planning.

The partial and piecemeal reforms implemented up to 1989 undermined the central planning system. This led to a deterioration in the economic situation, because the plan could no longer be fully enforced and most of the non-state economic activities thrived on the distorted pricing system still in use. The 1987 law that gave enterprises a modest degree of financial autonomy can be viewed as the end of the strict planning period, because enterprises could now evade constraints imposed from the 'centre' by initiating their own operations. This law loosened financial discipline and was thus the beginning of a considerable acceleration in the growth of the monetary overhang as documented in Section 11.3 below. But this law also increased the incentive to export to the West, which initiated a shift in the export structure of the former Soviet Union (FSU) that predates the collapse of the CMEA. Section 11.4 below shows that the shift in exports towards Western markets was already well advanced by 1991, so that the partial trade liberalisation of 1992 did not have a strong effect on trade patterns.

The general weakening of central control led, in 1989-90, to the widespread admission that the entire system of central planning had to be abandoned. During the summer of 1990, three competing comprehensive reform plans for the transition to a market economy were presented to the Supreme Soviet of the Union, which was to adopt the necessary legislation. The Supreme Soviet, however, refused to approve any of the three plans. Instead, it gave President Gorbachev broad emergency powers and authorised him to present a plan of his own. The compromise plan presented by the president, called "Basic Guidelines for the Stabilisation of the National Economy and the Transition to a Market Economy", was then approved by a large majority on 19 October 1990.

The president's guidelines, which were more general and political than the other three plans, became the official programme of the Union government, but their implementation was checked by the constitutional crisis that developed between the Union and the republics.[2] The economic situation continued to deteriorate. Prices had to be increased and a clumsy attempt by the Ryzhkov government in April of 1991 to confiscate large denomination notes was a complete failure. In May 1991, the Union government again presented a vague outline of a reform plan, concentrating on macroeconomic stabilisation.

The four major plans that dominated the discussion in 1990-91 all agreed on three final goals: a market economy, stabilisation, and the preservation of the Soviet Union as a unified economic space. Furthermore, all of these plans contained most of the necessary elements outlined in Section 11.3.[3]

None of these programmes could be implemented, however, as long as President Gorbachev did not really believe in a market economy. Moreover, even timid reform measures were impossible as long as there persisted the 'war of laws', under which each republic passed a declaration of sovereignty stating that its laws would take precedence over Union law, whereas the Union government insisted that Union law would take precedence. The implementation of reforms would

---

2. A law establishing a two-tier banking system and an independent central bank was approved on 1 November 1990, and survived the subsequent upheavals not only in Russia, but also in most other former Soviet republics.

3. For a comparison of various reform plans, see Commission of the European Communities (1992). There were important differences between the reform plans in the emphasis given to these goals and the speed with which they were to be attained. In general, the government programmes put more emphasis on macroeconomic stabilisation than on liberalisation, and they insisted, for obvious reasons, on more powers for the Union.

have required an agreement (in effect, a new Union treaty) that defined the powers of the republics and the Union. Such an agreement was reached in May of 1991, but the aborted coup of August of that year set in motion a chain of events that led to the dissolution of the Soviet Union.

Towards the end of 1991, it became clear that the central government would not be able to implement reforms. The Russian President Yeltsin then created a government with a group of economists, led by Yegor Gaidar, that was charged with the elaboration and implementation of a comprehensive reform plan. Since this new team was installed only late in 1991, and since the political environment was changing quickly, it is not surprising that the plan was elaborated in detail only in early 1992, *i.e.* after its key element, namely price liberalisation, had already been implemented. However, given that the deterioration of the economy accelerated with the overall breakdown of authority, the Russian government did not really have a choice.

11.3 Price liberalisation with a 'Big Bang'

11.3.1 The first disappointment

The liberalisation of prices that occurred in early 1992 was thus inevitable, given the accelerating loss of control on the part of the government, rather than a deliberate choice that could have been avoided. The most outstanding feature of price liberalisation in Russia is the size of the jump in price levels that occurred almost instantaneously. At the end of January 1992, the consumer price level was almost three times higher than at the end of December 1991 (an increase of 280%). Industrial producer prices increased by 100 percentage points over and above this level. However, even if one is only concerned with consumer prices, the Russian experience is extreme when compared with that of other reforming economies.

It is difficult to decide whether the entire impact of price reform should come within the first month or whether it takes longer for the monetary overhang to be eliminated. Table 11.1 shows what happened during the first month and the first quarter after price reform or price liberalisation. The table shows the percentage increase in both prices and money (cash in circulation) to segregate the impact of price reform from that of an expansionary monetary policy which might also have had an influence on prices. It is apparent that for the first month, the increase in money is so small compared with that of the price level that one can neglect its impact. However, after one quarter, the potential influence of monetary policy, while still small in most cases, can no longer be neglected.

The table presents data for three distinct periods in Poland, two of which were a combination of partial price liberalisation and administrative price increases under the last Communist government. These episodes represent a key to understanding what happened in Russia, as argued below. Thus the data show clearly

Table 11.1: The impact of price liberalisation

Country/(month of price reform)	Percentage increase in the PPI after price reform during the first:	
	Month	Quarter
FSU (4/91)	52 (7.3)	71 (21.7)
Russia (1/92)	296 (13.6)	518 (42.9)
Poland (8/89)	40	n.a.
Poland (10/89)	55 (18.3)	124 (63.4)
Poland (1/90)	80 (12.4)	115 (91.5)
Czechoslovakia (1/91)	26	41
Bulgaria (1/91)	123	n.a.

Note: The figures inside the parentheses represent the percentage increase in money over the same period, where money is defined as cash in circulation (where data were available).

Source: Koen and Philips (1993) and IMF, *International Financial Statistics*, various issues

that Russia had by far the highest price jump among the group of four economies undergoing rapid price liberalisation. The second highest increase was about 120% in Bulgaria. By contrast, in Poland it was 'only' 80% during the first month of final price liberalisation in January of 1990, which is usually considered to be the Polish 'big bang'. If one considers the first quarter following price liberalisation, the difference is even larger: in Russia, prices increased by 518%, almost five times as much as in Poland where the increase during the first three months of 1990 was 115%.

The extent of the price increase in Russia surprised the government (and most observers), although by the end of 1991, the ratio of free to controlled prices had reached multiples in the order of four to five (Koen and Phillips, 1993). For example, the IMF had calculated before the reforms took place that a jump in the price level of around 50% would be sufficient to eliminate the monetary overhang (see IMF, 1991 and Cottarelli and Blejer, 1992).

Gros and Steinherr (1995) argue that, with a better analysis of the historical data on money supplies and a closer examination of the Polish experience, the size of the jump in prices could have been anticipated to a large extent. The basic argument is that in Russia price liberalisation just allowed the rate of circulation of cash to return to the value it had in the 1960s, *i.e.* before the accumulation of the monetary overhang. The head-line jump in prices on 1 January 1990 in Poland that is commonly associated with the start of reforms there was much smaller, but it was not sufficiently appreciated that a large part of the monetary overhang had already been eliminated in Poland under the Communist regime during 1989. In Poland the total increase in prices over the five-month period that started with the partial price liberalisation in August 1989, and ended just before the final price liberalisation in January of 1990, was 400%, whereas the increase in the money supply during the same period was 123%; the amount of real money had thus already been halved. By contrast, the price increase of about 120% in the FSU between April and December 1991, before the price liberalisation of 1992, did not really dent the monetary overhang since the money supply had increased by about the same amount (110%) (Gros and Steinherr, 1995).

The *Solidarnosc* government in Poland thus inherited a much better starting position than the Gaidar team in Russia, because a large part of the monetary overhang had already been eliminated.[4] This explains why the price increase in January 1990 turned out to be 'moderate' in Poland, at least in comparison with Russia.

The much larger than expected price increase in Russia was not just an embarrassment for economists; it also constituted a severe setback for all the other reform measures that were planned for 1992. The extreme and sudden increase in prices gave a lot of ammunition to the conservative opponents of Yeltsin who came to dominate the Russian parliament which then effectively blocked many reforms until the crisis of September-October 1993.[5]

11.3.2 The political economy of price liberalisation in Russia

The perceived fall in living standards that came with price liberalisation became a major argument against further reforms. Part of the popular discontent with the reformers was undoubtedly due to the fact that as consumer prices rose almost threefold in January of 1992, measured real wages were cut to about one-third of their (measured) end of 1991 level. The anti-reformist camp obviously seized this apparent fall in real wages as the best proof that the reforms were 'misguided' or 'hasty'. In other countries, notably Poland, similar arguments had also been used, but the size of the price increase in Russia meant that, given that wages did not rise along with prices in January of 1992, *measured* real wages also fell by much more in Russia than in other reforming economies.

Measured real wages fell in Russia to about one-third of their previous level (*i.e.* comparing December 1991 with January 1992), more than in Poland where measured real wages fell to about one-half and in Czechoslovakia where they fell by only about 20%. However, it is by now generally accepted that these reductions in real wages were mostly a statistical artefact since in the last years, sometimes months, of the socialist system workers obtained large increases in nominal wages with which they were not able to buy anything more since production was

---

4. A prominent expert on Eastern European economies is widely quoted as saying that "the best thing the Communist government could do for Poland was to increase prices and then resign".

5. The new parliament that was elected in December 1993 after the violent confrontation between the old Supreme Soviet and President Yeltsin, however, was not much different; this was the main reason why most of the reformers (especially Gaidar and the finance minister Fyodorov) preferred to leave government in early 1994.

already declining. This had been particularly pronounced during the last days of the Soviet Union.

It is thus clear that one cannot compare wages deflated by the price level immediately before and after price reforms. A more appropriate comparison would use a base year in which shortages were minimal. Koen and Phillips (1993) argue that 1987 represents a good base year. If one thus compares real wages in 1992 with their level in 1987 the result is quite different. In Russia, real wages stabilised after an initial strong dip at about 20% below the measured 1987 level. Most of the huge cuts in measured real wages that one finds by looking at the first months thus disappear if one uses a more appropriate base period.

The drop in real wages in Russia, using 1987 as the base period, was similar to the one that occurred in the Central European countries. However, this should be viewed as an anomaly because in principle one could have expected a stronger recovery of real wages in Russia than in other transforming countries. This is because, with the dissolution of CMEA, the price of energy deliveries to Central Europe went to the world market level and, with the dissolution of the Soviet Union, Russia no longer had to subsidise the other republics with cheap energy and raw materials. The latter did not happen immediately, but a process started in 1992 and by the end of 1993 most former Soviet republics were charged world market prices for energy deliveries (although most 'paid' only in arrears). Russia thus reaped a considerable gain in terms of trade. By contrast, the Central European countries had to accept a loss in terms of trade. Hence, real wages should have been able to increase during 1992 and 1993 in Russia. However, if anything, they have declined even further, along with the decline in production.

In Russia price liberalisation, while inevitable given the lack of effective government control over the economy, could not become popular given the continuing fall in production. The immediate gains from price liberalisation can only be small, as this act per se does not increase the size of the overall cake to be distributed – only its distribution. In Poland a flexible agricultural sector immediately increased the supply of food, but this was not possible in the unreformed Soviet type agriculture of Russia. Moreover, Polish enterprises quickly switched production to new products and markets (in the West). This quick change was the result of external competition, since privatisation took much longer to implement. The Russian reformers were, of course, aware of the need for external liberalisation, which was part of their platform. However, the next section will show that in this area reality was quite different from perception and serious errors were made.

It is sometimes argued that external liberalisation should be less important for such a large country as Russia. However, the Russian economy is as open to trade as the Polish economy. The ratio of trade (average of exports and imports) to GDP is around 25% for both economies (in Russia it varies much more with the exchange rate for the rouble).

11.4 External liberalisation

11.4.1 Liberalisation of international trade

Full external liberalisation can in principle be achieved by a stroke of a pen. However, this was not the case in Russia in 1992. In most evaluations of the Russian reforms, it is stressed that imports were almost completely liberalised, in the sense that in January 1992 quantitative restrictions were abolished and only in July was a flat import tariff of 5% levied. The problem with the policy on imports was not trade barriers, but in a sense the opposite, namely the huge budgetary subsidies given to state trading organisations that paid only a fraction of the world market price for their imports. During 1992, these subsidies amounted to over 10% of GDP. As shown (see Gros and Steinherr, 1995), the distortions caused by these subsidies led to welfare losses of possibly up to 10% of GDP. Fortunately, these import subsidies had already been reduced considerably in the course of 1992 and completely phased out in 1993 (Konovalov, 1994).

However, even more serious problems arose on the export side as the initially very liberal stance on imports contrasted starkly with the regime that was retained for exports of raw materials and energy and which had to be controlled because domestic prices of these goods had not been liberalised. The government evidently feared that most of the large industrial enterprises would go bankrupt if they had to pay world market prices for energy and other raw material inputs. The reasons for this decision are not important for this section. What matters is that these products accounted for about 75% of all Russian exports. In view of the 'Lerner symmetry theorem' (Lerner, 1936), which states simply that an export tariff is equivalent to an import tariff) one cannot speak of trade liberalisation if most exports are subject to restrictions.

The maintenance of restrictions on the export side was necessitated by the price controls on energy (and other raw materials) that continued in 1992 and 1993. (See Annex 11.1 on the importance of raw materials for the Russian economy.) Although the official prices of oil, gas and electricity were increased from time to time, their dollar equivalent did not always come closer to the world market price. The ratio of domestic prices to world prices was thus highly variable for these goods, but the domestic price was typically only a fraction of the world market price as shown in Gros and Steinherr (1995).

It is difficult to find the precise reason for the price difference for each product as only in some instances were there explicit export taxes and/or export quotas that could account for it. Instead of going through the official records of export regulations, one can simply use the proportional price differential as a crude approximation of the (*ad valorem*) export tariff that would have been equivalent to the export restrictions that were actually applied. This approximation is not exact since it neglects transport costs and exchange rate fluctuations that make it difficult to determine the exact world price to compare with the price quoted on the Russian commodity exchanges. However, the orders of magnitude that this exercise yields are revealing.

Gros and Steinherr (1995) calculate that the implicit export tax on energy-related products must thus have exceeded 100% most of the time. Since energy alone accounted for 50% of overall exports and since for other raw materials (like aluminium, which accounted for another 25% of exports) a similar differential between domestic and world market prices existed, about 75% of all exports were thus implicitly taxed at this rate. In view of the equivalence between export and import tariffs mentioned above, one can only conclude that the liberalisation of Russian trade in 1992 was partial, at best.[6]

11.4.2 Fiscal consequences of porous borders

It proved impossible for the Russian government to enforce the official restrictions on raw material exports. The main reason was that initially Russia did not have a customs service along its borders with other former Soviet republics. The huge difference between the domestic Russian price and the world market price for oil and other raw materials meant that large gains could be made by transporting these commodities to other former republics and then re-exporting them for hard currency. On top of that, one has to add the notorious corruption of the Russian civil service, which was exposed to extraordinary temptations. The price difference on a simple shipment of 20,000 litres of fuel on a single truck would be worth 2,000 dollars, several times the annual salary of a Russian customs official.

How much in potential government revenue was lost? This is difficult to estimate precisely since the official tariffs changed over time. However, a crude calculation can indicate the order of magnitude: in 1992 Russia exported about 20 billion dollars worth of energy products and other raw materials. Given that the implicit export tariff was about 100%, as shown above, the Russian government should have been able to collect at least 10 billion dollars (50% of export sales at world market prices) in tariff revenues from these exports. At the average 1992 exchange rate of about 250 roubles to the dollar, the loss of revenue was thus equivalent to 2.5 trillion roubles. This should be compared with total government revenues of about 5.3 trillion roubles and an official deficit of 650 billion roubles (3.3% of revised GDP). The official 1992 budget deficit could thus easily have been covered from this source alone, which would have increased government revenues by 50%. This is, of course, a very crude calculation. Nevertheless, it serves to indicate the order of magnitude of the problem. Revenue losses of a similar, but somewhat smaller magnitude could be calculated for subsequent years as well.

---

6. It is also interesting to note that the domestic price of wheat (of which Russia is a net importer) stabilised at 54% of the world market price after the wheat market was liberalised at the end of 1993.

Who obtained the revenues the government lost? This is impossible to determine precisely; most went presumably to producers and agents in the energy trade. A significant part was also given away directly as the government granted many exemptions to particular regions or producers.

11.4.3 Export performance

'The proof of the pudding is in the eating.' The proof of a substantial liberalisation of foreign trade is the strong growth in exports and imports. On this account the picture is mixed, but compatible with the view that trade liberalisation came on later when (implicit and explicit) export restrictions were abolished. There are no reliable trade data for the years surrounding the break-up of the Soviet Union. Russian export statistics suggest that the exports of Russia were flat in 1992 and 1993, but jumped by almost 80% between 1993 and 1997. This delayed reaction is quite different from the Polish experience. Polish exports increased considerably already during the first year of reforms, as even state-owned enterprises were not blind to the profit opportunities that arose when wages were only about 100 dollars per month.[7] Since most of Russia's exports are raw materials whose supply does not react strongly to wages and the real exchange rate, one should perhaps look at exports of manufactured goods only. However, as documented in Gros and Steinherr (1995), exports of manufactured goods from Russia also did not react to the official trade liberalisation and the low dollar wages.

It is often argued that a major achievement of the liberalisation of foreign trade was a re-direction of trade away from the 'bad' trade with the socialist economies and LDCs that did not pay for their imports of Soviet weaponry, towards 'good' trade with Western economies based on market principles. However, as documented in Gros and Steinherr (1995), this re-direction of trade had already started much earlier. This can also be seen from Figure 11.1, which shows the evolution of the share of the European developing countries and industrial countries[8] in the exports of the FSU (until 1991) and of Russia (after 1992). During the former period, the first group of countries corresponds roughly to the CMEA, whereas the second group of countries corresponds roughly to the market economies.

It is apparent that between 1986 (when the law on the partial financial liberalisation of enterprises mentioned above began to take effect) and 1991, the share of CMEA fell by one-half, from about 40 to 20% of overall exports. During the same period, the share of market economies approximately doubled, from about 30 to 60%. By 1991, the adjustment was thus complete. In a sense this should

---

7. The export boom went hand in hand with a boom of imports from the industrialised countries. As foreign financing became more widely available, imports increased more than exports and most Central European countries developed a trade deficit. But this development has nothing to do with the overall expansion of trade generated by trade liberalisation.
8. Both in the IMF *Direction of Trade Statistics* definition.

Figure 11.1: Geographical distribution of Russian/FSU exports and imports
(Percentages)

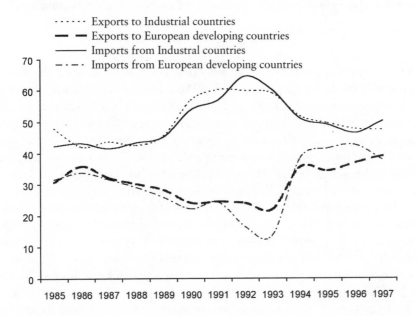

Source: IMF, *Direction of Trade Statistics.*

not be surprising, since the CMEA had ceased to exist by then. However, subsequent developments are more surprising. After 1992 the share of 'developing European countries' began to increase again. This group became more heterogeneous as the Central European countries became market economies, whereas some other CIS countries could not really be classified in this way. Some pick-up of trade with Central Europe might have been justified by market forces as these economies grew rapidly after 1993, but it is difficult to understand why the share of industrialised countries in Russian exports fell so strongly, from almost 60% to less than 50%.

In the Polish case, the share of industrial countries in exports (and imports) jumped after the reforms and continued to increase to above 70%. In the case of Russia, one could argue that the existing pipeline system limits the degree to which exports can be re-directed by market forces to new destinations, but for Russia the shares of the two country groupings in imports show a very similar time profile as exports. A more thorough analysis on the basis of the gravity model, which takes into account market size and distance (see Chapter 4) presented in Brenton (1999), comes to a similar result: the geographical distribution of Russian exports does not correspond to the pattern one would expect if Russia were a fully fledged market economy. For example, the share of the EU in Russian exports should be 42%, but is only 33%, conversely the share of other CIS countries (and rather soft markets, with which a lot of trade is still on the basis of barter) is still close to 20%, whereas one would expect that given the small size of these economies, its equilibrium share should only be about 6% when the transition is complete.

11.4.4 The foreign exchange market

More progress was made on the issue of convertibility, which can also be achieved by a stroke of the pen (as long as the exchange rate is not fixed), since all that the government has to do is to allow anyone to buy or sell foreign currency without restrictions. Full current account convertibility was not permitted immediately, but in July of 1992 the various exchange rates were unified and anyone with an import contract could then participate in the increasingly frequent auctions for foreign exchange. This implied that from July 1992 onwards, the rouble was convertible for current account transactions. Given the laxity of controls, one could even argue that *de facto* convertibility also extended to capital account transactions. A large degree of capital account convertibility was officially permitted when, in the summer of 1993, non-residents were allowed to open rouble accounts which they could also use for investment purposes.

Gros and Steinherr (1995) document that the foreign exchange market became quickly efficient in the technical sense by testing the so-called 'weak' form of market efficiency (which implies that information on past prices cannot be used to make more by predicting future prices). Formal tests of market efficiency indicate that the foreign exchange market in Russia was efficient almost from the start. Efficiency in this context means that the exchange rate did not follow any predictable pattern in general. This finding shows not only that financial markets adjusted quickly to the new environment. However, the crucial importance of *de facto* capital mobility became apparent only much later, namely during collapse of the rouble in the summer of 1998.

11.5 Macroeconomic instability

As documented above, the reforms in Russia began with an increase in the price level of more than 250% at the beginning of 1992. This was not the end of the story, however. Prices continued to increase at two-digit levels and the monthly average for the year, excluding January, was close to 20%; the average for 1993 was at a similar level. Average inflation fell below the one-digit level (always on a monthly basis) only in early 1994. Stabilisation thus took over two years, much longer than in Central Europe, where inflation never took off (see Figure 11.2 for the evolution of the inflation rate).

The ultimate cause of high inflation is almost always a large fiscal deficit that is financed by the central bank. Russia is no exception to this rule, but its fiscal accounts are in such a mess that it is impossible to document the underlying

Figure 11.2: Inflation and seigniorage in Russia

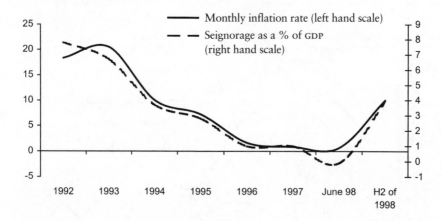

deficit.[9] Reported figures for the fiscal deficit during 1992 range from official Russian figures of 4.8% of GDP, to IMF estimates of 7% and private sector esti-mates of over 9%. All these estimates leave out the import subsidies of 15% of GDP that were discussed above. In the case of Russia, one can therefore use just two statistics: cash in circulation (or more comprehensively the monetary base, from the balance sheet of the Central Bank of Russia (CBR) and credits from the IMF. The first gives an indication of monetary financing (seigniorage), the second gives an indication of the amount of foreign aid that contributes to non-infla-tionary financing of the deficit.

Printing money obviously creates inflation. The very close link between infla-tion and seigniorage can be seen in Figure 11.2, which shows (scale on the right) also seigniorage (the increase in the monetary base) as a percentage of GDP. Seigniorage amounted to over ten percent of GDP during 1992, but fell to little above 1% during 1996 and 1997 and was actually slightly negative during the first half of 1998. During this latter period, the Russian government was thus able to finance its (continuing) deficit through non-inflationary means and this led to the reduction in inflation.

Where did the non-inflationary finance come from? At the start of the reforms it was expected that the West would support the reformers decisively. However, support for the budget of Russia through the IMF came rather late. Figure 11.3 shows the two sources of financing for the budget (IMF lending and increases in the monetary base) in terms of billions of dollars. It is apparent that during the first two years of the reforms, IMF lending was negligible (around 1 billion dol-lars) compared with monetary financing of over ten billion dollars. This changed only later, basically during 1995/96 when IMF lending rose to almost 3 billion dol-

---

9. For a thorough analysis of fiscal policy in Russia, see López-Claros and Alexashenko (1998).

lars per year. However, it remained always modest compared with the scale of monetary financing at the start of the transition, as can be seen from Figure 11.3.

Figure 11.3: Seigniorage and IMF support
(In billions of US dollars)

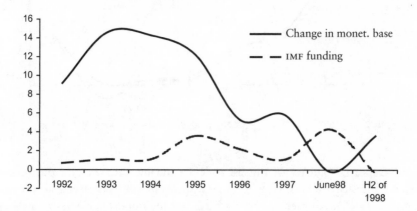

It was access to private capital that allowed the Russian government to finance its deficits through non-inflationary means on a grand scale. However, given the openness of the capital account this implied that Russia was exposed to sudden withdrawals of foreign capital, in other words, to speculative attacks.[10] Was the sudden collapse of stabilisation in 1998 just the result of a speculative attack? The literature on speculative attacks emphasises that under certain conditions highly indebted countries can fall into a low credibility trap. This occurs when a government is judged not to be credible by financial markets. It then has to pay a risk premium in terms of higher interest rates. The higher debt service burden that results, if inflation is kept low, makes it even more likely that the authorities will abandon the attempt to stabilise and will try to reduce the real value of the debt through a surprise inflation. Hence this further increases the risk premium demanded by financial markets, possibly leading to a spiral of increasing interest rates, until the government caves in.

However, the debt trap is not the only state of equilibrium. The same country could also end up with low interest rates if it can start a virtuous circle of high credibility and low interest rates. All that is needed to reach this state of equilibrium is that markets think *a priori* that the government will be tough on inflation. It will then pay lower interest rates and thus will have, at the same inflation rate, a lower debt service burden to carry. This in turn could validate the initial assump-

---

10. See Komulainen T. (1999) for a survey of the currency crisis theories and the application to the Russian case.

tion. Hence there could be two equilibria in financial markets and a mere shift in expectations leading to the bad equilibrium would have to be validated even by a hard-nosed government.

The experience of Russia provides a good illustration of both equilibria. After basic stabilisation was achieved, large capital inflows allowed the government to finance a continuing fiscal deficit at lower interest rates. At first, the real *ex post* interest was very high, but this did not matter much since the stock of debt was also minuscule. As low inflation persisted, nominal interest rates fell throughout 1996 and into early 1997. At interest rates of around 20% *per annum*, the Russian government was able to service its debt. This was the good equilibrium. In the meantime, the debt-to-GDP ratio kept increasing, and with the onset of the financial crisis in Asia capital flows to emerging markets in general fell dramatically. Investors could also see that the Russian government would not be able to service its debt at much higher interest rates (and still keep inflation under control). The CBR could not really tighten monetary policy, because increasing interest rates increase the fiscal deficit even further. This was the bad equilibrium. When foreign capital stopped coming in, the Russian government could not service its debt and could no longer support the exchange rate, which fell precipitously from about 6 to about 24 roubles per dollar.

The August 1998 financial crisis led to a new increase in inflation (for a brief period at above 100% at an annual rate) and thus threatened the hard-won stabilisation. However, Russia did not collapse; the lesson that hyperinflation has very high social and political costs had been learnt even by the new old leadership, including the president of the central bank of Russia, Mr. Gerashenko, who had presided over the inflationary early 1990s.[11]

11.6 Who lost Russia?

The evolution of the Russian economy is closely followed in the Western press, and, starting in 1992-93, the G-7 economic summits devoted a lot of their time to discuss how to help Russia. In 1999, Russia was even included in this club of the major economic powers. From all this one could gain the impression that the Russian economy is somehow important for the global economy. This would be completely wrong, however. That Russia is important for non-economic reasons may be obvious. However, it is not widely appreciated how small the Russian economy really is. Translated at market exchange rates, the Russian GDP oscillates around 250-350 billion dollars, depending on the exchange rate. This puts Russia only in the same league as Brazil.

---

11. See Gaidar (1999) and Havrylyshyn (1999) on the determinants of growth in transition economies.

It is often argued that one cannot translate the Russian GDP at the market exchange rate and that one should use a purchasing power exchange rate to measure the Russian economy. The debate about the appropriate purchasing power exchange rate is really beside the point, since the numbers mentioned above just serve to measure the weight of Russia in the world economy; they have little to say about just how poor the Russian population is. To measure the latter, one would indeed have to apply a purchasing power corrected exchange rate. However, in order to avoid this argument one can also measure the weight of Russia by its international trade. Even from this point of view, Russia is small: its exports are now running at about 80 billion dollars (statistically recorded imports much less), about the same as Sweden, less than Mexico. In terms of exports of manufactured goods, Russia is much smaller than either of these two countries (and somewhat smaller even than Poland).

Despite its small size, the Russian crisis of 1998 did have a strong impact on the world economy. In this sense all the attention devoted to Russia turned out to be justified. However, the impact of the Russian crisis on the world economy came through financial markets and not through the short lived collapse of Russian imports (which implied a fall in demand of about 20 to 30 billion dollars which is negligible compared with the volume of world trade). It is ironic that the political attention devoted to Russia during the two crucial periods of 1992/93 and August 1998 is the reverse of the economic impact on the West. During the early reform period it was perceived to be politically very important that the reforms in Russia should succeed, but the economic impact of success or failure would have been negligible. In 1998, the impact on the Western economy was much stronger, but politically Russia had been written off.

11.6.1 1992/93: the wrong form of aid?

The debate about aid to Russia during 1992/93 became sterile: Western officials pointed to the large amount of aid actually delivered (over 10% of GDP and 40% of imports in 1992), whereas the critics pointed out that this was the wrong kind of aid and that the Russian government did not receive what it needed most, namely direct budgetary support (Lipton and Sachs, 1992). Gros and Steinherr (1995) actually show that both sides were right (and wrong) if one analyses more closely the economic mechanisms at work during the early period of incomplete reforms.

The basic point is that the critics of Western aid policy towards Russia during 1992/93 were even more right than they suspected, since the credits to finance Russian imports probably did actually harm the Russian economy because the Russian government subsidised imports at the same time. If the Russian government had adopted different policies (taxing imports instead of subsidising them), it could have used these credits to stabilise the economy. The basic argument (explained in more detail in Gros and Steinherr, 1995) is a straightforward application of standard welfare theory in a second-best situation.

Regarding the welfare from emergency credits, one has to start from the fact that credits to finance imports do not constitute a gift; they have to be repaid at some point in the future. Consumers in an economy that does not have access to (private)[12] world capital markets gain from these credits because it allows them to smooth consumption. Emergency credits should thus increase the welfare of the recipients, even though they have to be repaid. However, this is necessarily the case only if there are no distortions in the receiving economy. If the government subsidises imports, additional credits magnify the losses from an existing distortion. One then has to set the gain in terms of the smoothing of consumption against the standard welfare losses from the import subsidies applied by the Russian government during 1992.

Gros and Steinherr (1995) present a small model that can be calibrated to the data, and which suggests that the net effect of the emergency assistance to Russian in 1992 was probably negative, resulting in a welfare loss, equivalent to anywhere between 1% and 7% of GDP for 1992. Causing welfare losses of this magnitude, of course, does not constitute a desirable result of foreign aid.

One can certainly discuss the details of the calculations based on such a crude model, but the central point is quite clear: the export credits lavished on Russia in 1992 probably helped to *reduce* the welfare of the average Russian citizen. This was not the fault of the West, since the cause for this unintended effect was the under-pricing of imports through massive subsidies operated by the Russian government. However, this example shows that sometimes helping a severely distorted economy can have unintended negative side effects.

Why did the West accept the bad policies of the Russian government? It should have taxed imports. In this way it would have avoided the welfare losses and the resulting receipts would have allowed it to stabilise the economy much earlier.

These considerations show that both the West and the Russian government are to blame for the fact that the substantial assistance that was given during the early reform period did not lead to a quick stabilisation. Stabilisation started much later, not only because of the impressive efforts of the new finance minister Fyodorov to cut credit emission, but also because the environment for aid changed: import subsidies had been abolished and import tariffs were gradually introduced so that the declining amounts of import credits did have a positive effect. Moreover, some limited amounts of the 'right' type of aid were slowly forthcoming.

The West also lost an opportunity in the sense that, even given the bad policies pursued by the Russian government, a moderate amount of the right aid, namely budgetary assistance to the government, could have helped to achieve stabili-

---

12. There was a need for official credits because private lenders were not willing to extend credits to Russia in 1992-93 (on the contrary, they even asked for reimbursement of old debts coming due). In this situation the only way to maintain imports until exports could pick up was to use official credits.

sation. How large should direct assistance to the government have been in order to achieve stabilisation? The proper criterion should be the level of support from the West that would have allowed the authorities to avoid creating too much money. It was argued above that the relevant part of seigniorage was worth about 2,000 billion roubles; approximately 8 billion dollars at the average 1992 exchange rate. Buying stabilisation in this way would have been more expensive in 1993 when the increase in the cash in circulation was worth about 12 billion dollars. However, this would still have been less than the export credits that were given in 1992. This is not surprising: providing a country of 140 million people with international purchasing power is an expensive proposition, but providing the government with internal purchasing power to cover its deficit is cheap if the real exchange rate is low.

11.6.2 The crisis of 1998

Stabilisation thus eventually came to Russia, even if somewhat late. The 'right' form of aid (from this point of view IMF credits) also came late, perhaps so late that it had again unintended perverse effects. A good indicator of external official balance-of-payments assistance is the amount of fund credit, because an IMF programme is usually a condition for other institutions, notably the World Bank. Most of the assistance from the IMF came only during 1995 as documented above. It helped to achieve stabilisation. Nevertheless, there was again a catch, which was, however, not visible immediately. At first sight the stabilisation of 1994/95 was impressive. Starting from early 1995 the nominal exchange rate was held constant. Inflation continued, but at a much lower rate, so that the deterioration in the real exchange rate seemed tolerable, especially as the current account remained in surplus. Then came the collapse of the exchange rate in August of 1998 and inflation started to accelerate again. Was the West to blame for this disaster as well?

Table 11.2 shows that the cumulative current account over the five-year period 1994-98 was actually about 35 billion dollars. However, despite continuing current account surpluses, the external debt of Russia kept on increasing, by over 31 billion dollars. The figures for the current account imply that, if one trusts the data (and assumes that the Russians did not make large unilateral transfers), Russian economic agents were accumulating claims on the rest of the world worth about 35 billion dollars. At the same time, the liabilities of the Russian government were increasing instead of falling.

The difference between the cumulative current surplus and the increase in foreign debt could be called capital flight.[13] It amounted to 66 billion dollars over a

---

13. As the foreign exchange reserves of the CBR did not change over this period, they were neglected here. See Dooley (1999) for a model and different estimate of capital flight.

Table 11.2: Factors influencing Russian foreign debt, 1994-98
          (In billions of dollars)

Cumulative current account balances	35
Cumulative net errors and omissions	30
Increase in external debt	31
Difference between current account and debt	66
Memo: Total credits disbursed by IMF	10

Source: Institute for International Finance, all figures rounded

five-year period. This is the key problem still facing Russian policy makers today: they are left servicing an ever increasing debt while their own citizens accumulate huge assets abroad. According to official statistics, most foreign direct investment in Russia now comes from Cyprus. Most of this capital is presumably owned by Russian citizens. There are also newspaper reports that a large fraction of the eurobonds issued by the Russian government are now owned by Russian citizens (via their offshore investment vehicles).

It is often argued that IMF funding ended up financing capital flight. This is likely, although it is not possible to say what would have happened in the absence of IMF lending. However, it is also clear that the little over 10 billion dollars of funds from the IMF during this period could at most have financed a small part of the total capital flight that took place. The aftermath of the 1998 crisis marked the first time the Russian government really faced a hard budget constraint. As IMF and foreign funds were cut off for a time, the only way out was either to cut spending and increase revenues or to revert to printing money. As the costs of the latter option were clear from the 1992/93 experience, successive Russian governments were forced to undertake the arduous task of actually enforcing some discipline on tax payers.

11.7 Conclusions

The particular aspects of 10 years of transition in Russia that have been highlighted in this Chapter suggest that a closer analysis quite often reveals a significant gap between perception and reality. The specific instances discussed in this chapter (price liberalisation, external trade liberalisation and stabilisation) show that most economic policy measures were at first implemented only partially and thus contained internal contradictions. Over time, however, the initial shortcomings were slowly made up. In a certain sense one can therefore conclude that the 'big bang' lasted rather long in Russia. The most serious mistake of the reformers was not to have increased energy prices and not to have eliminated import subsidies immediately. Later on, their freedom of manoeuvre was more circumscribed and further reforms became more difficult. The next mistake was to rely excessively on foreign financing of continuing fiscal deficits, which in effect allowed Russian citizens to accumulate huge assets abroad while the government had to service an ever increasing foreign debt.

What does all this imply for the future? The critical analysis of ten years of the reform process, which did not start only in 1992 as is often assumed, has shown that the policies actually implemented during the initial 'big bang' (as opposed to the policy announced) had serious negative welfare effects. This can explain why the constituency for reforms was initially rather weak. However, since most of the initial errors were slowly corrected, the welfare gains from the elimination of import subsidies and the reduction of export controls were probably only dimly perceived by the population at large and this might be the main factor why the reforms never stopped. Nevertheless, as the initial errors were corrected, the country was putting its stability in the hands of international capital markets by a combination of excessive opening of financial markets, imprudent fiscal policy and a corrupt banking system. This mixture proved almost lethal when private capital inflows suddenly stopped and a classic currency plus banking crisis followed.

However, the lesson that reforms and stabilisation improve the economy and pay off politically in the long run was not lost on the political system. This is the key reason why Russia did not descend into hyperinflation and disintegration after August 1998. For the near future one can therefore expect a continuation of the slow, but imperfect progress that has been the hallmark of developments in Russia so far.

The Russophoria of 1996/97 and the over-reaction of financial markets to the crisis of 1998/99 show a tendency to exaggerate developments in Russia in both directions. In order to put the current excessively negative picture of Russia into perspective it seems appropriate to conclude with the quote from the noted economist cited at the start of this chapter:

> "If one is to make any generalisation in present conditions, it must be this – that at a low level of efficiency the system does function and possesses elements of permanence".
>
> J.M. Keynes

References

Brenton, P. (1999), *Trade and Investment in Europe: The Impact of the Next Enlargement*, Centre for European Policy Studies (CEPS), Brussels.

Cottarelli, C. and M.I. Blejer (1992), 'Forced Saving and Repressed Inflation in the Soviet Union, 1986-90', IMF *Staff Papers*, Vol.39, No.2.

Dooley, M. (1999), 'A Model of Crisis in Emerging Markets', *The Economic Journal*, forthcoming.

Gaidar, Y. (1999), 'Lessons of the Russian Crisis for Transition Economics', *Finance and Development*, June 1999, Vol.36, No.2, International Monetary Fund, Washington, D.C.

Gros, D. and A. Steinherr (1995), *Winds of Change Economic Transition in Central and Eastern Europe*, Addison, Wesley Longman, London.

Havrylyshyn, O. and Th. Wolf (1999), 'Determinants of Growth in Transition Countries', *Finance and Development*, June 1999, Vol.36, No.2, International Monetary Fund, Washington, D.C.

International Monetary Fund (various dates), *International Financial Statistics*, Washington, D.C.

Keynes, J.M. (1992), 'A Short View of Russia, 1972, Essays in Persuasion', *The Collected Writings of John Maynard Keynes*, Part IX, London and Basingstoke.

Koen, V. and S. Phillips (1993), 'Price liberalisation in Russia', *Occasional Papers*, No.104, International Monetary Fund, Washington, D.C.

Komulainen, T. (1999), *Currency Crisis Theories – Some Explanations for the Russian Case*, Discussion Paper, No.58, University, Potsdam.

Konovalov, V. (1994), 'Russian Trade Policy', in: D. Tarr (ed.), *Trade in New Independent States*, World Bank, Washington, D.C.

Layard, R. and J. Parker (1996), *The Coming Russian Boom*, Free Press, New York.

Lerner, A.P. (1936), 'The Symmetry Between Import and Export Taxes', *Economica*, No.3, pp. 306-13.

Lipton, D. and J. Sachs (1992), 'Prospects for Russia's Economic Reforms', *Brookings Papers on Economic Activity*, No.2, pp.213-65.

López-Claros, A. and S.V. Alexashenko (1998), 'Fiscal Policy Issues during the Transition in Russia', *Occasionial Papers*, No.155, International Monetary Fund, Washington, D.C.

Liberalisation and Economic Development in Ukraine

Victor Pynzenyk[1]

12.1 Introduction

Ukraine is undergoing an extremely difficult and painful process of transformation of the economic system. Unlike other countries in Central and Eastern Europe, where significant progress has been made, the Ukrainian economy does not show any signs of recovery. The country faces very serious fiscal and structural problems. These became particularly acute in 1998 when, after a lengthy period of stability of the exchange rate, in just a few months the national currency was devalued by 80%. Ukraine goes its own, unique way of transformation from a planned economy to a market economy. This does not refer to the popular idea in Ukrainian political circles about the uniqueness of the Ukrainian situation and the need for inventing specific Ukrainian remedies to treat the diseases of the Ukrainian economy. The uniqueness of the Ukrainian situation is of a different nature. The leaders of the country act on the principle: the best mistakes are your own mistakes. Moreover, in order not to forget these mistakes one has to repeat them every now and then. The experience with Ukrainian reforms demonstrates this rather well.

12.2 Ukrainian economic development

Ukrainian economic development can be divided into three periods. The first period was characterised by the Ukrainian way to independence. The second period was marked by a desperate economic situation at the end of 1994 and the need for radical stabilisation measures. The third period started with the financial crisis of 1998.

Searching for the Ukrainian way or confusion with independence

Unlike many other countries, Ukraine had to face two rather complicated problems at the same time: establishing the institutions of an independent state and

---

1. This chapter was translated from the Ukrainian language.

carrying out economic reforms. The institutions of power, inherited after the collapse of the former Soviet Union, were part of the complicated system of a planned economy. At the same time, the centre, from where this system was operated, was located outside the borders of the independent state. The mentality of the civil servants had been formed in a time when the state held the controlling function of organising all aspects of economic life and when money served just as an accountancy tool. In these conditions it was unavoidable that a strong opposition within the state apparatus was formed against any measures aimed at removing or restricting the role of the state and its direct participation in economic life. In addition, the role of money was neglected, as was reflected in demands to conduct an accommodative monetary policy. The democratic forces which came into the Parliament on the wave of anti-communism and the ideas of independence, got stuck in euphoria and excitement with the serious economic potential of Ukraine, which, in their opinion, could be easily realised now that the country had gained independence.

However, the liberalisation of the prices for energy imported by Ukraine from the Russian Federation brought the economy into a state of shock. The traditional trade relations with the partners in the former Soviet Union began to break down. Ukrainian companies, which were used to operate with chronic deficits, faced a new, and until then, unknown problem: a crisis in the demand constraint and hence difficulties in selling products. Even those products, that had always been in shortage, suddenly became impossible to sell.

The presence in the Ukrainian Parliament of a strong political lobby of directors of companies and the unwillingness of the state institutions to work in the new conditions were the main causes for the hyperinflation in the period 1992-1993. 'Peculiarities' of the Ukrainian economy and 'insufficient' money in circulation were the major factors prompting the decision to pump ever-increasing amounts of money into the economy. As a result of such a policy, prices increased by 28.9% on a monthly basis in 1992, and by 47.1% in 1993. A quick fall in the monetisation of the economy from 50% at the end of 1992 to 26.5% by the end of 1994 was 'treated' by printing more money. Another reason for increasing the money in circulation was the wish of politicians to 'protect' the citizens from rising prices. The consequence of this 'protection' was a threefold fall in real wages in 1993 alone.

In the period 1992-1994 Ukraine was confronted with serious budget problems. The government revealed its main fiscal problem: a lack of financial resources to cover the expenditure deficit was financed with direct credits from the National Bank of Ukraine. Very often emissions were made not by the National Bank, but by the Ministry of Finance. While keeping separate revenue and expenditure accounts with the National Bank, the Ministry of Finance financed budget expenditures without settling the expenditures on the revenue account.

In the situation of constant printing new money, attempts to cut government expenditures did not improve the budget situation. In 1992-1994, Ukraine faced a chronic shortage of hard currency funds needed to make external payments. As the reserves of the National Bank were insufficient, the trade deficit was mainly covered by not paying for energy supplies from Russia. In fact, during this period a significant amount of the external debt was created. Unpaid energy supplies constituted external debts for the Ukrainian government.

The Ukrainian economy experienced particularly serious problems in connection with the introduction of the official exchange rate for the national currency, which three times exceeded the market exchange rate. This, as well as many other similar Ukrainian 'inventions' of the Ukrainian way of crises settlement, was motivated by the need to stop the constant increase in nominal prices for energy sources, mainly obtained through import.

After several partial attempts to liberalise prices, with respect to both internal and foreign trade, the country was pulled more and more into an administrative regime. The search for a 'Ukrainian model' of macroeconomic policy had sad results. In the period 1992-1994, both GDP and industrial production decreased by 40% and consumer prices increased sharply (see Table 12.1). The consolidated budget deficit exceeded 10% of GDP. Having no hard currency reserves, the balance of payments deficit was covered exclusively by not paying for imports which, in the first place, consisted of energy supplies from Russia. The country was on the brink of a financial collapse.

Table 12.1: Ukrainian economy 1992-1998, % change compared with the previous period

	1992	1993	1994	1995	1996	1997	1998	1999 January-April
GDP	-9.9	-14.2	-22.9	-12.2	-10.0	-3.2	-1.7	-4.1
Industrial production	-9.0	-7.4	-28.2	-12.7	-5.1	-1.8	-0.5	-2.7
Agricultural production	-8.3	1.5	-16.5	-3.6	-9.5	-1.9	-9.8	n.a.
Inflation (Dec. to Dec.)	2,106	10,255	501	282	140	110	120	106
Consolidated budget deficit	-12.2	-6.5	-10.5	-7.9	-4.6	-7.1	-2.3	-0.4

Radical stabilisation measures and financial stabilisation

The desperate economic situation at the end of 1994 forced the authorities to take radical stabilisation measures. This marked the second period of development in the country's economic situation: the period of financial stabilisation. It was the only period of decisive reform acts by the Ukrainian government, supported by IMF and World Bank credits. The government carried out a large-scale liberalisation of prices with respect to both internal and foreign trade. In a short period of time, rents increased sharply. The state subsidies on rent were replaced by subsidies for the poorest. All these measures, as well as the reduction of state orders for agricultural products and the cancelling of direct state support for loss making companies, allowed a significant reduction in the consolidated budget deficit. In 1996, it decreased to 7.9% of GDP, in 1997 to 4.6% (compared with 10.5% in 1994). Apart from that, starting in 1995 the government began to cover the budget deficit by means of issuing T-bills. From 1996 onwards, the National Bank of Ukraine stopped direct financing of the budget deficit.

The stabilisation measures quite quickly brought positive results. Average monthly inflation rates went down from 47.1% and 14.4% in 1992-1993 to 9.0% in 1995, 2.8% in 1996 and 0.8% in 1997 (see Figure 12.1). At the beginning of 1998, the real exchange rate for the national currency rose by 2.5 times compared with October 1994 when the stabilisation programme was started. In the period 1996-1997, the nominal exchange rate remained practically unchanged, which allowed a successful currency reform to be carried out in the autumn of 1996.

The turnover in the currency market started to increase sharply. In the period 1995 to 1998 the turnover in US dollars increased by 3.3 times, in D-marks by 5.9 times and in Russian roubles by 3.1 times. For the first time since the independence, the Ukraine experienced a significant inflow of hard currency (see Table 12.2). This allowed the National Bank of Ukraine to replenish its currency reserves. Especially significant purchases were effected during the first half of 1997.

Table 12.2: Inflow of hard currency

	Changes in reserves (million US dollars)
1995	- 6,238
1996	+ 2,753
1997	+ 16,986
1998	+ 13,946

Following the period of hyperinflation in 1992-1994, starting from 1996 the amount of household deposits increased as a result of the renewed confidence in the national currency. In 1996-1997 the volume of deposits in nominal figures rose by 3.2 times, including fixed deposits by 4.2 times. The growth in real terms was 67% and 174% respectively.

The financial stabilisation in the period 1995-1997 created the necessary conditions for economic growth in Ukraine and large-scale investments in the economy. The climate for private investors, however, remained extremely unfavourable. Although the government took important steps towards the liberali-

sation of prices and trade, completed small privatisation and privatised a significant part of the large and medium-sized companies, the investment risks remained
high. This was caused by the following circumstances:

1. Complicated procedures for starting up a business. In fact, Ukraine uses a system for investments based on permits. To establish any kind of company,
   including those with the participation of foreign investment, permits from
   many civil servants are needed, which takes much time. An extremely large
   number of activities need a license or special permission. The procedure for
   obtaining permission for new building activities is very complicated.
2. Over-regulation for running a business. This is reflected in restrictions on the
   right to open accounts in different banks, in different regimes for cash and non-
   cash payments, in the right of a dozen appointed state bodies to control company activities and in a special regime of management of expenditures in case
   a company has debts.
3. Absence of legal protection in relations between the state and private business.
   The current legislation in Ukraine allows for the confiscation of accounts and
   property without court decision.
4. Unclear bankruptcy mechanisms and mechanisms for dividing or restructuring
   existing companies, which increases risks of losses in relations with partners in
   Ukraine and promotes barter deals.
5. High tax pressure, especially the high level of pay-roll tax, which exceeded
   50% in 1996-1997, the complicated and unclear system of taxation and the
   constant changes in tax legislation.

In 1996 an attempt was made to introduce a package of structural reforms, supported by the international financial organisations. A package of bills called 'Economic growth', which envisaged large-scale deregulation, an almost two-fold
reduction in the level of taxation, the regulation of the procedures on bankruptcy and a significant cutting of government expenditures was presented to the Parliament of Ukraine. It turned out that there was in Ukraine no political will to
approve such decisions. Most bills were rejected by the Parliament. The foundation for the next period of economic development was laid in 1996-1997, *i.e.* the
years of stagnation and the years of the rejection of absolutely obvious and utter-
ly necessary decisions, required to achieve real results.

From stabilisation to financial crisis

Without structural reforms and changes at the micro-level, the basis for financial
stabilisation turned out to be very weak and unstable. No conditions were created
to increase state revenues without jeopardising the growth of economic activity.
Moreover, the policy of supporting unprofitable and non-competitive production
(direct support was replaced by indirect support) came at the expense of the viable
sectors of the economy. The lack of possibilities for structural reforms with respect
to outdated production owing to severe budget constraints gave, and still gives,

ground for serious objective arguments to exert political pressure on the government and demand new, additional subsidies. Such subsidies were, and still are, allocated by writing off or rescheduling tax indebtedness and the granting of tax privileges, the issuing of subsidised credits out of non-budget funds or international credit lines, that were never returned by the borrowers and formed an additional heavy burden on the budget. The Ukrainian way of writing-off revenues from the account of a debtor offered a remarkable mechanism to avoid paying taxes. Banks only kept account of ever growing tax indebtedness.

The absence of a mechanism for securing responsibility for the fulfilment of mutual financial obligations created a Ukrainian hybrid of a private owner: a deformed owner, whose aim is to steal, not to multiply. All these circumstances have an extremely negative influence on taxpayers, inducing them to divert activities to the regime of the shadow economy. It is therefore not surprising that in Ukraine mainly shadow activities in the economy are possible and these activities are continuously growing in size. An indirect confirmation of this phenomenon is the growing amount of money circulating outside the banking sector.

Further complication of the budgetary situation was not only caused by the growing pressure of debt servicing. After reaching financial stabilisation, politicians lost the desire to continue cutting budget expenditures. The period of reducing the real budget deficit in Ukraine was very short. Later, the budget deficit was cut on a cash basis. This did not at all mean a decreasing demand or decreasing expenditures in budget sectors. Balancing the budget was realised at the expense of the financial state of 'viable' sectors in the economy simply by not paying them for services or activities provided. Therefore it is not surprising that co-operation with the budget sector is most unreliable in Ukraine. Payments can be delayed for years or are not effected at all. No decision was taken in order to reduce the network of budget institutions that receive money out of the budget. On the contrary, opposite decisions were taken on expanding, increasing and enlarging the structure and the number of employees of executive bodies or on raising their wages. Starting from 1996 onwards, the arrears in the budget on payments of pensions and wages of medical personnel, teachers, academicians and military personnel began to grow. By 1 January 1998 payment arrears for pensioners alone made up close to 2% of the GDP.

In these circumstances, data on the cash deficit of the Ukrainian budget statistics are rather unreliable. The real deficit is much higher because of the unfulfilled responsibilities towards state institutions and organisations, and payment arrears on wages of employees in the budget sector.

Because of the existence of a seriously complicated budget situation, a significant part of the government's funds is spent outside the budget (the so-called off-budget funds) or is otherwise passed through the treasury as special purpose funds. A number of Ukrainian institutions have such a large volume of off-budget funds that they could easily qualify as commercial companies rather than state institutions. Searching for additional funds became their major activity. This concerns in the first place the tax administration, which channels 30% of unpaid tax-es, once revealed, not to the state budget, but to its own budget.

While not proceeding with structural reforms and cutting budget expenditures, the government continued to solve the problem of a lack of funds by borrowing. By mid-1998 the situation became critical. Debt servicing absorbed an ever-grow-ing part of the budget revenues. In 1995, debt servicing took 1.4% of the state budget, in 1997 this was 4.2% and on the eve of the crisis (the first seven months of 1998) it became 12.2%.

Before the introduction of T-bills, the National Bank was the only centre for regulating the exchange rate of the national currency. With the appearance of T-bills another centre appeared: the Ministry of Finance. Budget policy became an important factor with respect to the exchange rate. As long as the budget situa-tion did not raise alarm and there was still hope for renewed economic growth in connection with the package of bills labelled 'Economic Growth', sent to the Par-liament for approval, there was a continuing inflow of hard currency into the country. This did not only support the value of the national currency, but helped to accumulate the reserves of the National Bank. At the same time, the price of attracting funds in the market by the government came down. In September 1997 the interest rate dropped to 22%. After the 'Economic Growth' package was rejected by the Parliament, a financial crisis became unavoidable.

At that time the steep devaluation of the Ukrainian hryvnya went along with the devaluation of the Russian rouble, and this was seen by politicians as ground to search for Russian roots in the Ukrainian crisis. In 1998 for the first time in recent years, the real exchange rate of the dollar on the Ukrainian market start-ed to rise. In the period January-June 1998, consumer prices rose by 2.1% and the selling price of dollars rose by 10.8%. Despite disinflation in June (-0.9%) the government issued a loan, with an enormous effort, at an interest rate of 70%. The National Bank managed to control the situation in the currency market by spending 60% of its currency reserves.

The real cause of the Ukrainian crisis was the neglected 'disease' of the coun-try's economy. The Russian financial crisis only reinforced this neglected disease. The crisis in Ukraine was possibly less destructive than that in Russia. The extent of devaluation, however, was enormous. By the end of 1998, the Ukrainian cur-rency had been devalued by 80%. The confidence in the national currency that had been gained with such effort disappeared rapidly. After a lengthy period of a pretty fast increase of deposits in banks, now the withdrawal began. In the peri-od August-October 1998 around 18% of all household deposits were withdrawn from bank accounts, including 10% of common deposits and 22% of fixed deposits.

The devaluation of the national currency had a negative impact on production. The tendency towards a flat growth of GDP, noticeable in the period May-June 1998 (from +0.1% to +0.5%), immediately turned in the opposite direction. In 1998 as a whole, production dropped by 1.2%. In 1999 the situation became worse, the GDP declined by 3.5% in the period January-May. The reaction of the government to the financial crisis resembled the behaviour of a poor physician. As the sick Ukrainian economy had a 'temperature', the Ukrainian doctors tried to fight the thermometer itself. The administrative regulation of the exchange rate and the introduction in certain sectors of state control of prices led to a curtailment of economic activity, especially of small businesses. These measures were renounced pretty soon, as they stimulated shadow activities and activated the withdrawal of hard currency from the country.

It was not only the lack of action and of political will on the part of the Ukrainian authorities that was responsible for the economic developments in Ukraine. The policies of the international financial organisations, in the first place the IMF, were also to blame. The IMF mainly concentrates on solving the problems of macroeconomic stabilisation and pays little attention to structural reforms. In any case, according to the ideology of the IMF, structural reforms should follow stabilisation and cannot be carried out simultaneously. The position of the IMF with regard to keeping the budget deficit at an accepted level, not on a real basis but on a cash basis, is short-sighted as well. It is abundantly clear that without taking real steps to cut state expenditures, this approach will ruin macroeconomic stability.

Lately, the activities of the IMF resemble the activities of a charity organisation with serious political colouring. It is difficult to say exactly what it is that the IMF supports in Ukraine: an imitation of reforms or its own reputation. Only because of the 'humanitarian' assistance received in March and June of 1999, did Ukraine manage to avoid a second serious collapse. Such external support does not help the country, it only extends the agony, drives problems into a corner and delays solving them to future, more complicated times. The relations between the IMF and Ukraine in past years resemble attempts to help a drowning person. The latter takes the helping hand with only one aim: to take another breath of fresh air before he finally, with renewed efforts, sinks to the bottom.

Those countries that open international credit lines with state guarantees and provide technical assistance are also partly responsible for the situation in Ukraine. In credit relations, the government acts as the creditor. The inefficiency of such banking activities on the part of the government is confirmed by the following figures: In 1996, borrowers did not return 85% of the credits issued with state guarantees. This implied a heavy burden on the Ukrainian budget. In reply to the behaviour of the West, Ukraine exported corruption to the West. It seems as if the West does not want to acknowledge the fact that, with participation from the Ukrainian side, special international corporations were formed, specialised in attracting funds under international credit lines.

The processes that are currently taking place in the world are characterised by the globalisation of not only financial markets, but consumer markets as well. The economies of the countries of the former USSR became more open. The breakdown of the old system of economic ties, based on the administrative distribution of products, and the deterioration of the economic situation in a number of countries, substantially changed the geographical structure of trade. In 1995 more than half of Ukrainian exports went to the CIS countries and the share of exports to other European countries was only 21.2%. In 1998 the volume of exports to the European countries exceeded exports to the CIS countries. Similar tendencies took place in the geographical pattern of imports (see Table 12.3). The period of financial stability broadened the possibilities for imports from Europe.

In these conditions, the transformation, taking place in Ukraine and other countries of the former USSR is not only an internal problem for these countries. They affect the interests of the European Union as well. The financial crisis in Ukraine did not only affect the national economy. Companies in the West, from which exports were directed to the Ukraine, were hit as well.

Table 12.3: The geographical distribution of Ukrainian foreign trade

	1995	1996	1997	1998	1999
Exports as a % of total exports to					
CIS	54.7	53.3	40.8	35.1	26.1
Russian Federation	43.4	38.7	26.2	23.0	18.2
Europe	21.2	22.2	24.2	29.8	32.6
Asia	18.8	18.8	26.9	23.7	28.4
America	3.1	4.2	4.6	6.8	4.2
Africa	1.9	1.5	3.3	4.4	7.1
Imports as a % of total imports from					
CIS	66.1	65.1	60.0	56.4	67.3
Russian Federation	53.3	50.1	45.8	48.1	49.5
Europe	24.5	24.8	29.5	31.5	23.4
Asia	3.5	3.8	4.9	6.0	4.7
America	4.8	5.3	4.7	5.1	3.4
Africa	0.6	0.8	0.8	0.8	1.1

The European countries should have provided more support to the countries that are in a process of transformation. In the first place, this concerns the lifting of non-tariff import restrictions and the reduction of tariffs on imports. This would not only help economies in transformation. At the same time, it would support the process of reforms in the European countries. Not once has the example of the European countries served as an argument against the reduction of import duties or the mitigation of subsidies to the agricultural sector. Entanglement between Ukraine and Europe should be a mutual process. Ukraine is interested in the first place. But there is also an economic stake for the European countries. The dynamic process of growing exports to Ukraine during the period of financial stabilisation is convincing enough.

12.3 Ukrainian reform perspectives

It is difficult to remain optimistic while analysing the developments in the economic situation in Ukraine. At the same time, Ukraine today is closer to a serious break-through in reforms than ever before during the years 1996-1997, the period of financial stability. This conclusion may seem both surprising and unfounded. To think like this is only possible if the technical side of the problems is analysed: what has been done and what has not.

The Ukrainian experience, as in many other countries, confirms that crises are of a political nature. Hopeless or dead-end situations do not exist. They become hopeless because of the unwillingness or unreadiness of politicians to proceed with real reforms. This is confirmed by the example of the hyperinflation of 1992-1993. Many analysts considered the situation as hopeless. Very few believed in the possibility that financial stability would be achieved. However, the situation itself resulted in very decisive actions having to be taken, and these brought reasonable results. The financial crisis of 1998 did not teach the politicians a lesson. Ukraine will probably have to go through another financial shock before the lesson is learned. The actions currently taken point towards the development of such a scenario. Instead of conducting a policy aimed at achieving a non-deficit budget, as is needed in such situations, the government sent a draft budget with a significant cash deficit and a hidden deficit for approval to the parliament. Instead of a radical cut in expenditures and large-scale deregulation, the government decided to write off or reschedule tax indebtedness, to exempt critical imports and the agricultural sector from paying VAT, and to introduce a number of laws on free economic zones with significant tax privileges.

The restructuring of the government's debts in 1998 did not relieve, but only postponed, the existing problems. Already this year the government may fail to meet its debt responsibilities. The debt burden is still growing. In the first four months of 1999, debt servicing took almost 25% of the state budget. Already this year, the volume of the external payments exceeded 2 billion dollars. The available reserves of the National Bank and the expected external borrowings may be insufficient for a timely payment of the debts. The situation was 'saved' several times by the IMF, which took political decisions by granting new tranches and new credits. But even in the unlikely case that financial stability can be maintained in 1999, default cannot be avoided next year. The sum of payments out of the state budget exceeds its annual revenues and a major share of debt servicing consists of external payments. Radical decisions have still not been taken to resolve this extraordinary situation.

Ukraine lost the momentum to carry out reforms in the way that has led many Central and Eastern European countries on the road to economic growth. The necessary conditions were not used. Ukraine did not go through the economic reforms, and now it has to pay a much higher price compared with other countries. The political leaders showed their unwillingness and inability to carry out reforms and their fear of taking decisive reform-oriented measures. The lengthy blocking of structural changes gave birth to a new, unique type of reform opponents. It is often thought that it is mainly left wing forces that are opposed to reform. Unfortunately, the opponents also include number of the so-called new capitalists: people who want capitalism but only for themselves. These new capitalists do not want changes and therefore block them. Ukrainian businesses in gas, energy, and agricultural sectors can hardly be called businesses. It was established and developed as a result of a dangerous merger between businessmen and civil servants by severely monopolising certain activities through procedures that can only be described as a game without rules. The reform-oriented forces in Ukraine do not have sufficient political support, which makes it impossible to achieve a decisive break-through in reforms. The citizens of Ukraine do not understand reforms. The reform-coloured rhetoric of the leaders of the country, masking inaction, generates the logical question: "What are all these reforms for if they only worsen our living standards?" The West contributes to the strengthening of these ideas by supporting the imitation of reforms in Ukraine rather than real reforms.

The Ukrainian society needs serious pressure. Only pressure can force the politicians to take radical actions. Without the pressure of hyperinflation in the period 1992-1993, financial stabilisation would have been unlikely. It was the continuous daily pressure of the critical economic circumstances that forced the political leadership to take decisive steps. Without a financial collapse, it is impossible to break the resistance of capitalist clans. Their funds are utilised exclusively for personal enrichment, for bribing civil servants, for control of the mass media and for buying votes at the time of elections. Only a financial crisis can change the attitude of citizens who, having lived in a crisis situation for a long time now, quite naturally lost their confidence in changes for the better and do not take part in elections or get caught by the demagogic, populist slogans of the left or by the handouts of business clans. There is no way back. More than once, Ukraine has demonstrated that any attempts to reverse developments turn into a marking time and an abrupt deterioration of the economic situation. It was the extremely critical economic situation of Ukraine that made the country take the route of fast radical reform. It is a pity that Ukraine made this choice. However, when other variants do not help, a shock can serve as a good impetus for decisive action and progress.

12.4 Conclusions; lessons of Ukraine

1. Financial stabilisation and corresponding measures involving fiscal and monetary policy should be carried out simultaneously with structural reforms. The implementation of stabilisation and structural decisions cannot be effected separately in time. Financial stabilisation that is not reinforced with structural reforms weakens the attention of politicians and creates the illusion of the pos-

sibility of continuous political manoeuvring. This illusion is extremely dangerous in conditions where the necessary political will and a clear understanding
of the essence of structural reforms are absent. Such a policy is doomed to fail.

2. The untimely implementation of structural reforms creates a specific, unique
type of reform opponent: a part of the private sector, which satisfies its own
interests by monopolising certain sectors of the market. Inflation causes a redistribution of wealth, and financial stabilisation hampers this redistribution. By
not regulating structural problems, new powerful channels of such redistribution are created. The business clans bring unique phenomena into political life,
such as commercialisation of political activities and privatisation of political
parties.

3. Transition countries with insufficient political will for reforms do not have the
right to afford the luxury of a budget deficit. At the same time, equilibrium
with respect to government finance appears only to be possible in the finan-
cially most complicated periods. The Ukrainian experience of 1994-1995 confirms that in such periods things can be done that later cannot be achieved in
years. In a stable financial situation it is impossible to settle the whole complex
of budget problems that Ukraine is confronted with today. It is sufficient to
bring into mind that the bills adopted by the parliament will need funds that
exceed the revenues of the consolidated budget by a factor three.

4. Radical changes in the economy are impossible without administrative
reforms. One has to start with decisions that are well understood by the population and thus clear the way for the necessary transformations as well. It is
difficult to explain to the population the need for certain restrictions while the
number of civil servants and the expenditures for the executive power keep
increasing. Even more important is the following: if the old administrative
management system, which was oriented towards planned management methods, is preserved, this creates insurmountable obstacles on the path to reforms.
Steps towards reforms under these conditions are more an exception than a
rule. In the end, a dead person will grab and pull down a living one.

5. International financial organisations should not follow the principle that since
the early reform activities were supported, support cannot now be suspended.
This approach does not prevent shocks occurring, or a serious deterioration of
the situation. It only addresses the symptoms of the disease and postpones the
necessary treatment, meanwhile feeding the opinion among the population that
there is a connection between reforms and the worsening of the Ukrainian
economy.

6. The country has to go through a process of reforms, which have to be understood and supported by society. This problem is not so acute in countries which
have taken decisive reform steps. In Ukraine, where reforms were interrupted
by attempts to reverse them and by open inactivity, where effective reforms are
replaced by imitations of reforms and where the idea of reforms is devalued, it
will be impossible to make a decisive break-through without a further deteri-

oration of the situation and a financial collapse. There is no other way when for many years now politicians have been trying to bury their heads in the sand to avoid existing problems, and when inactivity and political manoeuvring are considered better than decisive reform-targeted action. Shocks do not only relieve the politicians from fear, they also eliminate the main obstacles for reforms in those countries that are not moving forwards: the power of oligarch clans.

The Integration of Russia and Ukraine into the World Trading System

Constantine Michalopoulos[1]

13.1 Introduction

A country's trade policy is a key link in the transmission of price signals from the world market to domestic resource allocation and to the economy's effective integration in the world trading system (see Chapter 4). Thus, it is not surprising that countries in Central and Eastern Europe and the former Soviet Union (FSU) wishing to increase consumer choice and escape the inefficiencies of central planning, made trade policy reform an early and important component of broader price and market-oriented reforms.

Integration in the world trading system depends on whether policies and institutions are established in a country and its trading partners which are conducive to the mutually beneficial exchange of goods and services based on specialisation and comparative advantage. So, effective integration of Russia and Ukraine in this system involves not only their own trade policies and institutions but also those of their trading partners which affect market access and the terms of trade.

Integration also involves abiding by the rules of conduct that govern the multilateral trading system. These rules have been established and are being implemented in the context of the agreements administered by the World Trade Organization (WTO). Thus, membership in the WTO is an essential element, perhaps even a necessary condition for full integration in the world trading system.

In the aftermath of the collapse of central planning and the break-up of the Soviet Union, most countries in the former Soviet Union (FSU), including Russia and Ukraine in 1993, applied to accede to the GATT and then the WTO.[2] Almost six years later, only two countries from the FSU, Kyrgyzstan and Latvia have joined the WTO, and several more countries are close to completing the accession process.[3] But these do not include Russia and Ukraine.

---

1. Views expressed in this paper are entirely those of the author and should not be attributed in any manner to the World Bank or its member government's institutions. The author wishes to thank Gilles Moser of the WTO for his assistance in the preparation of the statistical analysis of the paper (18 June 1999).
2. The WTO was established as a successor organisation to the GATT in 1995.

The purpose of this study is to analyse the problems and prospects of integration into the multilateral trading system for Russia and Ukraine, with a focus on the question of their accession to the WTO. The emphasis is on the present and future challenges facing these countries rather than on a historical review of their policies and efforts to accede to the WTO.

The chapter is organised as follows. First, there is a review of trade patterns, policies and institutions in Russia and Ukraine as they relate to WTO accession. Next, market access issues for the two countries, especially regarding the US and the EU are discussed. This is followed by several sections on WTO accession which address the benefits of WTO membership, the WTO accession process and the problems and prospects of these countries' accession to the WTO. The last section contains conclusions and recommendations on steps Russia, Ukraine and the international community should take to improve the prospects for these countries' more effective integration into the multilateral trading system.

13.2 Patterns of trade and policy reform

With the break-up of the Soviet Union in late 1991, all 15 countries started more or less with the same state planning apparatus for the control of international trade. From this common beginning, the patterns of trade policy soon diverged. The Baltic States quickly dismantled the state trading apparatus and started shifting their trade orientation to the European market economies. At the other extreme were countries like Turkmenistan and Uzbekistan, whereas late as mid 1994, state organisations continued to control the bulk of foreign trade. Russia and Ukraine were in between, with Russia closer to the Baltic States and Ukraine closer to the countries in Central Asia in terms of trade controls. Russia introduced trade reforms early but retained a significant but declining role for the state in the control of key commodity exports. As late as 1994, Ukraine continued to impose significant controls on exports (Michalopoulos and Tarr, 1994).

13.2.1 Reforms in early transition

Following the demise of central planning, the main aspect of the integration of Russia, Ukraine and other FSU countries into the multilateral trading system involved the reorientation of trade away from each other and towards the rest of the world. There were several reasons for the decline in intra-FSU trade during the early years of the transition. Probably the most important was the collapse of the payments system. Also, some trade, which was clearly uneconomical, collapsed from the introduction of foreign competition. And some declines resulted from

---

3. Countries with good chances to accede in 1999 include Croatia, Estonia and Georgia. Armenia, Lithuania and Moldova are also close to accession.

conscious shifting of exports of raw materials and, especially, energy, away from countries in the FSU, which could not pay, and towards countries in the West, which could.

Except for the Baltic States, the main policy response to the intra-FSU trade decline in the beginning of the period was the establishment of a network of state trading agreements akin to the previous Council of Mutual Economic Assistance (CMEA) arrangements, as well as the establishment of a so called 'free trade' area for the Commonwealth of Independent States (CIS).4 At the same time, export controls were imposed on raw materials, intermediate inputs, food and energy for several reasons: to implement a shift in the direction of trade, to keep domestic prices of these inputs artificially low as a means of providing support to industrial users and consumers or as a source of huge rents to those controlling the exports (Aslund, 1999a).

On the import side, controls were few initially: tariffs were typically low and domestic producers were shielded from international competition by the highly depreciated exchange rates. But Ukraine also used foreign exchange controls then and later.

In 1994-1996, as countries started to introduce their own currencies and stabilisation programmes began to take hold, and as they also initiated broader market-oriented reforms, the trade regimes that are in place today started to emerge. The transition had several dimensions: first, the exchange rate appreciated for various periods and at various times in different countries, giving rise to pressure for protection through more traditional means – *e.g.* through the introduction of differentiated tariff schedules. Second, export controls on raw materials and energy were progressively dismantled. Third, the state trading agreements that attempted to stabilise trade among the CIS countries were progressively abandoned. Efforts continued, however, especially by Russia, to strengthen preferential arrangements through the conclusion of a customs union with Belarus, Kazakhstan, Kyrgyzstan – recently joined by Tajikistan. Throughout the period a key element of trade policy was its instability: there are numerous examples of decrees prohibiting or taxing a specific export or import in both Russia and Ukraine. Perhaps the most extreme example is a Ukrainian decree of 4 May 1994, fortunately not implemented, according to which import duties were to be reviewed on a weekly basis.5

---

4. Michalopoulos and Tarr (1994) contains a detailed discussion of trade policies in these countries through 1994, based on seven country case studies.
5. Drabek (1996) analyses a number of examples of trade policy instability in Eastern Europe.

13.2.2 Trade patterns

Figures 13.1 to 13.4 show the changes in the orientation of trade and increasing participation in the international markets for Russia and Ukraine in the period 1991-1998 in US dollars, using market exchange rates. Clearly, much of the apparent decline in 1991-1992 was due to exchange rate depreciation. However, there were large real declines in the volume of trade among the FSU countries during this period as well (see Michalopoulos and Tarr, 1994).

Russia's trade dominates the total trade for the FSU. It accounted for 52% of total trade – exports plus imports – of the FSU in 1998. By comparison Ukraine's share was about 19% for total trade and much smaller (less than 10%) for exports. Intertemporal and intercountry comparisons are difficult because of the lack of consistent data and the very sharp depreciation of the rouble in 1992. Nonetheless, there is a sense that trade both within the FSU and with the outside world picked up after the initial shock and that both countries increased their total exports after the sharp drop in 1992.

Figure 13.1: Merchandise exports Russia
(In billions of dollars)

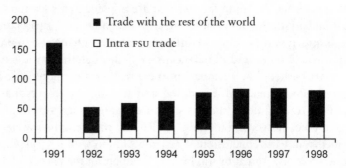

Source: IMF, *Direction of Trade Statistics*, for 1994-1998 and for 1991-1993, Michalopoulos and Tarr (1994 and 1997)

The Baltic States and Russia were the countries which reoriented their exports to the rest of the world the fastest. However, Russia's exports to the rest of the world, after rising by 50% between 1992 and 1995, have essentially stagnated since then. Indeed, 1998 exports to the rest of the world were less than in 1995. Ukraine's exports to the rest of the world were slow to pick up but have increased steadily in the last four years (see Figure 13.3). Thus, for the whole period from 1992 to 1998 Ukraine's growth rate of around 7% *per annum* was slightly higher than Russia's, and its rate of growth of imports was substantially larger still (see Figure 13.2 and 13.4).[6] Post-1992 growth rates of exports by the two countries to the FSU were very similar, around 8%. But import growth in Ukraine was much higher at about 17% (compared to 9% for Russia) reflecting in good part the

Figure 13.2: Merchandise imports Russia
(In billions of dollars)

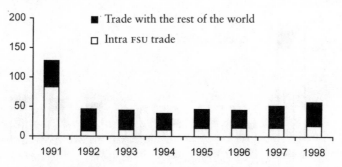

Source: IMF, *Direction of Trade Statistics*, for 1994-1998 and for 1991-1993, Michalopoulos
and Tarr (1994 and 1997)

Figure 13.3: Merchandise exports Ukraine
(In billions of dollars)

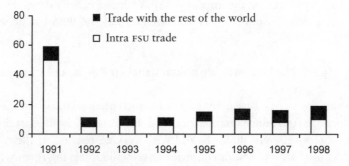

Source: IMF, *Direction of Trade Statistics*, for 1994-1998 and for 1991-1993, Michalopoulos
and Tarr (1994 and 1997)

increasing payments for energy imports from Russia and Turkmenistan.

As a consequence of these developments, at the end of the period Ukraine continues to be far more dependent on trade with the FSU – including both exports
and imports – than either Russia or the Baltic States. This is due in substantial
part to Ukraine's composition of trade. Unlike Russia, whose exports contain a
large proportion of raw materials and fuels, which are readily marketed in OECD
countries, Ukraine's exports are dominated by ferrous metals, machinery and
chemicals. These three groups of products accounted for over 55% of Ukraine's

---

6. As there was significant real appreciation of the ruble and the hrivna, especially following
1994, the subsequent increases in the dollar value of trade are somewhat less impressive. For
more general discussions of trade reorientation of transition economies, see Brenton and Gross
(1997) and Havrylyshyn and Al-Atrash (1998).

Figure 13.4: Merchandise imports Ukraine
(In billions of dollars)

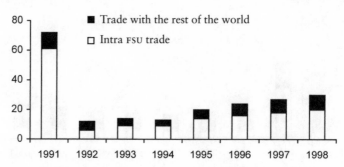

Source: IMF, *Direction of trade Statistics*, for 1994-1998 and for 1991-1993, Michalopoulos and Tarr (1994 and 1997)

total exports in 1994-1997 (Michaely, 1998). Indeed some of the exports have been seriously affected by anti-dumping actions in foreign markets (see below Section 13.3.4). Similarly, on the import side, Ukraine is heavily dependent on energy imports, which account for over 50% of the total and whose main sources are in the FSU.

13.2.3 The current trade policy stance in Russia and Ukraine

Throughout the 1990s Russia and Ukraine and other countries of the FSU pursued efforts to introduce market-oriented reforms as well as stabilise their economies with different intensity and with varying results. At the time of this writing, reform efforts in both countries have stalled, leaving them with a large unfinished agenda for transition (Aslund, 1999b, Gaidar, 1999). Perhaps, more progress has been made in trade policy than in other areas. But in both countries the trade regime is under attack from protectionist interests. And the institutions established to support trade, *e.g.* banking and customs, are weak. Both the stalled overall reforms and the weak constituency for liberal trade have adversely affected the countries' efforts to accede to the WTO.

The role of state trading

Any discussion of trade policy in previously centrally planned economies must start with a discussion of the residual role, if any, of state trading entities whose operations may introduce distortions in trade. Progress on this front depends a great deal on two factors: the extent of broader market liberalisation; and the existence or not of 'important' or 'strategic' commodities, whose trade governments feel they need to control for one reason or another.

Considerable progress has been made on this issue in both countries: it has been variously estimated that the private sector accounts for over 75% of output in Russia and a slightly smaller proportion in Ukraine. At present, there is probably even less specific state involvement in terms of setting of prices or in the provision of other special advantages to state trading entities that may fall within the definition of state trading enterprises that require to be notified under Article XVII of the GATT. A review of the situation in Russia in 1997 (Drebentsov and Michalopoulos, 1998) suggested that up to 26% of Russian trade turnover (exports plus imports) may have been affected by enterprises involved in state trading. The main such enterprises included Gazprom, Almazyuvelir (diamonds), and Roscontract. Subsequently, many of these enterprises were to be privatised, leaving state trading to account for perhaps 14-16% of total turnover, much conducted on commercial terms. While upon entry into the WTO, such enterprises would need to be notified under the provisions of GATT Article XVII, their existence in no way suggests that Russia would qualify as a country in which the government has complete or substantially complete monopoly of its trade as required in order to qualify as a 'non-market' economy for purposes of anti-dumping action under the WTO (see below).

There is little systematic information on the extent of state trading still prevailing in Ukraine. There is a general sense, that while private trading entities conduct the bulk of the trade, there is extensive government interference – possibly greater than in Russia. But here also, the former controls have been substantially weakened and government intervention, while intrusive through a variety of licensing and other arrangements, would also not qualify Ukraine as a 'non-market' economy.

Tariff and non-tariff measures on imports

Broadly speaking, tariffs in both countries do not provide for a large degree of protection, although there is significant variation by sector. Russia's import-weighted applied tariff rates average 13.6% with highs of 50% in beverages. A recent study of the Russian tariff suggested significant tariff escalation only in a few sectors (Tarr, 1998). This is not significantly different than applied rates in many developing countries at comparable level of *per capita* income (Michalopoulos, 1999).

Ukraine's tariff schedule is similar with import weighted applied tariff rates averaging 11% and weighted by domestic production 16% with the highest tariffs of 60% on foodstuffs. But the large majority of imports come in at very low or zero duties (Michaely, 1998).

Both countries also do not use extensively traditional non-tariff barriers such as as quotas to control imports at the border.7 However, in Ukraine, more so than in Russia, there is still extensive government intervention through various kinds of licensing and involvement in markets especially agriculture and major exports (Aslund 1999b).

Ukraine has also used the standard setting agency, *Derzhstandart*, as a vehicle for imposing significant *de facto* barriers to trade. Ukraine, in the interest of protecting consumers, requires universal compulsory adherence to Ukrainian 'standards' for all products. Frequently, it does not recognise standards employed by the countries of origin. This has resulted, for example, in *Derzhstandart* insisting on doing its own certification of widely sold imports from European sources, such as laundry detergents and automobiles (Michaely, 1998).

Finally, Ukraine recently imposed foreign exchange controls to limit imports in the context of balance-of-payments problems originating in the Russian rouble devaluation in 1998.

In the case of Russia, the federal structure of government combined with weak enforcement capabilities gives rise to a different set of problems: regulations regarding safety standards, labelling, and other potential technical barriers to trade exist both at the federal and at the local level, giving rise to uncertainty regarding which rules apply or will be enforced (OECD, 1999).

In the area of services there is no systematic analysis of existing restraints on modes of supply or on the provision of services in particular sectors. This is an important area where commitments will have to be made as part of the WTO accession process. The key issues in Russia (and to some extent also in Ukraine, for which even less information is available) appear to be the following. First, there are issues relating to the movement of legal and juridical persons across borders which appears to be subject to more restraints in Russia than in other WTO members. Second, there are issues regarding giving access to foreign investment to establish a commercial presence in Russia for the provision of services, *e.g.* in banking, insurance or telecommunications. Finally, there are problems that arise out of Russia's federal structure and the roles that are played by local authorities in the regulation of the service. These may well be even more significant than the problems that arise for the same reasons in the trade for goods (Smith, 1998).

The situation in Ukraine is probably similar, although there appears to be less sensitivity to movement of natural persons. There are limitations in the establishment of foreign bank branches and there are limits to foreign ownership in several sectors, *e.g.* insurance, where it can not exceed 49%.

In both countries very serious non-tariff barriers to trade of a different kind exist in the form of the general weaknesses of market support institutions, which appear to be pervasive but difficult to document and quantify systematically. Weaknesses exist both in general, for example concerning enforcement of contracts and property rights; as well as in particular areas critical to international trade, such as the availability of trade finance and insurance, or the transparency

---

7. In 1996, however, Ukraine issued a Presidential decree which would *de facto* result in a quota regime for all industrial products in which there is a "considerable violation of equilibrium between domestic and imported goods in the Ukrainian market". The equilibrium concept is nowhere defined. Fortunately, the decree has not yet been implemented.

of customs procedures. Because of weaknesses in the government and the judicial system of enforcement, there are problems, even when the laws and regulations are in conformity with international standards. Arguably, these weaknesses in the market mechanism tend to discriminate more against foreign suppliers and imports – just as they do against foreign investors.

Trade preferences

In 1992 a free trade arrangement (FTA) was concluded by the twelve CIS countries. This was followed by a number of other agreements of which the most important for the present is the customs union agreement noted earlier by Belarus, Kazakhstan, Kyrgyzstan and Russia (BKKR). The costs and benefits of this arrangement, as well as other FTAS among FSU countries, are discussed in Michalopoulos and Tarr (1997). In summary, the conclusion from that analysis is that FTAS and customs unions among the CIS members are likely to be inimical to the future trade and growth prospects for participating countries. This is in part because of the trade diversion costs entailed, but also, and perhaps most importantly, because such arrangements tend to lock in place production based on outmoded technology based on central planning.

While in principle a free trade arrangement providing for duty free treatment exists among all CIS members, the coverage of the FTA regarding individual products tends to vary, and it appears to be subject to extensive exemptions between different pairs of countries. On the other hand, a FTA, rather than a customs union appears to be in place for the BKKR countries; and a customs union (with some exemptions) appears to be in place between Belarus and Russia. The language used to describe these arrangements is tentative because information, as to what is actually in place, is hard to come by and often contradictory.

Although the BKKR countries signed a customs union agreement in 1996, a common external tariff was not fully agreed among the countries; and they decided to apply to the WTO as individual members with separate tariff schedules. Indeed, at present, Kyrgyzstan is a WTO member with a separate schedule of tariff bindings and different applied rates than those of the other three countries. There are several differences in the applied tariff rates between Kazakhstan and Russia, while there appears to be a close link between the Belarus and Russian tariffs.

Following the Kyrgyz accession to the WTO, Russia and Kazakhstan complained that the WTO commitments made by the Kyrgyz violated the commitments they had made to their customs union partners and would cause trade deflection, not only in goods but also in services, in the light of porous customs controls between Kazakhstan and Kyrgyzstan (Gabunia, 1998). The Kyrgyz authorities have engaged in consultations on this issue, but no definitive solution appears in prospect in the near future. Given the commitments Kyrgyzstan has made in the WTO, it would be very hard for it to maintain membership in a customs union with the other three countries, unless the Russian tariff (which was intended to be the basis for the external tariff of the customs union) is substantially modified.[8]

13.2.4 Market access issues

When fifteen countries emerged from the dissolution of the Soviet Union, they inherited the adversarial trade relationship that used to characterise that country with the OECD, including lack of MFN treatment. Matters changed quickly, however. First, the Baltic States and, soon thereafter, almost all of the fifteen countries obtained MFN status, and some were also extended preferential treatment under the Generalised System of Preferences (GSP) in a number of OECD markets.[9] The path of the Baltic States continued to diverge from that of the other countries later on as well. The signature of the Europe agreements provided them with preferential access in their most important markets in Western Europe. On the other hand, the remaining countries, including Russia and Ukraine, continued to face less favourable market conditions than most of their competitors in the European and US markets.

It should be underscored that for Russia, whose main exports consist of energy and raw materials, OECD markets are not significantly protected. In general terms, supply side issues rather than market access conditions have tended to be the major constraints to its overall export performance. There are far greater problems for Ukraine, whose export structure is different, and there are significant problems for both countries in specific export sectors, for example, metals, textiles, chemicals, and processed food, some of which have their origins in the cold war and the aftermath of central planning.

First, regarding access to the European markets, while both Russia and Ukraine have signed bilateral trade agreements with the EU, they face tariffs which typically put them at the bottom of the EU preference pyramid, below the ACP countries, the 'Mediterranean' agreements, the Andean pact, etc. (Stevens et al., 1999). On some products, the tariff differences are substantial: the average EU tariff on ethyl alcohol is 30 percentage points lower than what exporters from Russia and Ukraine face.

In the US, the problem is of a different nature: the MFN treatment extended by the US to CIS countries, as well as Albania, China and Mongolia is contingent on these countries' adherence to the provisions of the Jackson-Vanik amendment to the 1974 Trade Act regarding freedom of emigration. Belarus and China are subject to annual waivers. The rest, including Russia and Ukraine, have been found

---

8. In April 1999, Kyrgyzstan notified the WTO of its participation in the customs union which it said will adopt a common tariff in 2003 (WTO, 1999a).
9. For a discussion of market access issues during the early 1990s, see Kaminski (1994). Azerbaijan has had difficulties in obtaining MFN status in the US for reasons arising from its conflict with Armenia.

to be in full compliance and have received 'permanent' conditional MFN status. As long as the provisions of the act are in place, however, the US can not legally provide unconditional MFN status. This is an important issue, which raises a number of problems in connection with WTO accession for these countries, discussed below.

But perhaps the gravest market access problems these countries face arise when the EU, the US and other countries invoke trade 'remedies' against their exports. This involves primarily anti-dumping actions, the most common (and legal under the WTO) means of protection in the late 1990s; and to a secondary extent, safeguard actions. The problems in these areas arise in part because they are not members of the WTO. But in large part, they stem from the fact that they are still being designated as 'non-market' economies in the determination of anti-dumping and, in the case of the EU, also for safeguard actions. As a consequence of this designation these countries face less transparent and potentially discriminatory procedures against their exports.

There is evidence that both anti-dumping investigations and the imposition of 'definitive' anti-dumping duties is much more common against non-WTO members than against members. Table 13.1 presents recent evidence from the WTO data base on the frequency of the initiation of anti-dumping investigations – which themselves have been shown to have an adverse impact on exports – and the imposition of definitive measures, usually anti-dumping duties, relative to countries' shares in world exports for the period 1995-1997. The ratio of investigations or definitive measures to the share of total trade (Rad) is a measure that shows the tendency of a country's exports being subjected to anti-dumping actions relative to its share of world exports. Table 13.1 shows that Rad is much higher for non-WTO members than for members for both anti-dumping investigations and the imposition of 'definitive' measures, usually anti-dumping duties. It is still higher for so-called 'non-market' economies which are also not WTO members including, China, Russia, Ukraine and the rest of the CIS. Indeed Ukraine has the highest Rad for both investigations and final measures for any major country not in the WTO. Russia is also more prone to be subjected to anti-dumping measures, but in terms of investigations, its Rad is about the same as that for developing country WTO members, which is still much higher than that for developed countries.

There are many factors that contribute to these countries being much more likely to be the targets of anti-dumping actions, relative to their share in total world trade, by comparison to any other group of countries, developed or developing. The fact that they are not WTO members obviously does not help. WTO members can take actions against non-members without fear of being challenged through the WTO dispute settlement mechanism. The fact that their exchange rate has been often undervalued in recent periods makes them appear to have an unfair competitive advantage. Finally, Ukraine in particular, has an export structure dominated by products such as steel and chemicals for which there is excess capacity world-wide and which for that reason are prone to be subjected to anti dumping actions in major markets (Miranda *et al.*, 1998).

Table 13.1: Anti-dumping: Share of affected economies in total cases relative to share in world exports, 1995-1997 (in % and ratios)

Affected Economies	Share in world exports	Share in total anti-dumping investigations	Share in total definitive measures	Rad investigations	Rad definitive measures
WTO Members	87.7%	73.4%	63.9%	0.8	0.7
Developed	62.5%	34.1%	21.7%	0.5	0.3
Developing	22.0%	34.4%	36.1%	1.6	1.6
Transition & Other	3.2%	4.8%	6.1%	1.5	1.9
Non WTO Members	12.3%	26.6%	36.1%	2.2	2.9
Russia	1.8%	2.3%	6.1%	1.3	3.3
Ukraine	0.2%	1.3%	2.8%	6.8	14.1
China	4.5%	15.6%	22.3%	3.5	5.0
Other 'non-market'	0.4%	1.5%	0.9%	4.3	2.6
Other	5.4%	5.8%	4.0%	1.1	0.7

Rad: Share in investigations (Measures) / Share in world exports.

Source: WTO, Trade and Anti-dumping Data Base; Miranda (1998)

Once the target of an investigation, the procedures used to determine whether dumping has occurred in 'non-market' economies are usually different from those applied to other countries. Because it was assumed that prices and exchange rates in centrally planned economies, did not reflect true opportunity costs, 'surrogate' or 'analogue' countries' costs and exchange rates were and continue to be used for the determination of 'normal' value, against which the actual price is measured.[10] This introduces the possibility for arbitrariness and non-transparency. More importantly, these procedures make it easier to induce exporters to agree to minimum price undertakings such as those concluded with Russia on uranium and aluminium (Michalopoulos and Winters, 1997).

In the context of safeguards, the EU standards for taking action against 'non-market' economies are lower than for other countries which are WTO members. In the case of 'non-market' economies merely the coexistence of higher imports and injury to domestic producers as opposed to a causal link needs to be demonstrated; and there is no limit on the duration of the action, as required by GATT Article XIX (Michalopoulos and Winters, 1997). With regard to anti-dumping, the WTO provides legal justification for such practices through the reference of Arti-

---

10. The EU publishes annually a list of 'non-market' economies. The latest list (1999) includes Albania, Armenia, Azerbaijan, Belarus, Georgia, Kazakhstan, North Korea, Kyrgyzstan, Moldova, Mongolia, Tajikistan, Turkmenistan, Ukraine, Uzbekistan and Vietnam. In the US, the decision is made on a case-by-case basis, but the countries are mostly the same as in the EU and have included both Russia and Ukraine.

cle 2.7 of the Anti-dumping Agreement to the second Supplementary Provision to paragraph 1 of Article VI in Annex 1 to GATT 1994 which permits such different treatment "in the case of imports from a country which has complete or substantially complete monopoly of its trade and where all domestic prices are fixed by the State" (Palmeter, 1998, p.116).

These practices perhaps were fully justified when practically all trade was controlled by state trading enterprises or Ministries under central planning and prices were fixed by the State and hence could not be taken to reflect 'normal value'. But at present, although markets in Ukraine and Russia are quite imperfect, it is impossible to argue that these countries' governments have 'a substantially complete monopoly on trade' or that all domestic prices are fixed by the State. Continuation of the traditional EC and US anti-dumping practices in the new setting no longer appears justified for either Russia or Ukraine.

In early 1998, the EU announced liberalisation measures on this issue *vis-à-vis* Russia (and China, but not Ukraine) which terminated their designation as 'non-market' economies at the country level and would permit determinations to be made on a case-by-case basis, that would take into account the market conditions prevailing in each product in which dumping has been alleged. Such a case-by-case approach has also been used by the US. It is unclear whether this would result in a smaller number of anti-dumping actions against this country in the future: and what were the reasons for excluding Ukraine – or for that matter a number of other CIS countries.

13.2.5 Summary

The above review of Russian and Ukrainian trade policy and market access issues, suggests that, while the two countries have taken a number of steps to establish trade policies and institutions that would support their integration into the multilateral trading system, much remains to be done: a number of non-tariff impediments to trade exist, some of which are generic and reflect weaknesses in overall market supporting institutions and some which are specific to the institutions and policies affecting international trade. At the same time, in terms of market access, the international community continues to treat both countries much less favourably than others, especially regarding the use of anti-dumping measures affecting Ukraine's exports, thereby impeding their fuller participation in the multilateral trading system.

13.3 WTO accession

13.3.1 The benefits from WTO membership

The benefits from WTO membership fall in three main categories: (1) strengthening of domestic policies and institutions for the conduct of international trade in both goods and services which is needed before accession into the WTO can be accomplished; (2) improvements in the ease and security of market access to major export markets; (3) access to a dispute settlement mechanism for trade issues.

Domestic policies and institutions

Under central planning, the government of the Soviet Union controlled trade through ministries and state trading enterprises. The institutions governing other aspects of international exchange of goods and services, such as intellectual property rights, standards, phytosanitary provisions, procurement, *etc.*, were either different or non-existent. WTO membership requires that these policies and institutions be brought in line with the provisions of the main international agreements regarding trade in goods (General Agreement on Tariffs and Trade, GATT), trade in services (General Agreement for Trade in Services, GATS) and trade-related aspects of intellectual property rights (TRIPS). This involves dramatic and profound changes in the way trade was, and in some respects still is, conducted by Russia, Ukraine and the other FSU countries.

Perhaps most important of these changes is the need to introduce the laws and institutions for the operation of private enterprises and markets free from government controls and state trading practices.[11] Equally important is the introduction of greater stability in commercial policy, which is a consequence of adherence to WTO rules and legally binding agreements. Stability is important both to domestic producers and to exporters from other countries wishing access to the markets of Russia and Ukraine.

WTO membership also offers the opportunity for new members to lock in trade regimes with legally binding obligations regarding tariff levels and commitments on services under the GATS. This not only permits them to enjoy the benefits of liberal trade, but also gives them a first line of defence against domestic protec-

---

11. During the cold war, the issue of compatibility of central planning with the WTO and GATT was heavily influenced by political considerations: Hungary, Poland and Romania were admitted to the GATT, essentially for foreign policy reasons under special arrangements and despite serious concerns as to whether their commitments, for example regarding tariffs, were meaningful in the context of central planning (Haus, 1992). At the same time Czechoslovakia and Cuba maintained their original membership in the GATT although their central planning systems made their commitments relatively meaningless.

tionist pressures that are on the rise in both Russia and Ukraine and which inevitably are present in all market economies.

Market access

There are two main dimensions of market access of importance to transition economies. First, is the extension of permanent and unconditional MFN status, that comes with WTO membership. While, as noted earlier, transition economies have been granted MFN treatment voluntarily by major trading partners, there is nothing that guarantees that they will be continued to be awarded such treatment, for example in the US. Second, WTO membership could help but not guarantee the termination of designating Russia and Ukraine as 'non-market' economies by major trading partners such as the EU and the US.

Dispute settlement

Access to an impartial and binding dispute settlement mechanism, whose decisions have a significant chance of being enforced, is a very important potential benefit for all countries participating in international trade. This is especially important to both Russia and Ukraine as their exports appear to have been affected by WTO member practices on anti-dumping that may or may not be consistent with WTO rules. The dispute settlement mechanism under the WTO, in the short time since its establishment, has been shown to provide significant opportunities for any member, large or small to get satisfaction on grievances stemming from practices of other members that cause injury to its trade.

13.3.2 The accession process

The process of accession to the WTO has been complex, prolonged and difficult for most countries. The average time for accession was more than five years for the last six countries which became WTO member. The process has two major components: (a) a fact-finding phase, which aims at determining whether the acceding country has in place laws and regulations consistent with obligations that it will be assuming under the WTO agreements; (b) a negotiation phase, in which countries are asked to make 'offers' of legally binding commitments regarding their tariff schedule on all goods, a separate set of commitments on agriculture (which includes a more complex set of commitments involving *e.g.* aggregate domestic support), and services. After these 'offers', as modified through negotiations, have been accepted by the WTO members, they become part of the protocol of WTO accession and result in legally binding commitments.

Formally, the discussions are conducted under a 'Working Party' established by the WTO, but at the negotiation phase, they involve a large number of bilateral negotiations with important trading partners. At the end of the process the

Working Party issues a draft report for consideration and approval by the WTO Council.[12]

The negotiations tend to be one way only. With very few exceptions, the sole focus of discussion is the policies, laws and institutions of the acceding country, not those of the existing members. The burden is almost totally on the acceding country to persuade WTO members that it has met WTO conditions and it has made reasonable offers. An acceding country, however, may seek in bilateral negotiations an understanding, outside the formal accession protocol, regarding the way one or more WTO members implement their WTO commitments, which has a bearing on its commercial interests – not in the commitments themselves. This is rare, and depends a great deal on the leverage an acceding country may have because of the size of its market.

Accession thus depends, in the first instance on the acceding country satisfying the WTO members that it has put in place and is able to implement the laws and regulations required for conformity with WTO Agreements. Delays and problems have arisen for all transition countries in this phase of the process. Some are due to the inherent complexities of enacting legislation and regulations that bring into conformity the regimes of transition economies with WTO rules. These extend far beyond the obvious such as the Law on Customs, the tariff schedule and related regulations on imports and exports. They also include items such as the laws on joint stock companies, the central bank and credit institutions, licensing of economic activity, domestic taxation, regulations on food and alcoholic beverages, veterinary medicine and pests subject to quarantine, patent and copyright protection, consumer protection, *etc*. Design and enactment of all this legislation and regulations are quite demanding on the institutions of the acceding countries. But the WTO accession process provides a useful stimulus for the review and consistency of a lot of these matters which may not have otherwise happened.

There are some issues, which are especially difficult in transition economy accessions, which have also caused delays. These include the degree of privatisation in the economy and the extent to which government agencies involved in the regulation of economic activity do so on the basis of transparent rules and criteria as opposed to administrative discretion. Both of these concerns emanate from the dominant role that the state previously played – and in some cases, *e.g.* Belarus, still does – in the economies of these countries. While the WTO agreements have no explicit requirement that a member must have fundamentally a market economy,[13] such a requirement is being imposed *de facto* by existing members as

---

12. For a detailed discussion see Michalopoulos (1998); for a recent update, WTO (1999b).
13. GATT Article XVII calls for notification of enterprises engaging in state trading practices. However, Article XVII had never been intended to address problems that come up when the bulk of external trade was controlled by the state. Indeed the old GATT accommodated under special protocols several countries, *e.g.* Romania and Czechoslovakia, which at the time had centrally planned economies.

part of the leverage they have in the accession process for new members. A key issue for enterprises that are expected to remain state owned is whether they operate under market conditions or enjoy special monopoly rights and privileges.

In many cases, there have also been concerns relating to the jurisdiction and capacity of national agencies to implement policies on which commitments are being made. The fundamental concern is one of governance. Do the government agencies have the authority and capacity to implement the commitments that they are making in the context of WTO accession regarding the laws and regulations that concern the conduct of international trade? A related concern arises about the role and jurisdiction of local authorities and whether they have the right and opportunity to nullify the commitments made by the national authorities in the context of accession negotiations.

Accession also depends on a country reaching an agreement with WTO members on its 'offers' for binding commitments in tariffs, agriculture and services. The latter in turn depends on how liberal its trade regime is and how demanding WTO members are regarding the degree of access they expect in the acceding country's markets for goods and services.

Experience has shown that the smaller the country, and hence the more dependent on international trade, and the more rapidly it has moved to introduce market-oriented reforms and liberal trade policies, the easier it is to accede to the WTO. This is because small countries have little leverage in the negotiations and much to lose by protectionist policies and by remaining outside of the WTO. Latvia and Kyrgyzstan which have already become members, as well as the other Baltic States, Armenia and Georgia, which are close to acceding, are all small countries with relatively open trade regimes. By contrast, the countries in Central Asia which are laggards in market-oriented reforms are also lagging in terms of WTO accession.

13.4 The status of Russia's and Ukraine's negotiations for WTO accession

Russia and Ukraine originally applied for accession to the GATT in 1993, and working parties (WP) to consider their applications were established in June and December of that year respectively. The first substantive steps involving the preparation of a memorandum on their foreign trade regimes were taken in March and July of 1994 respectively (see Table 13.2). With the establishment of the WTO in 1995, the accession discussions were continued under the auspices of the new Organisation.

In the six years since their original application, there were numerous WP meetings (nine in the case of Russia and six for Ukraine) to discuss various aspects of their foreign trade regimes covering various aspects of their domestic and foreign trade policies and institutions ranging from standards, to privatisation and tax legislation linked to the accession process (WTO, 1999b). In support of these discussions the countries have had to prepare voluminous documentation on all aspects of their domestic laws and regulations that impinge on the implementation of their future obligations under the wto agreements.[14]

The formal working party process has been characterised by a question and answer format: wp Members would pose specific questions usually in writing, but also verbally, to which the governments produce answers in writing. The process is cumbersome and lengthy: if a member does not feel it has received an adequate answer to a question, it resubmits it for the next wp meeting. And the governments have had to make numerous presentations dealing with changes occurring in their evolving trade regimes and progress they have made in enacting appropriate legislation.

While there has been extensive discussion of many aspects of the Russian and Ukrainian trade regimes over the last five years, many issues regarding the institutional and legal aspects of the regimes are unresolved including such questions as legislation affecting foreign direct investment as it relates to commitments in GATS; implementation of the TRIPs Agreement; in the case of Russia, questions of implementation of a VAT, based on the destination principle for imports from all sources; jurisdiction between federal and local authorities in the area of standards; in both countries, but especially on Russia, issues related to the workings of regional preferential agreements. Some of these questions may not be fully resolved until the last stages of negotiations and as part of an overall agreement that includes the offers on tariffs and services, as well as commitments on support to agriculture.

In parallel with the formal wp discussions, both Russia and Ukraine have made preliminary offers on tariff bindings for goods in 1998 and 1996 respectively, which have been the subject of initial bilateral negotiations with wto members. Ukraine has also made initial and revised offers on services. Thus, formally at this stage both countries (with the major exception of Russia not having made a service offer) have entered the last phase of discussions regarding accession to the wto. Unfortunately, experience has shown that this last phase can be a protracted one and depends very much on the trade regime for goods and services in each country, their negotiating stance regarding the kind of binding commitments in both goods and services they offer, and the attitudes of wto members regarding their expectations for access they obtain in these countries' markets.

13.4.1 Acceding government strategy and tactics

Within the rules and disciplines of the wto, each country has considerable scope as to how restrictive or liberal its trade regime will be, consistent with the overall wto disciplines. The key decision Russia and Ukraine have to make relate to

---

14. At the time of this writing, the last formal Russia wp meeting had occurred in December 1998, and in the case Ukraine, June 1998. Just the listing of the documents produced on Russia covers six pages.

Table 13.2: Timetable of accessions to the WTO

Government	WP establishment	Memorandum	Tariff offers	Service offers	Draft working party report
Former Soviet Union					
Armenia	12/93	04/95	01/99	10/98, 01/99	02/99
Azerbaijan	07/97	04/99	-	-	-
Belarus	10/93	01/96	03/98	-	-
Estonia	03/94	03/94	08/95, 02/99	04/95	11/98
Georgia	07/96	04/97	02/98, 12/98	02/98, 09/98	4/99
Kazakhstan	02/96	09/96	06/97	09/97	-
Lithuania	02/94	12/94	10/95, 02/99	04/95	10/98
Moldova	12/93	09/96	03/98, 01/99	02/98, 10/98	-
Russian Federation	06/93	03/94	02/98	-	-
Ukraine	12/93	07/94	05/96	07/98, 10/98	-
Uzbekistan	12/94	09/98	-	-	-
Other Countries in Transition					
Albania	12/92	01/95	05/97, 01/99	05/97, 11/98	-
Cambodia	12/94	-	-	-	-
China	03/87	02/87, 09/93	04/94	09/94, 11/97	12/94
Croatia	10/93	06/94	04/97, 04/98	05/97, 11/98	08/98
FYR Macedonia	12/94	04/99	-	-	-
Laos	02/98	-	-	-	-
Vietnam	01/95	09/96	-	-	-

Source: WTO (1999b)

the level at which they bind their tariffs, the support they provide to agriculture and the range of commitments in the liberalisation of the service trade.

Russia and Ukraine have felt that significant levels of protection are necessary during a transition period during which restructuring of inefficient state enterprises and service sectors can be undertaken.[15] Accordingly, they have presented initial offers that propose to bind tariffs at rates much higher than those currently applied, ('ceiling bindings') and, in the case of Russia, leave a number of tariffs unbound. This strategy is also motivated by tactical considerations. Since at accession applicants can not typically negotiate improvements in their own market access, it may be desirable to try to maintain significant levels of protection, which they can use as bargaining chips to obtain improved access in future negotiating rounds. Their strategy appears to involve liberalising as little as minimally necessary to ensure accession.

---

15. See Gabunia (1998).

There are serious dangers to such a strategy, however. Unbound tariffs and ceiling bindings are an open invitation to lobbies in both countries to seek additional protection. They also create uncertainties for foreign suppliers regarding the stability of market access. Binding tariffs at close to applied rates provides governments with political cover against domestic protectionist lobbies and increase stability and credibility in the trade regime. Increased protection to 'safeguard' against injury to domestic industry is permitted under WTO rules – but it is supposed to be decided on the basis of a detailed and transparent investigation to demonstrate which is then notified to the WTO and subjected to the scrutiny of other members. Unfortunately, all this appears to be too complicated and transparent for the powerful protectionist interests which influence trade policy in both countries at present.

Russia's offer, made in February 1998, led to some preliminary and rather difficult negotiations. Russia was invited to put forward an offer on services, but as of mid-June 1999 had not done so. There is a strong evidence that for a variety of reasons, both political and economic, Russia's accession has lost its dynamic: struggles between the executive and the *Duma* over legislation, the rising influence of economic elite in the service sector – whose interests might adversely be affected by a liberal service offer, and continued uncertainty in the relations between the centre and the regions are key reasons (Buchalova, 1998). Government instability throughout 1998 and early 1999 also set back the accession process.

Ukraine has been pursuing a similar, though separate approach to its negotiations. In some respects its discussions are more advanced, since it has tabled an initial and revised offer on services; but its tariff offer on goods is a preliminary one, dating to 1996; and the discussions on it were only of a general nature. Prospects for their resumption in the immediate future are clouded by the impending presidential election.

13.4.2 WTO member attitudes and policies

Acceding countries are not solely responsible for the delays in accession. WTO members have played their part as well. In many respects the demands made for newly acceding countries are greater than the disciplines on existing members at similar levels of development (Michalopoulos, 1998). Acceding countries are typically requested to meet all commitments at entry, for example with regard to TRIPs, customs valuation, standards or sanitary and phytosanitary regulations; without time limits, such as those available to existing members at similar levels of development; and regardless of whether institutional weaknesses make it difficult for them to fulfil such commitments. These weaknesses relate broadly to aspects of the operations of a market economy, where it takes time to establish the proper institutional infrastructure that would enable them to discharge their responsibilities properly under the WTO agreements. There are many examples of such areas: the development of appropriate legislation and institutions for intellectual and other property rights protection, the establishment of a suitable regulatory environment for standards or phytosanitary controls, regulatory aspects of provision of financial services, *etc*. In agriculture, which both Russia and Ukraine did not support, but rather penalise, the requests they face for reductions in aggregate support may not be warranted; and in any case meaningful calculation of commitments in this area is subject to serious statistical difficulties.[16]

While the insistence of WTO members on a liberal commercial policy at entry is likely to serve both acceding countries' long-term economic interests as well as WTO members' commercial objectives, insistence on adherence to all the WTO commitments at entry and without transition periods in areas such as customs valuation, TRIPs, standards and SPS (sanitary and phytosanitary measures) where there are obvious institutional weaknesses in Russia, Ukraine and other transition economies, raises problems. Effective implementation can be realistically expected only some time in the future. But both countries may be prone to agree to meet these commitments at entry to get the negotiations concluded, leaving themselves open to future complaints.

Perhaps the most important factor for the delays associated with WTO negotiations is that the political economy of international trade policy is dominated by particular commercial interests in all countries. While at a general policy level WTO members might agree that accession of Russia and Ukraine to the WTO is of paramount importance to their foreign policy interests, accession can not occur until the particular commercial interests in all countries are satisfied. And that takes time. However, the WTO accession discussions with both Russia and Ukraine have not yet reached the stage where delays are occurring because of the need to satisfy particular commercial interests in the acceding country or in WTO members.

13.4.3 Issues that Russia and Ukraine should raise with WTO members

While the leverage any acceding country has in obtaining modifications in existing member policy is extremely limited, there are two issues that both Russia and Ukraine have to raise in connection with their accession to the WTO, with the US, the EU and a number of other developed countries members of the WTO.

The first concerns solely the US and involves the repeal of the provisions of the

---

16. Accession involves in part commitments to aggregate measures of support to agriculture relative to a 'representative' period, usually the three years prior to the application for accession. Such commitments are most often based on data which contain serious statistical and economic pitfalls. For example, the three years prior to the accession application frequently coincide with the early 1990s when these countries were in the midst of hyperinflation and their exchange rates were unstable and could hardly be viewed as representing 'equilibrium'. Similar problems arise if the late eighties are used as 'representative'

Jackson-Vanik amendment to the 1974 Trade Act regarding freedom of emigration. As long as the provisions of the act are in place, however, the US can not legally provide unconditional MFN status. Russia and Ukraine must obtain iron-clad guaranties. Indeed, probably they should obtain a US commitment that the legislation is repealed before they accede to the WTO. If the legislation is not repealed, these countries, as well as others on the US list, might find themselves in the uncomfortable position of having had extended negotiations on their trade regime with the US, only to have the US exercise its right of non-application under WTO's Article XVIII.

This is what happened with Kyrgyzstan and Mongolia. Both countries were given an understanding by the US in the context of their accession negotiations that it will seek Congressional amendment to the Jackson-Vanik legislation. This has not occurred yet. In the meantime, the US invoked Article XVIII of the WTO for both, which means that it does not provide these countries with unconditional MFN – or for that matter with any other WTO rights – and thus *de facto* the US does not accept their membership in the WTO.

The second, and perhaps even more difficult, question both countries need to raise with the US, the EU and a number of other developed countries, in the context of their accession negotiations, is their designation as 'non-market' economies. As noted above this issue arises when the EU, the US and other countries invoke trade 'remedies', especially anti-dumping actions against their exports.

WTO membership could inhibit the most egregious excesses in anti-dumping practices against which a non-member has no recourse, as the WTO dispute settlement mechanism, albeit with some limitations, can be utilised for this purpose. WTO membership would also address the problem 'non-market' economies have regarding the different standards imposed by the EU on safeguards. WTO membership, however, would not automatically terminate the designation of countries in transition as 'non-market' economies, nor completely terminate the problems they have with anti-dumping. In 1999, the EU continues to consider both Kyrgyzstan and Mongolia as 'non-market' economies, although they are WTO members and the role of the state in their economies is probably less than in many developing country WTO members.

Thus, Russia and Ukraine need to reach an understanding in the context of their accession negotiations as to whether they will continue to be treated as 'non-market' economies. They should try to obtain guarantees that they will not be, even on a case-by-case basis. The standards of accession have evolved in such a way as to provide WTO members with assurances that a newly acceding country fundamentally is run on market principles, however imperfect its markets, making current anti-dumping practices, if not illegal, demonstrably unfair and inconsistent with current WTO provisions. It can be reasonably assumed that Russia and Ukraine would not secure WTO membership unless they could demonstrate that their trade was fundamentally based on market transactions. And on that basis, they should seek to obtain assurances (outside the formal protocol) that they will no longer be designated as 'non-market' economies.

13.5 Challenges for the future

Given where Russia and Ukraine stand in their negotiations for WTO accession, they will not be able to become members before the end of 1999. They have not yet reached an understanding regarding the implementation of the rules and disciplines contained in the WTO agreement. They are at early stages of negotiations regarding their offers on tariffs, services and agriculture. And they have a number of issues that they would want to raise about WTO member practices. This means that they will not be able to participate fully in the upcoming WTO multilateral trade negotiations expected to be launched at the Seattle Ministerial Meeting in November 1999. This has implications regarding their accession strategies, their participation in these negotiations and their longer-term integration in the multilateral trading system.

The momentum for market and trade reforms in both countries has stalled. While their trade regimes are not especially restrictive, weaknesses in the operations of fundamental market institutions inhibit effective integration in the trading system. It is not that the state is controlling prices or output decisions. Rather that the market-support systems as well as the systems of governance are weak, resulting in *de facto* barriers to trade. These problems, combined with persistent protective pressures, have inhibited progress and accession to the WTO.

Both countries need to reinvigorate their accession efforts, in the context of wider market reforms. As long as the overall market-reform process is lagging, it is very difficult – and less meaningful – to move forward in trade. In addition, they need to take stock of where they stand in the enactment of legislation and implementation of regulations that are needed to meet WTO requirements and take the appropriate steps to make sure that the needed legislation and regulations are put in place. This will not be easy, but it is essential for accession. Finally, they need to get on with bilateral negotiations on tariffs, services and agriculture. They should be prepared to revise their offers with a view to binding all tariffs at levels reasonably close to those they apply, and be forthcoming in liberalising services and providing a market environment for agriculture. All these steps would promote their long-term economic interests as well as be helpful in speeding up the accession process. In the context of the bilateral negotiations, they should be willing to 'give up' these 'concessions' – which are likely to be in their long term economic interest in any case – in order to get WTO members to change certain of their policies, *e.g.* with regard to anti-dumping which are quite harmful to Russia's and Ukraine's export interests.

While the bulk of the reform and adjustment effort must be made by Russia and Ukraine, WTO members, and especially the US and the EU, which take the leading role in accession negotiations, need to make some changes as well. First, both need to review their policy regarding 'non-market' economies as it relates to anti-dumping and in the EU case, safeguards. The review should ensure that countries where market decisions prevail – however imperfect the markets may be – are not designated as 'non-market' economies and thus subjected to even more opaque and non-transparent procedures than those normally associated with anti-dumping practices, nor encouraged to enter into cartel like price fixing arrangements. This should be done immediately and should apply to countries in the process of acceding to the WTO.

Second, countries that are members of the WTO should be automatically judged to be 'market' economies and should be excluded from the 'non-market' procedures applied in anti-dumping and safeguard measures.[17]

Third, consideration should be given to extending the time frames – but not deviating from the principles – regarding the implementation of commitments in WTO areas where Russia's and Ukraine's institutions are weak, e.g. TRIPs, phytosanitary and other standards, customs valuation. Whereas more technical assistance than currently provided to these countries to strengthen their capabilities in this area may be needed, it should be recognised that technical assistance alone does not build institutions, and that the latter take time to put in place and become effective.

Finally, as neither Russia nor Ukraine will be able to become members before the launching of the new WTO Round of multilateral negotiations, arrangements will have to be made for their effective participation in the Round as observers. There are precedents for this under the GATT Uruguay Round of multilateral trade negotiations. Such arrangements would probably require that they commit to a standstill in trade measures, just like other participants in the Round. While they may not be able to participate in the give and take of the actual negotiations, it would be possible for both countries to follow the negotiations and adjust their own policies as necessary, so as to permit them to become members at the end of the Round. It is conceivable that they could accede during the Round, but it would be difficult, especially because once the Round gets under way the focus of attention shifts to the negotiations under the Round. One way or the other however, they need to ensure that they do what it is necessary to ensure accession at least by the end of the next Round, so as to be able to participate more effectively in the multilateral trading system.

---

17. The US has a special problem which it needs to address as well, namely the repeal of the Jackson-Vanik amendment, without which it can not make credible commitments of providing MFN treatment to many transition economies acceding to the WTO.

References

Aslund, A. (1999a), *Why Has Russia's Economic Transformation Been so Arduous*, Annual Bank Conference on Development Economics, World Bank, April, Washington, D.C.

Aslund, A. (1999b), *Problems with Economic Transformation in Ukraine*, paper presented at the 5TH Dubrovnik Conference on Transition Economies, June.

Brenton, P. and D. Gros (1997), 'Trade Reorientation and Recovery in Transition Economies', *Oxford Review of Economic Policy*, Vol.13, No.2.

Buchalova, M. (1998), *The Role of Internal Factors in Delaying Russia's Accession to the* WTO, Occasional Paper, No.48, Carleton University, Ottawa.

Drabek, Z. (1996), 'The Stability of Trade Policy in the Countries in Transition and their Integration in the Multilateral Trading System', *World Economy*, Vol.19, No.6.

Drebentsov, V. and C. Michalopoulos (1998), 'State Trading in Russia', in: T. Cottier and P.C. Mavroidis (eds.), *State Trading in the Twenty-First Century*, The University of Michigan Press.

Gabunia, G. (1998), 'Reasonable Protectionism', *Expert*, Vol.33, September.

Gaidar, Y. (1999), *The Legacy of the Socialist Economy: The Macro and Microeconomic Consequences of Soft Budget Constraints*, paper presented at the 5TH Dubrovnik Conference on Transition Economies, June.

Haus, L. (1992), *Globalizing the* GATT, The Brookings Institution, Washington, D.C.

Havrylyshyn, O. and H. Al-Atash (1998), *Opening Up and Geographic Diversification of Trade in Transition Economies*, IMF Working Paper, No.22, Washington, D.C.

Kaminski, B. (1994), 'Trade Performance and Access to OECD Markets', in: C. Michalopoulos and D.G. Tarr (eds.), *Trade in the New Independent States*, Studies of Economies in Transformation, No.13, World Bank, Washington, D.C.

Michaely, M. (1998), *Ukraine: Foreign Trade and Commercial Policies* (processed), World Bank, Kiev.

Michalopoulos, C. (1998), 'WTO Accession for Countries in Transition', *Post-Soviet Prospects*, Vol.6, No.3.

Michalopoulos, C. (1999), 'Trade Policy and Market Access Issues for Developing Countries', World Trade Organization, forthcoming.

Michalopoulos, C. and D.G. Tarr (1994), 'Summary and Overview of Developments Since Independence', in: C. Michalopoulos and D.G. Tarr (eds.), *Trade in the New Independent States*, Studies of Economies in Transformation, No.13, World Bank, Washington, D.C.

Michalopoulos, C. and D.G. Tarr (1997), 'The Economics of Customs Unions in the Commonwealth of Independent States', *Post-Soviet Geography and Economics*, Vol.38, No.3.

Michalopoulos, C. and L.A. Winters (1997), 'Summary and Overview', in: P.D. Ehrenhaft *et al.*, *Policies on Imports from Economies in Transition*, Studies of Economies in Transformation, No.22, World Bank, Washington, D.C.

Miranda, J., R. Torres and M. Ruiz (1998), 'The International Use of Anti-Dumping', *Journal of World Trade*, Vol.32, No.5.

OECD (1999), *Round Table on the Interface Between the Central and Sub-National Levels of Government in Russia's Trade Policy*, March 1999, Novgorod Velikiy.

Palmeter, D.N. (1998), 'The WTO Antidumping Agreement and the Economies in Transition', in: T. Cottier and P.C. Mavroidis (eds.), *State Trading in the Twenty-First Century*, The University of Michigan Press.

Smith, M.G. (1998), 'Russia and the General Agreement on Trade in Services (GATS)', in: H.G. Broadman, *Russian Trade Policy Reform for WTO Accession*, World Bank Discussion Paper, No.401, Washington, D.C.

Stevens, C., M. McQueen and J. Kennan (1999), *After Lome IV: A Strategy for ACP-EU Relations in the 21st Century*, Paper presented at the Joint Commonwealth Secretariat, World Bank Conference on the Small States, 17-19 February, St. Lucia.

Tarr, D.G. (1998), 'Design of Tariff Policy for Russia', in: H.G. Broadman, *Russian Trade Policy Reform for WTO Accession*, World Bank Discussion Paper No.401, Washington, D.C.

World Trade Organization (1999a), *Accession of the Kyrgyz Republic to the Customs Union between the Russian Federation, Belarus and Kazakhstan*, Notification, April, WT/REG71/N/1.

World Trade Organization (1999b), *Technical Note on the Accession Process*, March, WT/ACC/7.

Conclusions

Guido Biessen and Frans Engering

The primacy of politics

At the moment the idea was born to prepare a book on the prospects for European integration after ten years of transition, newspapers were dominated by the awful news of the Kosovo-crisis, after the NATO intervention in the region. The terrible war and the revival of nationalist sentiments and inter-ethnic conflicts in former Yugoslavia have come at great cost to the local population and have shocked the world. It provoked a number of commentators to remind the public of the original aims of European integration: political stability and peace. As Van den Broek clearly states in Chapter 5: "European integration brought remarkable political stability and a spectacular increase in well-being". Suggestions were made to speed up the process of enlargement, to extend negotiations to the second group of accession candidates, for instance Bulgaria and Romania, and to start a discussion on how to incorporate (parts of) former Yugoslavia into the process of European integration. In this context, the European Commission has proposed that Stabilisation and Association Agreements be established with five South-Eastern European countries, *i.e.* Albania, Bosnia-Herzegovina, Croatia, FYR Macedonia, and the Federal Republic of Yugoslavia.

In Chapter 9, Rosati pays ample attention to the political benefits of economic integration and classifies the benefits into four categories. First, integration enhances international security. The well-known proposition of interdependence is that economic relations are costly to break, which may prevent political tensions getting out of hand. Second, membership of the EU enhances the internal stability in the candidate countries. The adoption of Western European concepts of rule of law and the introduction of Western European market-oriented institutions foster economic growth and political stability. Third, the process of accession to the EU reinforces the reform process in the Central and Eastern European countries (CEECs), and restricts tendencies towards populism, nationalism and a reversal to authoritarian rule. Fourth, the geographical location of the CEEC-10 between Western Europe and the CIS is of strategic importance, and, once an integral part of the EU, the CEEC-10 may serve as a useful bridge between Western Europe and the CIS.

European integration appears to have strong attractiveness to the countries surrounding the EU. The coming round of eastern enlargement is essential in building the new Europe in the post Cold-War era. The primacy of politics in the process of European integration is underlined. As Baldwin *et al.* (1997) rightfully conclude: "economic integration is the means, not the end". A focus on the pure economic benefits and budgetary consequences of the enlargement to the East discredits the principal idea behind European integration. Given the huge political interests and the large economic advantages in all its aspects, a pure bookkeeper's interpretation of an eastern enlargement is entirely out of place.

The importance of economics

Economics does matter though. In order to integrate successfully into the world economy, progress with respect to market-oriented reforms is of key importance. Although the region is far from homogenous, it has been pointed out at several places throughout this book that the progress that has been made with respect to transition to a market economy is remarkable. The larger part of GDP is now accounted for by the private sector. Growth has resumed in a large number of countries after the initial severe depression at the start of the transition process. The countries that seek accession to the EU have to satisfy a number of conditions. As Van den Broek emphasises in Chapter 5, the countries have to meet the three Copenhagen conditions. One is a political criterion, *i.e.* being a stable democracy. There is also an *acquis* criterion, *i.e.* taking on the obligations of full membership. Additionally, there is also an important economic criterion, *i.e.* having a functioning market economy that is able to cope with the competitive pressure within the EU. Analogously, Michalopoulos concludes, in Chapter 13, that weaknesses in the operation of fundamental market institutions are the main obstacles to Russia and Ukraine becoming fully integrated in the world trading system, and that they prevent their accession to the WTO.

With respect to macro-stabilisation, substantial progress has been achieved. Stern and Wes note in Chapter 2, that the countries, in general, were successful in reducing the high levels of inflation that were common at the onset of the transition process. Inflation rates dropped from extremely high levels in the early 1990s, to much lower levels in the second half of the 1990s, although in some countries a reversal could be observed. As extremely high inflation has an obvious negative effect on economic growth and efficiency, the containment of high inflation is a necessary condition for the resumption of economic growth.

Stern and Wes also draw attention to the fiscal aspects of transition. Raising tax revenues remains an important challenge for the future. Particularly in Russia and other CIS countries, tax collection is a huge problem, and hampers macroeconomic stabilisation efforts. Tax evasion is widespread. Extensive barter trade makes effective tax collection on these transactions virtually impossible. Tax avoidance is common. Tax exemptions and tax breaks are given to enterprises in a rather arbitrary way. Soft budget constraints take the shape of large tax arrears for enterprises which, especially in Russia, are extraordinary high.

An important aspect of transition is reintegration in the world economy. Note-worthy is the reorientation of trade. Trade of the CEECs shifted from their former principal trading partners in Eastern Europe, in particular Russia, towards West-ern markets, in particular to the European Union and especially Germany. In Chapter 4 it is shown, based on a gravitational analysis, that the level of trade between the countries of the EU and three Central European countries has increased substantially. The gap existing in the 1980s between the 'potential' level of trade and the actual level of trade within Europe between East and West has been narrowed to a considerable degree during a decade of transition. In 1997, in general, Western European countries were exporting close to their potential, but imports were still significantly below the 'potential' level. In coming years, a further flow of goods from Central Europe to Western Europe is to be expected.

Hence, the process of opening up was accompanied by substantial trade deficits. Stern and Wes (Chapter 2) suggest that current account deficits are a nor-mal phenomenon for a country in transition when foreign savings are used for domestic restructuring. Foreign capital inflows are important for restructuring the economy. Nevertheless, rapidly increasing current account deficits exceeding 5% of GDP, a threshold often used as a 'rule-of-thumb' warning signal, may prove to be unsustainable. They may trigger investors to withdraw capital from the coun-try at a rapid pace, leaving the central banks struggling with the exchange rate. While the inflow of foreign capital is important, it is equally essential to increase domestic savings to finance the necessary investments.

A related issue, which Stern and Wes mention as being yet another challenge for the second decade, is the development of real exchange rates. The authors expect real exchange rates to appreciate during the transition, because of still higher inflation rates. This, however, might have an adverse effect on the com-petitiveness of firms on foreign markets, leading to even larger current account deficits. Therefore, an increase in productivity is necessary, stemming from con-tinuing reforms and increasing investments.

Important progress has also been achieved with respect to the dismantling of the institutions typical to the system of central planning and the introduction of institutions characteristic of a market economy. Nevertheless, important chal-lenges for the future remain. In Chapter 3, Bos, Gelauff and De Mooij identify four main co-ordination mechanisms for economic behaviour, *i.e.* control (the power of an agent to take decisions and impose these on others), competition (rivalry between agents striving for something not obtainable by all), common values (congruent sets of preferences within a group of economic agents) and co-operative exchange (bargained co-operation between independent agents with different preferences). They analyse the progress in institution building within this framework of co-ordination mechanisms. According to the authors, most coun-tries have achieved substantial progress in introducing and reforming the compe-tition and control mechanisms. In the initial phase of the transition, an emphasis was put on the development of a competition mechanism. Prices have been liberalised to a considerable degree, the CEECs have opened up for international trade, privatisation efforts have been impressive and the private sector contribution to GDP has increased sharply. However, also in this area challenges persist. Despite the progress made, the financial sector in most transition economies is still relatively underdeveloped. With respect to the control mechanism, the authors note that progress is substantial, but, at the same time, there are worrisome developments. The quality of public administration is a cause of concern, the shadow economy is large, and corruption in some CEECs is a persistent problem. The appropriate legal frameworks may have been established, but enforcement remains a matter of concern. The other two mechanisms, common values and norms and co-operative exchange, are relatively underdeveloped in all CEECs. According to the authors this is a consequence of the low level of inherited 'social capital'. Initial conditions do matter in institutional design, and it takes time to implement new institutions, particularly the informal ones.

To sum up, from the macroeconomic and institutional perspective, much has been achieved, but the CEECs have clearly not reached the end of the road.

The process of European enlargement

At present, there are thirteen candidates who have submitted applications, and ten of these countries are CEECs (see Chapter 5). With five CEECs, Poland, Hungary, the Czech Republic, Slovenia and Estonia, actual accession negotiations began in 1998. Van den Broek argues in Chapter 5 that the term 'accession negotiations' is in fact misplaced: "the *acquis* is not negotiable. The only real purpose of the negotiations is threefold: to determine whether the candidate country has fully grasped the meaning of the *acquis*, to verify that it is able and willing to implement it, and to discuss transition arrangements. In a limited number of areas it may be desirable either for the candidate country or for the incumbent member states that the *acquis* is phased in gradually".

The above implies that accession is an inherently complex process, rather than an event. All relevant parts of the *acquis* should be implemented, and this process is screened with precision. The authors of this book agree that some transitional periods are necessary, and that transitional arrangements are not necessarily undermining the functioning of the internal market. Nevertheless, it is obvious that the countries are joining a club that has certain rules with respect, for instance, to the free movement of goods, services, capital and labour, and to fair competition, and that these rules cannot be violated to any great extent. As Van den Broek states in Chapter 5, "Casting this principle aside for the benefit of rapid enlargement – in other words, allowing new entrants major and lengthy dispensation from the common rules – would help no one. The current members would suffer because the essence of what has been a successful venture would be destroyed, and the new members would not gain from joining something that has been destroyed by the manner of their joining".

The case of the Portuguese accession to the EU provides relevant lessons for the CEECs. Mateus, in Chapter 8, shows that the Portuguese accession certainly was a great success. It gave the Portuguese authorities a strong incentive to pursue reform policies. After accession, the economy showed a remarkable recovery, with GDP growing substantially. A strong disinflation program, a healthy fiscal policy and a strict monetary policy supported this development. Moreover, structural reforms have underpinned the recovery. Privatisation, opening up of the economy and financial sector reform were measures crucial to recovery. An interesting observation of Mateus is, though, that, with the benefit of hindsight, most Portuguese negotiators are of the opinion that "requests for derogations were too many and unnecessarily broad".

Rollo and Smith (Chapter 6) view the enlargement from a different angle. The authors argue in essence that accession to the EU is part of the transformation process. Therefore, the accession should foster the political and economic transformation and stimulate growth and development. Rollo and Smith make a clear distinction between those parts of the *acquis* that will support the transformation, and will enhance economic growth and those parts that incorporate a huge burden for the CEEC-10. For the latter, derogations are appropriate, especially if they are not essential to the working of the single market. Thus, they argue: "as a matter of general strategy the urgent issues are those where adjustment to the EU's norms will provide economic disciplines, market access, and competition that will contribute to growth and efficiency; while adjustment to policies that are likely to be a burden on the CEECs' economies should be slow and should be accompanied by financial support from the EU".

With respect to free trade in goods and services, complete application of the *acquis* is deemed necessary, as it avoids comprehensive border controls, which increase the administrative burden. This also holds for trade in agricultural products.

With respect to the free movement of capital, derogations may be necessary. Wellink concludes in Chapter 7 that "adequate sequencing of short-term capital liberalisation may be required in order to gain time for adjusting the domestic financial sector to the competitive pressures that follow from capital liberalisation". However, he also sees that considerable progress has been made with respect to capital liberalisation, and that transitional arrangements are unlikely to be required. With respect to membership of the EMU, also part of the *acquis*, and membership of the ERM-II, Wellink is cautious. Fixing exchange rates at an early date of accession may be unwise, as productivity increases cause exchange rates to appreciate.

With respect to the free movement of labour, it is, as Inotai observes in Chapter 10, the EU that may call for a derogation. The fears for a large outflow of labour from the CEECs to the present EU members seem to be unjustified. A dynamic development of the domestic economy will limit the incentive for migration, despite huge income differentials. According to Inotai: "Hungary's migration potential is and will remain limited, provided enlargement takes place quickly and broad economic and social progress materialises. It is not quick enlargement that may increase the migration potential but just the opposite, the delaying or post-poning accession. In recent years, Hungary has been one of the main beneficia-ries of labour market rigidities in Western Europe. Since capital works in a glob-al framework, while manpower is seriously restricted to national (and regional) levels, international capital started to join Hungarian labour". Also Rosati (Chap-ter 9) is of the opinion that fears for large inflows of a low-wage workforce are largely unfounded. Moreover, labour outflow may come at great cost, not for the present EU members, but for the CEECs themselves, if it takes the form of a 'brain drain'.

Difficulties arise in the area of environmental and social policies. For example, the CEECs face a legacy of huge pollution and environmental mismanagement. On the one hand, taking on board all the obligations and requirements of the *acquis*, brings along tremendous costs for the CEEC-10, and will require huge financial assistance from the EU. On the other hand, levelling the playing field requires that the CEECs' firms have to compete with Western firms on an equal basis, and that derogations have to be limited. In this respect, the idea of Rollo and Smith is to make a clear distinction between those parts of the *acquis* that will support the transformation and those parts that incorporate a huge burden for the CEEC-10. For the latter, derogations are appropriate, especially if they are not essential to the working of the single market. The approach of Rollo and Smith, although sympathetic, incorporates the danger that it may violate the working of the inter-nal market, and may pass the problem of unfair competition onto the enlarged market. It is clear that in the longer run the CEEC-10 should adhere to the envi-ronmental policies of the club they seek to join. In the short run, a balance must be found between the costs of cleaning up and unfair competition.

Given the complex process of the implementation of the whole *acquis*, delays in enlargement have to be feared. Delays may stem from the side of the EU. The institutional framework of the EU has to be reformed in order to be able to absorb a large group of new members in an efficient way. In addition, as is widely known, the CAP has to be reformed, such that the newcomers can be equal partners here. Delays may also stem from the side of the newcomers. The implementation of the *acquis* might be stalled. Moreover, too many requests for derogations may show that, in fact, the newcomers are not ready yet. As Inotai observes in Chapter 10: "The overriding government approach should be that no derogation is worth delaying accession. Any delay would result in tangible economic, financial and, under certain circumstances, also security, losses, the extent of which would be several times greater than the most serious potential damage any forceful and pre-mature adjustment may generate". Timing is an important aspect of the enlarge-ment. A sometimes forgotten issue is that the popular support in the CEECs for enlargement is diminishing, as Rosati has shown for the Polish situation.

To sum up, there is a trade-off between a rapid enlargement and the political and economic benefits that go with it, and the degree of unfair competition that derogations bring along. Obviously, transitional periods should be clearly defined in terms of duration and content. However, no derogations at all would unavoidably lead to a delay in the eastern enlargement. The best is the enemy of the good.

Integrating Russia and Ukraine into the world economy

While the countries that seek membership of the EU have, in general, reported substantial progress with respect to the transition, the situation in the CIS, also Russia and Ukraine, looks entirely different. A country like Poland is realising substantial growth now for the eighth consecutive year, and in the last five years the economy has grown between 5% and 7% yearly. In sharp contrast is Ukraine, where growth rates have been negative from the outset of transition. Russia realised marginal growth only in 1997, and in all other years the economy shrunk. Living standards have been falling sharply, life expectancy has dropped, income inequality has become extreme, and for large groups in the society the economic situation looks grim. It remains an important and intriguing question why the outcomes of transition are so different. What are the causes of this, as Gros calls it, "Lost Decade"? Even more important, what can be done to reverse this dreadful development?

In essence, the worse outcome in Russia, Ukraine, and other countries of the FSU, has two principal causes: worse initial conditions and half-hearted policies (see also Wolf 1999). The initial conditions in Russia and Ukraine, and for all other countries of the FSU, were considerably less encouraging than in other CEECs. What is more, the disintegration of the Soviet Union had a considerable negative impact on all economies concerned. This also holds for the Baltic States, where the initial decline in output was much more severe than in countries like Poland. One could however expect that Russia, being the largest looser within the Soviet Union, and the CMEA for that matter, would have gained economically from this disintegration process, now that it could charge world market prices for the formerly heavily-subsidised energy exports within the CMEA and Soviet Union. This brings us to the policies pursued.

Gros (Chapter 11) concludes, after analysing the price liberalisation, external trade liberalisation and stabilisation processes in Russia, that the policies pursued were, at least in the beginning, incomplete and inconsistent. According to the author, one of the most serious mistakes the reformers made in the initial reform episode of 1992, was not to have increased energy prices and not to have eliminated import subsidies immediately. The price controls on energy and, hence, the concomitant existence of a huge price differential between domestic prices and world market prices, made restrictions on the export side a necessity. However, as the authorities were unable to enforce the restrictions on energy exports, especially along the borders with other former Soviet republics, the Russian government lost a tremendous amount of tax revenues. According to Gros, these lost revenues could have easily made up for the fiscal deficits.

The Russian government was, and still is, unable to force enterprises to pay their taxes. Huge fiscal deficits are the result. According to Gros, another serious policy mistake was to finance the fiscal deficit with foreign capital, as a result of which "the country was putting its stability in the hands of international capital markets by a combination of excessive opening of financial markets, imprudent fiscal policy and a corrupt banking system. This mixture proved almost lethal when private capital inflows suddenly stopped and a classic currency plus banking crisis followed".

One could easily add other instances of mismanagement to the account of Russian leaders. The privatisation process took the form of 'nomenklatura privatisation', (or 'spontaneous privatisation', see Chapter 3) in which the former elite changed the administrative power over state assets into ownership. Wolf (1999) mentions that state assets were sold far below their true value. Not only was this development dramatic for the current condition of the state budget, but it also encourages a society of lawlessness and corruption. In addition, it engenders an unhealthy entanglement of state and business, it hampers the dismantling of monopolies and discourages the development of a market economy based on competition.

Despite the fact that Gros describes the ten years of Russian transition as a lost decade, he remains in a sense optimistic: "the lesson that reforms and stabilisation improve the economy and pay off politically in the long run was not lost on the political system. This is the key reason why Russia did not descend into hyperinflation and disintegration after August 1998. For the near future one can therefore expect a continuation of the slow, but imperfect progress that has been the hallmark of developments in Russia so far".

Pynzenyk draws in Chapter 12 a quite similar picture for Ukraine. A dramatic decline of GDP, steep falls in agricultural and industrial production, the inability of the government to raise tax revenues and the appearance of huge inflation. There appears to be too little political support in the country for true reform. The author also questions the ways of privatisation in certain sectors in Ukraine, and, as in Russia, he observes, in the gas, energy, and agricultural sectors, "a dangerous merger between businessmen and civil servants by severely monopolising certain activities through procedures that can only be described as a game without rules". Given the developments of the past decade, Pynzenyk finds it hard to remain optimistic about the prospects for Ukraine, but at the same time, he feels that Ukraine is on the eve of true reforms.

Pynzenyk warns for Western support for quasi-reforms. Support for quasi-reforms postpones true reforms, and has a prolonging effect on the painful transformation. This, at the same time, encourages the feeling amongst the population that there is a causal relation between reforms and worsening living standards. In Chapter 11, Gros also questions the effectiveness of Western aid during the early reform period. According to Gros, most of the aid to Russia was given in the form of trade credits. As Russia was in fact subsidising imports, aid that encouraged imports made matters worse. According to the author, Western governments and institutions could have assisted in a more effective way, despite the bad policies pursued in Russia, if budgetary assistance had been given to the government, in order to achieve stabilisation.

The discussion on the effectiveness of aid brings the 'Trade, not aid' concept again to the fore. It is of the utmost importance to further integrate Russia and Ukraine into the world economy, and, especially, in the European economy. In Chapter 13, Michalopoulos addresses the prospects for Russia and Ukraine for joining the WTO. His basic message is clear. Both Russia and Ukraine went a long way in establishing trade policies and institutions that support their integration into the multilateral trading system and their membership of the WTO. However, Michalopoulos does not foresee their membership before the upcoming WTO multilateral trade negotiations. Although their trade regimes are not especially restrictive, there are flaws in the functioning of market institutions that obstruct effective integration in the trading system. The *de facto* trade barriers stem from weak market support systems and from inadequate systems of governance. While Russia and Ukraine have to address these issues in order to become more integrated in the world economy, Michalopoulos and Pynzenyk are of the opinion that the WTO members, notably the US and the EU, are with respect to trade policy too restrictive towards these countries. They continue to treat the countries much less favourably. Ukraine is particularly affected by a much more frequent use of non-transparent anti-dumping procedures. Obviously, this is not very helpful.

To conclude

This book serves as food for thought for policy-makers, and seeks to address the key policy issues and policy dilemma's Europeans face in the process of further integration on the continent. Now that the first decade of transition has come to an end, the Kosovo-crisis has once again made clear how important further integration can be in fostering peace and prosperity on the old continent. The war in Kosovo has led some to argue that the process of EU enlargement should be accelerated, and that the Balkan countries should be included in negotiations for accession as quickly as possible. This is however too simplistic a view. A number of countries are far from satisfying the conditions for membership. Such an enlargement of the EU must not be brought about at the expense of the achievements of the EU so far, which would benefit no one. At the same, permitting no derogations at all would unavoidably lead to delays in the eastern enlargement. Such delays are clearly undesirable, as the EU has both a responsibility for and an interest in the process of further integration on the European continent. This book underlines the importance of further integration and the complicated dilemmas and trade-offs that the CEECs and the EU face in the process. The EU should stimulate the transformation in the economies of our Eastern and South Eastern neighbours in the most effective way, in order to make sure that candidate countries qualify as quickly as possible. Furthermore, the EU has to transform itself in such a way that it is able to welcome and absorb qualified newcomers. Dealing with these dilemmas involves skilled manoeuvring of both the EU and the CEECs. Certainly, it entails avoiding the *Scylla* of a premature accession that could endanger the achieved level of integration in the EU. But it also calls for a firm hand on the steering wheel to avoid the *Charybdis* of a lack of perspective for the CEECs to become members of the EU in the near future. Only then can a second decade of transition lead to more peace and prosperity in the whole of Europe.

References

Baldwin, R., J. Francois and R. Portes (1997) 'The costs and benefits of EU enlargement to the East', *Economic Policy*, No.24, pp.125-176.

Wolf, M. (1999) 'Caught in the Transition Trap', *Financial Times*, 30 June.

List of Abbreviations

ACP	Africa, Caribbean, and Pacific
BKKR	Belarus, Kazakhstan, Kyrgyzstan, and Russia
CAP	Common Agricultural Policy
CBR	Central Bank of Russia
CEC	Central European Countries
CEEC	Central and Eastern European Countries
CEI	Commission for European Integration
CIS	Commonwealth of Independent States
CMEA	Council of Mutual Economic Assistance
CMS	Constant Market Shares (analysis)
CPSU	Communist Party of the Soviet Union
CSE	Consumer Subsidy Equivalent
CU	Customs Union
DNB	Dutch National Bank
EBRD	European Bank for Reconstruction and Development
EC	European Community
ECB	European Central Bank
ECU	European Currency Unit
EFTA	European Free Trade Area
EMU	Economic and Monetary Union
ERM	Exchange Rate Mechanism
EU	European Union
EUE	European Union Enlargement
FDI	Foreign Direct Investment
FSU	Former Soviet Union
FTA	Free Trade Area (Free Trade Arrangement)
FYR	Former Yugoslav Republic
FYROM	Former Yugoslav Republic Of Macedonia
GATS	General Agreement for Trade and Services
GATT	General Agreement on Tariffs and Trade
GDP	Gross Domestic Product
GNP	Gross National Product
GSP	Generalised System of Preferences

IGC	InterGovernmental Conference
IFI	International Financial Institution
IMF	International Monetary Fund
IPN	International Production Networks/Networking
LDC	Less Developed Country
MFN	Most Favoured Nation
MNC	MultiNational Corporation
MTOE	millions of tons of oil equivalent
NATO	North Atlantic Treaty Organisation
OECD	Organisation for Economic Co-operation and Development
PPP	Purchasing-Power Parity
PSE	Producer Subsidy Equivalent
RSFSR	Russian Soviet Federated Socialist Republic
SME	Small and Medium Enterprises
SPS	Sanitary and PhytoSanitary measures
STF	Strategic Task Force
TRIP	Trade Related aspect of Intellectual Property Right
UNCTAD	United Nations Conference on Trade And Development
VAT	Value Added Tax
WP	Working Party
WTO	World Trade Organisation

About the Authors

Guido Biessen
Dr. Guido G.A. Biessen (1960) graduated in economics from the University of Amsterdam in 1987, where he became a research assistant in the same year. He was a lecturer at Leiden University from 1991 to 1997. From 1989 to 1990, he was affiliated to the Institute of Economic Science of the Polish Academy of Sciences and in 1995 to the Foreign Trade Research Institute of Warsaw. At present, he is Deputy Head of the Foreign Markets Analysis Division at the Dutch Ministry of Economic Affairs. He has had his work published in journals varying from the *Journal of Comparative Economics* to the *Staatscourant*. His main publications are in the field of foreign trade, trade policy, countries in transition and European integration.

Marko Bos
Marko Bos (1954) graduated in economics from the University of Groningen in 1980. Between 1980 and 1986, he was affiliated to the international branch of the Economic Research Department of the ABN Bank in Amsterdam. He joined the secretariat of the Social and Economic Council (the independent, tripartite advisory body to the Dutch government) in late 1986 and is currently its Deputy Director for Economic Affairs. He is involved in the preparation of advisory reports on various subjects of economic policy, including European integration. He is currently employed part-time by the University of Leiden to teach the economics of European integration. His publications include articles on European integration, Eastern Europe and the consultation economy.

Ruud de Mooij
Dr. Ruud A. de Mooij (1968) graduated in econometrics at the Erasmus University in Rotterdam in 1992. He then combined a part-time job as an economist at the Ministry of Economic Affairs with a fellowship at the Research Centre for Economic Policy (OCFEB). Since 1995, he has been affiliated to the CPB Netherlands Bureau for Economic Policy Analysis. He has had several articles on taxation and labour markets published in international journals, including the *American Economic Review* and the *Journal of Public Economics*. In 1999, he received his Ph.D. with a thesis on environmental taxation. Currently, Ruud de Mooij

heads the European Comparative Analysis unit at the CPB. Major research areas include European labour markets, the subsidiarity principle, taxation and EU enlargement.

Frans Engering

Frans A. Engering (1943) completed his studies in general economics at the Catholic University of Tilburg. He was affiliated to the economics faculty of Tilburg University from 1969 to 1978. From 1978 to 1984 he worked at the Dutch Ministry of Finance, where he was Head of the International Monetary Affairs Division and Director for Foreign Financial Relations. Frans Engering has been Director General for the Foreign Economic Relations Department at the Dutch Ministry of Economic Affairs since 1984. He is a member and chairman of various committees (EEC, OECD, ECSS) and acts in an advisory capacity to other committees (IMF/IBRD, ADB/IDB). He has published work on monetary theory and policy, public finance, international economic relations, trade policy, European integration and Eastern Europe.

George Gelauff

Professor Dr. George M.M. Gelauff (1955) graduated in 1977 in econometrics at the Erasmus University in Rotterdam. During 1979-1992, he worked at the CPB Netherlands Bureau for Economic Policy Analysis on empirical macroeconomic models and applied general equilibrium models to the Dutch economy. In 1992 he received his Ph.D. at the Catholic University of Brabant with a thesis on a model that focuses on taxation, social security and the Dutch labour market. Between 1993 and 1997 he co-ordinated CPB's comparative study of German and Dutch economic institutions (*Challenging Neighbours*, Springer Verlag, 1997). Since 1998, George Gelauff is professor of German Studies at the University of Nijmegen. As head of the Institutional Analysis Department at CPB he is involved in economic research on European issues, knowledge, technology, regulation and competition, and long-term scenarios for the world economy.

Daniel Gros

Dr. Daniel Gros is originally from Germany. He attended school in Italy, where he obtained a Laurea in *economica e commercia*, as well as in the United States, where he earned his M.A. and Ph.D. Upon completion of his academic studies, he went on to work at the International Monetary Fund in the European and Research Departments (1983-1986), and as an Economic Advisor at the Directorate-General II of the European Commission (1988-1990). He has also taught at various Universities across Europe, including the Catholic University of Leuven, the University of Frankfurt, Bocconi University, the Kiel Institute of World Studies and the Central European University in Prague. Currently, Daniel Gros is the Deputy Director of the Centre for European Policy Studies in Brussels, where he has been employed since the early eighties. At present, his interests lie within the EMU; transition towards market economies in Central and Eastern Europe; enlargement of the EU; stability of the European Banking system. His most recent publications include *Winds of Change in Central and Eastern Europe* (textbook, 1995); *European Monetary Integration, from the EMS to EMU* (textbook, 1997) and *Macroeconomic Policy in the First Year of Euroland* (First Annual Report of the CEPS Macroeconomic Policy Group, 1998).

András Inotai

Professor Dr. András Inotai (1943) was born in Szombathely, Western Hungary. He has been on the staff of the Institute for World Economics of the Hungarian Academy of Sciences since 1967 and has been its general director since 1991. He has also headed the Hungarian government's Strategic Task Force for European Integration since 1996. He is a professor of the College of Europe, Bruges and Warsaw. Professor Inotai has served abroad on several occasions (in Germany and Peru, and at the World Bank in Washington, D.C.). His main research fields include regional integration schemes, the European Union, economic modernisation in Central and Eastern Europe, international flows of direct capital, and Hungary's adjustment to the international economy. András Inotai has published numerous articles and books. His most recent publications include *On the Way, Hungary and the European Union* (1998); *The EC'92 Program and Eastern Europe* (forthcoming).

Abel Mateus

Professor Dr. Abel M. Mateus (1947) is presently adviser to the Board of the Banco de Portugal and an Associate Professor at the New University of Lisbon. Previously, he was a member of the Board and Executive Director of the Banco de Portugal, a member of the Monetary Committee and a member of the Economic Policy Committee of the European Commission. As a member of the Board of the Banco de Portugal for six years, he was responsible for monetary policy in Portugal and for bringing the country into the single currency. For eleven years, he was a senior economist at the World Bank. At the World Bank, he was mission leader and responsible for a structural adjustment program for Morocco and a large decentralisation and regional development project for Mexico, besides being a macroeconomist for several countries. He also worked on the social sectors, safety nets and agricultural sectors of several North African and Latin American countries. In addition, he has worked extensively on tax reforms. He holds a Ph.D. in Economics from the University of Pennsylvania, USA and has taught at the New University of Lisbon, the Catholic University of Portugal and the Free University of Lisbon. He has published extensively.

Constantine Michalopoulos

Dr. Constantine Michalopoulos is Special Economic Advisor in the World Trade Organization on secondment from the World Bank. In this capacity, he directs analysis and research on trade policy issues of developing countries and countries in transition. Among the various positions he held previously with the World Bank were those of Director for Economic Policy Analysis and Senior Advisor for Operations in Russia and Central Asia.

Prior to joining the World Bank, Dr. Michalopoulos served as Chief Economist of the US Agency for International Development. He has also taught economics at several universities, most recently as Adjunct Professor at the American University in Washington, D.C. He has been educated in Greece and the US and holds a Ph.D. degree in economics from Columbia University. Dr. Michalopoulos has published extensively on trade and finance issues related to development and economies in transition. His most recent papers include 'The Developing Countries in the WTO', 'WTO Accession for Countries in Transition' and 'State Trading in Russia'.

Harry Oldersma

Harry Oldersma (1956) studied econometrics at the University of Groningen. He entered the service of the Dutch Ministry of Economic Affairs in 1985. Since 1989, he has been employed at the Foreign Markets Analysis Division of the Directorate-General for Foreign Economic Relations at the Ministry of Economic Affairs. He has written several studies on the economic structures and positions of nations around the world. His publications range from specific studies of sectors and countries to articles in several journals, mainly in the field of international economic relations.

Victor Pynzenyk

Professor Dr. Victor Pynzenyk studied economics at Lviv University, after which he finished his Ph.D. in 1989 at Moscow University. From 1989 to 1992, he was professor at Lviv University. Between 1990 and 1992 he was the Director of the Lviv Management Institute. Since 1991, he has been a Deputy in the Ukrainian Parliament. In 1994, he became Deputy Prime Minister of Ukraine with responsibility for Economic Reform, a position he held until 1997. Since 1997, he has been the Head of the Institute of Reforms. As to other previous positions he has held, he has been Head of the Ukrainian Reform Support Foundation, and Deputy Head of the Economic Collegial of State Duma under the President of the Ukraine. His publications include three books and over 200 articles.

Dariusz Rosati

Professor Dr. Dariusz K. Rosati at present holds a chair in international economics at the Warsaw School of Economics. He also is a member of the Monetary Policy Council of the National Bank of Poland. He completed his Ph.D. and habilitation degree at the Warsaw School of Economics. Previously he worked as a consultant for several international organisations (including UNIDO, ILO, World Bank and EU), and was a Partner at Ernst & Young TKD Consultants Ltd. From 1991 to 1995, he was the Head of the Transition Economies Section of the United Nations Economic Commission for Europe in Geneva. In 1995, he became Minister for Foreign Affairs in Poland, a position he held until 1997. He has published extensively on macroeconomic policy, trade policy, financial analysis, international trade and finance, problems of economies in transition.

Jim Rollo

Professor Dr. Jim Rollo holds a chair in European Economic Integration at the University of Sussex and is Co-Director of the Sussex European Institute. He is external Professor of Economics at Nottingham University. Until December 1998, he was Chief Economic Adviser in the British Foreign Office. Before that, he was director of the International Economics Research Programme at the Royal Institute of International Affairs in London. He has published widely on international economic issues, principally in the field of EU and commercial policy. Lately, he has been responsible for economic analysis of global financial crisis at the British Foreign Office. Recent publications include work on Regionalism and the world trading system and on EU enlargement.

Alasdair Smith

Professor Dr. Alasdair Smith was born in 1949 on the Isle of Lewis, Scotland. In 1969, he finished his M.A. in Mathematics and Political Economy with first class honours at the University of Glasgow. He further studied at the London School of Economics (MSc, 1970, in Mathematical Economics and Econometrics) and Oxford University (DPhil, 1973, in international trade theory). Since July 1998, he is a Vice-Chancellor at the University of Sussex. Previously, he has been a Lecturer in Economics at University College, Oxford (1970-72), Lecturer in Economics, London School of Economics (1972-81), Professor of Economics at the University of Sussex (since 1981), and Dean of the School of European Studies at the University of Sussex (1991-94). Professor Smith has held visiting positions at Columbia University, the University of Rochester, the University of California in San Diego, the University of Michigan, the College of Europe, Bruges and Natolin, and the European University Institute in Florence. He is the author or editor of four books and the author of over sixty articles in journals and books, mostly concerned with international trade, European trade policy, and European integration. His current research focuses on the effects of international trade on European labour markets.

Nicholas Stern

Professor Dr. Nicholas H. Stern took up the post of Chief Economist at the EBRD (where he is also Special Counsellor to the President) in January 1994. He was appointed to a Chair (subsequently the Sir John Hicks Chair in Economics) at the London School of Economics in 1986. He has taught and researched at Oxford and Warwick universities, the Massachusetts Institute of Technology, the Ecole

Polytechnique in Paris, the Indian Statistical Institute in Bangalore and Delhi, and the People's University of China in Beijing. He gained his BA from Cambridge and his doctorate from Oxford. He was elected to a Fellowship of the Econometric Society in 1978 (and is currently a Member of Council), to a Fellowship of the British Academy in July 1993, and to a Foreign Honorary Membership of the American Academy of Arts and Sciences in 1998. His books include works on tax reform, the economy of an Indian village, the theory of economic growth, the role of the state, and crime and the criminal statistics.

Nicolette Tiggeloove

Nicolette Tiggeloove (1965) graduated in economics from the Free University in Amsterdam in 1989. She became a research assistant at the Inter-university Centre for Latin American Research and Documentation (CEDLA) in Amsterdam in the same year. After completing a post-graduate course on Financial Economic Policy Making at the Faculty of Economics of the Erasmus University in Rotterdam in 1992, she entered the service of the Dutch Ministry of Economic Affairs. At present, she is a senior policy advisor at the Foreign Markets Analysis Division of the Directorate-General for Foreign Economic Relations. Her work focuses on foreign trade, direct investment flows and emerging markets.

Hans van den Broek

Hans van den Broek (1936) was born in Paris and studied law at the University of Utrecht. After practising as a lawyer in Rotterdam from 1965 to 1968, he became the secretary of the managing board of ENKA BV, Arnhem, a post that he held from 1969 to 1973, after which he became a commercial manager with the company from 1973 to 1976. He was a member of the Dutch Lower House of Parliament from 1976 to 1981, and was a member of the executive board of the Catholic People's Party from 1978. He was State Secretary for Foreign Affairs from 1981 to 1982 in the second Van Agt government and was re-appointed State Secretary for Foreign Affairs in the third Van Agt government in 1982. He was appointed Minister for Foreign Affairs in the first Lubbers government in 1982 and subsequently re-appointed Minister for Foreign Affairs in the second and third Lubbers governments in 1986 and in 1989 respectively. In 1993, he was appointed member of the Commission of the European Communities. From 1995 onwards, his responsibility as a Commission member included the external relations with the countries of Central and Eastern Europe, the former Soviet Union, Mongolia, Turkey, Cyprus, Malta and other European countries, and the common foreign and security policy, human rights (in agreement with the President), and external diplomatic missions.

Sweder van Wijnbergen

Professor Dr. Sweder J.G. van Wijnbergen was born in 1951 in Haarlem. He holds a Masters degree in Physics and Econometrics from the Universities of Utrecht and Rotterdam respectively. He completed his Ph.D. at the Massachusetts Institute of Technology in Cambridge MA, between 1977 and 1980. Between 1980 and 1993, he held several positions at the World Bank, including Lead Economist for Mexico & Latin America, and Lead Economist for Eastern Europe. Between 1993 and 1997, he held a Chair at the London School of Economics, and since 1993 he holds a Chair at the University of Amsterdam. Since 1997, he has been Secretary-General of the Ministry of Economic Affairs. He has published extensively on macroeconomic policy, trade policy, financial analysis, international trade and finance, problems of economies in transition.

Arnout Wellink

Dr. Arnout H.E.M. Wellink studied Dutch Law at Leyden University between 1961 and 1968. He completed his Ph.D. in economics in 1975 at the Erasmus University in Rotterdam. From 1965 to 1970, he taught economics at Leyden University, after which he started working for the Dutch Ministry of Finance. From 1977 until 1981, he was Treasurer General at the Ministry of Finance. In 1982, Dr. Wellink started working for the Nederlandsche Bank, of which he became the President in 1997. He has occupied, and still occupies, several other posts on the boards and committees of international organisations and financial institutions including the OECD, the European Central Bank, the European Commission, and the Bank for International Settlements. He has published several books and articles.

Marina Wes

Dr. Marina Wes joined the Office of the Chief Economist at the EBRD in November 1997. Prior to that, she was a lecturer at the University of Amsterdam, teaching post-graduate courses for the Masters in International Finance programme. She has also taught MBA courses at the Western University and at the State Economic Institute at Baku in Azerbaijan. She graduated from Trinity College, Cambridge University and the London School of Economics, and her undergraduate work was completed at Bryn Mawr College (USA). She has held a Royal Economic Society Junior Fellowship and has been a Foreign and Commonwealth Office British Chevening Scholar. She has also done work for the Bank of England, the European Commission, the Economic and Social Research Institute (Ireland), the Institute for Public Policy Research (UK) and the World Bank. Her work focuses on economies in transition, international trade and finance, and foreign direct investment.